Runaway Hollywood

*The publisher and the University of California Press
Foundation gratefully acknowledge the generous support of the
Constance and William Withey Endowment Fund
in History and Music.*

Runaway Hollywood

INTERNATIONALIZING POSTWAR PRODUCTION
AND LOCATION SHOOTING

Daniel Steinhart

UNIVERSITY OF CALIFORNIA PRESS

University of California Press, one of the most distinguished university presses in the United States, enriches lives around the world by advancing scholarship in the humanities, social sciences, and natural sciences. Its activities are supported by the UC Press Foundation and by philanthropic contributions from individuals and institutions. For more information, visit www.ucpress.edu.

University of California Press
Oakland, California

Library of Congress Cataloging-in-Publication Data

Names: Steinhart, Daniel, 1977- author.
Title: Runaway Hollywood : internationalizing postwar production and
    location shooting / Daniel Steinhart.
Description: Oakland, California : University of California Press, [2019] |
    Includes bibliographical references and index. |
Identifiers: LCCN 2018027843 (print) | LCCN 2018029394 (ebook) |
    ISBN 9780520970694 (ebook) | ISBN 9780520298637 (cloth : alk. paper) |
    ISBN 9780520298644 (pbk. : alk. paper)
Subjects: LCSH: Motion pictures—Production and direction—United
    States—History—20th century. | Motion picture industry—Economic
    aspects—United States. | Motion picture locations.
Classification: LCC PN1995.9.P7 (ebook) | LCC PN1995.9.P7 S695 2019 (print) |
    DDC 791.4309730904—dc23
LC record available at https://lccn.loc.gov/2018027843

Manufactured in the United States of America

28 27 26 25 24 23 22 21 20 19
10 9 8 7 6 5 4 3 2 1

For Clara Gómez Steinhart and John Steinhart

CONTENTS

ACKNOWLEDGMENTS

I want to begin with a convention of how movies are sometimes interpreted and promoted, which is to treat the subject of a movie as a metaphor for its making. Like the story of this book, its creation was an international venture, supported by many individuals and organizations in the United States and abroad.

The genesis of *Runaway Hollywood* began at UCLA in the Cinema and Media Studies Program, which shaped this project and my thinking about media in significant ways. Steve Mamber's sensitive attention to form and style informed my analysis of location shooting. Our conversations showed me how thought provoking and fun the study of cinema and media should be. Janet Bergstrom and her scholarship on transnational filmmakers served as a model of historical rigor and originality. I learned from her that cinema is not just an object of study but a culture to actively engage with. John Caldwell taught me that there is much to learn from the craft and labor of production work. His feedback provided me with a well of ideas I continue to draw from.

For its support, I thank the rest of the Cinema and Media Studies faculty. This project first took shape in a research seminar, taught with an avuncular touch by Teshome Gabriel. He is missed. I also learned a great deal from discussions with Giuliana Muscio, whose knowledge of the Italian industry got me thinking about Hollywood's international activities in new ways. I want to acknowledge the amazing work of the programmers and archivists at the UCLA Film and Television Archive, which was so central to my film education. For challenging me intellectually, I'm grateful to my PhD cohort, especially Brian Hu, Erin Hill, and Jason Skonieczny. Ross Melnick, Emily Carman, Rebecca Prime, and Aynne Kokas have shared their valuable wisdom over the years. Bernardo Rondeau has expanded my movie horizons.

Harrison Gish and Jason Gendler have been lively filmgoing comrades. And thanks to the many members of the now-defunct Crank film society, who gathered to watch glorious archival prints in the James Bridges Theater.

The historical scope of this book would not have been possible without the extraordinary work of librarians and archivists in the United States and Europe. At the Margaret Herrick Library, I'm indebted to its stellar staff and the assistance of Jenny Romero, Barbara Hall, Louise Hilton, and Faye Thompson. I also thank Sandra Joy Lee Aguilar, Jonathon Auxier, and Brett Service at USC's Warner Bros. Archive and Julie Graham at UCLA's Performing Arts Special Collections. At UCLA, I was lucky to view the production files of Twentieth Century-Fox before the studio recalled its records after a loan agreement expired—an unfortunate outcome for film historians. Files from the State Department developed my understanding of motion picture diplomacy, so I want to recognize the staff of the National Archives in College Park, Maryland.

One of the pleasures of researching this book was interviewing veteran production personnel who had worked on the films I was studying. This project aims to highlight the contributions of below-the-line crew members who are too often overlooked in film histories. During a visit to Las Vegas, production manager C. O. "Doc" Erickson was crucial to fact checking and bringing to life what I had discovered in archives. Sadly, he passed away in 2017. I thank his daughter, Dawn Erickson, for sharing photos of her father with me.

This project reaped the benefits of spending a year in Europe, which was made possible by a Fulbright Fellowship in France. I appreciated the assistance of the Franco-American Commission in Paris. François Thomas of Université Sorbonne Nouvelle—Paris 3 was generous for sponsoring my research. At the Cinémathèque française, where I researched and wrote by day and blissfully took in movies by night, Valdo Kneubühler of the Bibliothèque du film pointed me in productive directions. He also introduced me to script supervisor Sylvette Baudrot, whose insights into Hollywood production in France were illuminating. She in turn put me in touch with production manager Christian Ferry, a study in courtesy, who passed away in 2011.

My research in Rome would have been a bust if not for the generosity of Giancarlo Concetti of the Biblioteca Luigi Chiarini at the Centro Sperimentale di Cinematografia. Giancarlo helped arrange a number of interviews and acted as a patient translator. Cinematographer Sergio Salvati was key to granting me access to Cinecittà studios and the Istituto Luce. For sharing their time and experiences, I'm grateful to cinematographer Giuseppe Rotunno and set dresser Bruno Schiavi, whose workshop was one of my favorite sites in Rome. In London, the staff of the British Film Institute library gave me useful guidance. Director of photography Oswald Morris graciously welcomed me into his home for an interview. A master of color and light, he passed on in 2014.

During this period abroad, I valued the chance to share my work with the research group CinEcoSA and founding member Nolwenn Mingant at its film marketing conference in Paris. Petr Szczepanik and Patrick Vonderau were kind for inviting me to Stockholm to share my research at the 2011 conference "Lights! Tystnad! Azione! Practices, Sites and Careers in European Film Production." The feedback at these conferences sensitized me to international perspectives on Hollywood's runaway productions. Petr and Patrick also published some of the research that appears in chapters 2 and 3 in their edited collection *Behind the Screen: Inside European Production Cultures* (2013); it is reproduced here with the permission of Palgrave Macmillan.

I was able to finish researching and writing this book at the University of Oregon. In the Department of Cinema Studies, I've treasured the camaraderie of some amazing colleagues. Michael Aronson and Priscilla Peña Ovalle have been heroic leaders. Sergio Rigoletto has been an inspiring film enthusiast. Peter Alilunas and Erin Hanna have been terrific allies. And I've gained a lot from the community fostered by Michael Allan, Dong Hoon Kim, HyeRyoung Ok, Sangita Gopal, and Bish Sen. Our dedicated staff, Kay Bailey, Timothy McGovney, Michelle Wright, and Veratta Pegram-Floyd, have made departmental duties smoother and brighter. In the School of Journalism and Communication, I've appreciated the mentorship of Gabriela Martínez and Chris Chávez and the support of Janet Wasko. With the assistance of Julianne Newton and a Dean's Faculty Fighting Fund Research Grant, I was able to bring the final stages of this book's research to a close. The Media Studies graduate program was a fruitful source of research assistants. I owe a huge debt of gratitude to the diligent work of Zachary Roman, whose deep dive into the *American Film Institute Catalog* made this book's appendix feasible. Rachel Quick helped assemble the appendix, and Edwin Wang and Benjamin Adu Kumi assisted with *Catalog* research. My students, especially those in my Global Hollywood and Production Studies courses, have spurred me to clarify my ideas.

This project found a welcome home at University of California Press. Raina Polivka championed the book and patiently shepherded it to the finish line. I thank Elena Bellaart for her editorial assistance, Lindsey Westbrook for her smart edits, and Kim Robinson for backing the book. This project benefited from the input of various readers. Patrick Keating, whose own scholarship on film style is a model of rigor and precision, offered many helpful suggestions. Vicki Mayer's sharp-eyed assessment made the book stronger. Bridget Conor's early endorsement pushed the project forward. The keen editorial eye of Anitra Grisales improved the manuscript enormously. For help with the book's cover photo, I thank Derek Davidson of Photofest.

Finally, this project would not have been possible without the support of my family. Alex, Heidi, Sofia, and Elliot have been a source of rejuvenation wherever my research pursuits took me. Kana Kawai has provided joy and nourishment through long stretches of writing. My parents, Clara Gómez Steinhart and John Steinhart, met in Colombia in 1966 and instilled in me a curiosity about the world that is the DNA of this project. They are exemplary teachers both in and out of the classroom and good friends. This book is dedicated to them. I feel extraordinarily lucky to have Masami Kawai in my life. Her own gutsy film work has deepened my understanding of the art and technique of filmmaking. Her encouragement, humor, politics, and ideas have inspired this book and me.

Prologue

MOVIE RUINS

On a March morning in 2011, I met Italian cinematographer Sergio Salvati in front of Cinecittà studios on the outskirts of Rome. He had agreed to take me to the fabled Roman lot so that I could gain access to the Istituto Luce archive to view old Italian newsreels. I had meet Salvati several days before, down the road at the national film school, the Centro Sperimentale di Cinematografia. I had been doing research at the school's library, hunting for any kind of material related to Hollywood's postwar productions in Italy. I knew him from his work on Lucio Fulci's gory zombie movies and lurid thrillers. I soon learned that he was also a teacher at the Centro Sperimentale and the former head of the Italian Association of Cinematographers. A man of warmth and generosity, he was an excellent guide for my research aims.

Salvati helped me check in at the studio's front entrance and introduced me to the staff of the Luce archive. He then left me to spend the rest of the morning watching newsreels, such as *La Settimana Incom*, which reported on the "Hollywood on the Tiber" phenomenon with segments on the arrival of Hollywood stars and directors at Rome's Ciampino Airport. As is common in archival work, the footage was interesting, but it wasn't a gold mine. After a few hours, I finished and left the Luce offices only to find myself on the grounds of Cinecittà without an escort. I expected to be ushered out of the studio, but the place was deserted. The urge to wander around alone was impossible to resist. After all, here was a studio that figured prominently in my research project and movie imagination.

Established in 1937 by Benito Mussolini, Cinecittà would become the center of Italian studio production. During World War II, however, it was a target of Allied bombing and housed occupying German soldiers. The facility served as a refugee camp immediately after the war, but soon, filmmaking

FIGURE 1. A dilapidated set from the *Gangs of New York* (2002) production stands next to Cinecittà's water tank. (Photo by author, Rome, March 21, 2011)

activities resumed. Hollywood began undertaking productions at the studio in order to invest lire earnings that had been frozen by the Italian government, which intended to force US film companies to invest locally rather than repatriate this money. MGM used these frozen funds to help rebuild the lot's damaged structures so that it could produce its big-budget epic *Quo Vadis* (1951) there.[1] For much of the 1950s and into the 1960s, Cinecittà was home to countless Hollywood film shoots and an Italian production boom of genre pictures and movies by auteurs like Federico Fellini, whose work turned me on to the creative promise of cinema when I was a teenager.

As I made my way through Cinecittà, I came across artifacts of its legendary past. In a corner of the studio lot were the decaying remains of the towering statues from the Circus Maximus scenes in *Ben-Hur* (1959). I passed by Stage 5, the jumbo soundstage where Fellini conjured his dreamlike visions. In another section of the studio was the oversize Venusia half-head from *Fellini's Casanova* (1976), lying on the ground as if emerging from the earth. There were more recent relics, too. Against the back end of the lot, surrounding the studio's empty water tank, were the remains of the sets for

Martin Scorsese's *Gangs of New York* (2002, fig. 1). About a decade old, the crumbling buildings of "Five Points" New York looked like a ghost town. Even stranger were the remaining sets for the television series *Rome* (2005–7). Located about six miles from the real ruins of the Roman Forum, the fading TV fabrication of ancient Rome seemed uncanny. As with many of the postwar Hollywood productions I was studying, the producers of *Gangs of New York* and *Rome* opted to film in Cinecittà to take advantage of economic inducements and the Italians' celebrated set-building skills.

More than just evidence of Cinecittà's film shoots over the years, these movie ruins represented a hidden cinema history that I was trying to excavate.[2] Walking the desolate back lot that day, I was witness to the tangible remains of the interplay of postwar international politics, economics, and filmmaking practices that drove Hollywood to make movies around the world, in places like Cinecittà. Back in Los Angeles, my home at the time, there were casualties of this move. A film workforce had faced uncertain job opportunities partly due to the global production strategies of the US motion picture industry.[3] This tangled history of postwar Hollywood, foreign film industries, and changing production practices is the subject of this book. The excavation of these haunting movie ruins is its goal.

Introduction

"HAVE TALENT, WILL TRAVEL"

IN 1962, MGM RELEASED VINCENTE MINNELLI'S *Two Weeks in Another Town*, a film whose story reflected its own production. Partially shot in Rome, it tells the tale of a washed-up Hollywood actor who takes over directing duties on a US-Italian coproduction after the film's original director suffers a heart attack. In its depiction of production work, the film is a striking representation of a phenomenon that had been slowly reshaping Hollywood for more than a decade. Since the late 1940s, Hollywood had shot movies worldwide for a variety of industrial, financial, and aesthetic reasons. Called "runaway" productions by US labor groups, these motion pictures used both Hollywood and foreign production workers, a transcultural intermixing captured in Minnelli's film.

In one pivotal scene, the actor Jack Andrus (Kirk Douglas) visits Cinecittà studios, where Hollywood director Maurice Kruger (Edward G. Robinson) stages a sappy love scene on a boat (fig. 2). In reality, this Cinecittà is not the lot in Rome, but a replica re-created at MGM's Culver City studio. MGM's massive three-million-gallon process tank and five-story-high cyclorama stand in for Cinecittà's own water tank and backdrop (fig. 3).[1] In a surprising reversal of Hollywood's drive to make movies on location, this fictionalized version of the Roman studio reveals that after nearly fifteen years of Hollywood's runaway productions, the filmmaking trend had become so mythologized that a foreign studio was now reproduced in Hollywood. The movie's re-creation of production work is also significant. As Andrus watches the scene unfold, Kruger calls out over his megaphone for crew members to

The title above borrows from "'Have Talent, Will Travel' Retorts Tiomkin to Critics of 'Runaway,'" *Daily Variety*, August 31, 1962, 8.

I

FIGURE 2. A fictional multinational crew shoots a scene in the water tank at what is meant to be Rome's Cinecittà studios in *Two Weeks in Another Town* (1962).

FIGURE 3. The real crew filming the fictional crew around the water tank at MGM's Culver City lot. (Courtesy of the Margaret Herrick Library, Academy of Motion Picture Arts and Sciences)

turn on the wind and wave machines. A local, bilingual assistant director translates these instructions from English into Italian. Kruger shouts, "Action!" and the two lead actors, a troubled Hollywood leading man and an Italian diva, commence performing. The actor speaks English and the actress responds in a mix of Italian and English until the director yells, "Cut." The bad acting, the ham-fisted treatment of the love scene, and the artificial setting all betray Kruger's hackneyed approach to filmmaking.

While Minnelli delivers a satire of international production, he includes some noteworthy insights into the kind of global filmmaking process that Hollywood had been investing in. Characterized by an international division of labor, the film shows that certain key personnel—the director, the unit publicist, and the script supervisor—are English-speaking workers from Hollywood. Meanwhile, the rest of the crew members are an Italian-speaking labor force. At the center of the set is a bilingual Italian assistant director who translates the director's commands to the crew. We also get a bit of technical insight: the production will dub the actors' performances, allowing the lead actor from the United States and the lead actress from Italy to speak in their native languages during filming. *Two Weeks in Another Town* serves as an important reflexive moment when a Hollywood film portrayed a procedure that filmmakers had established to facilitate the collaboration of an international cast and crew in a foreign locale.

This book tells the story of how this process was instituted and how it developed from the late 1940s to the time of this film's release in 1962, a transitional era for the US film industry. It is a story of continuity and change that shows how Hollywood built up an international production operation to navigate the period's industry transformations by exporting specific studio system practices and conforming to certain conditions of foreign film industries. It is ultimately an account of Hollywood's global reach expressed in its adaptive ability to make films that had an international dimension but that were still decidedly Hollywood products.

THE PAST AND PRESENT OF HOLLYWOOD
INTERNATIONAL PRODUCTION

Hollywood's global production efforts weren't unique to the postwar era. Today, runaway productions are rampant. States with enticing tax credits and rebates vie with foreign countries that offer their own incentives to lure

Hollywood film and television work away from Southern California. The runaway phenomenon keeps Los Angeles–area film workers in a precarious employment position while it simultaneously grows regional production centers and workforces in the United States and abroad.[2] The film trades function as a de facto record of the costs and benefits of runaway production. Articles in the *Hollywood Reporter* and *Variety* track the fluctuating rate of Los Angeles–based film shoots in the face of cheaper out-of-state options while also reporting on the newest foreign studio facility that aims to entice a Hollywood production to contract out its work.[3] This push and pull of filmmaking reflects an industry always trying to negotiate flux and stability. *Runaway Hollywood* historicizes this moment of widespread runaway productions and the debates that they elicit across the motion picture and television industries. While postwar foreign production heralded some of the practices of today's runaways, particularly the outsourcing of film labor, the postwar phenomenon was different, emerging out of a set of conditions specific to the transitional moment of the late 1940s and early 1950s.

The wave of postwar runaway productions also differed from previous ventures in international production and location shooting that stretched back to the beginnings of the US film industry. In the 1910s, independent film companies based in New York and Chicago sent location units to travel throughout the United States, with the occasional jaunt abroad, in search of warmer and sunnier climates and more varied backgrounds for their fictional multireel films. Selig Polyscope, Essanay, and Lubin discharged filmmakers around the country to shoot authentic locations, especially during the winter months. Meanwhile, some companies traveled farther afield. The Vitagraph Company set up operations in Paris and Jamaica, while the Independent Moving Pictures Company deployed a unit to Cuba for exteriors. Intending to bring viewers stories set against distant backdrops, the Kalem Company, which didn't have its own studio, sent its filmmakers and players to Ireland, Egypt, and the Holy Land. Despite these international location trips, the future of US commercial production would take root domestically. Out of these companies' repeated location treks to Southern California, a film colony emerged that benefited from good weather, diverse environments, and an open-shop labor pool, eventually evolving into the production center of Hollywood.[4]

By the mid-1910s, Hollywood companies reduced off-the-lot shooting because of its expense and attendant logistical complications. Improved studio facilities and the growing mastery of lighting techniques and production design all contributed to a decrease in filming on location.[5] With the transition to sound in the late 1920s and into the early 1930s, the majority of Hollywood films moved indoors in order to control the recording of dialogue and to take advantage of the infrastructure that studios had invested in.[6] Foreign locales were replicated through set design, or studio process departments rear projected footage of lands abroad onto screens, which actors performed in front of. Filmmakers also fabricated foreign exteriors on the studio back lot, the studio "ranch," and in the wide-ranging environs surrounding Los Angeles. In 1957, industry analyst Dorothy B. Jones looked back on this studio filmmaking trend and summarized, "There used to be a saying in Hollywood that any place or any thing under the sun could be recreated on the back lot. Producers had reasoned: Why go to tremendous expense and become embroiled in the many difficulties inherent in taking a production unit abroad if it can be shot just as well or better on the back lot?"[7] The notion that the landscape in and around Los Angeles could fulfill any demand of story setting was embodied in the industry maxim: "A rock's a rock, a tree's a tree—shoot it at Griffith Park."[8]

Even during this period, though, some filmmakers ventured out of Southern California to shoot fresh scenery to add spectacle and realism to genres such as Westerns and adventure pictures. King Vidor's *Billy the Kid* (1930) was shot on location in the Southwest, while Raoul Walsh's *The Big Trail* (1930) was filmed in the Northwest and Southwest. MGM produced a series of "outdoor" pictures, including *Trader Horn* (1931) in British East Africa and the Belgian Congo, *Eskimo* (1934) in the Arctic, and *Mutiny on the Bounty* (1935) in the South Pacific. John Ford, who excelled at location shooting, balanced studio filming with exterior work throughout his career. In *Stagecoach* (1939) he portrayed Monument Valley located in the Navajo Nation, a territory that would become a cinematic icon in both his movies and popular culture.

During World War II, trends shifted as wartime restrictions on building movie sets forced some film companies to shoot on location. Additionally, with a shortage of lighting and studio space and an intensifying focus on realism in combat documentaries, more filmmakers opted to shoot movies in authentic locales.[9] After the war, even though the limits on set building were eased, location filming both in the United States and abroad continued to increase due to some critical disruptions within the industry. In 1948, the Supreme Court's Paramount Decision forced studios to separate their production and distribution operations from their domestic theatrical chains. The breakup of vertical integration coincided with a drop in audience numbers and the rise in competition from television and new leisure-time activities. As part of the postwar retrenchment effort, studios began cutting overhead and selling off their back lots. As another cost-saving solution, film companies found that labor expenses were cheaper outside of California. Developments in faster film stock and more portable camera and sound equipment also advanced the move to locations.[10]

But location shooting was not a quick fix for all studios, since making a film off the lot, especially in a distant foreign location, could be expensive. Some companies tried to shorten location-filming schedules to cut down on costs, while others opted to curtail location treks and instead reconstruct foreign exteriors domestically.[11] Twentieth Century-Fox changed plans on a pair of films to be shot in North Africa to economize. For the international production of *The Desert Fox* (1951), North African scenes were re-created in California, while Arizona stood in for North Africa in *David and Bathsheba* (1951).[12] Still, certain postwar filmic trends reflected a growing naturalism that was heightened by working on location. In 1945, Fox studio and producer Louis de Rochemont made *The House on 92nd Street* and initiated a cycle of films referred to as "semi-documentary" that included Henry Hathaway's *13 Rue Madeleine* (1947) and Elia Kazan's *Boomerang!* (1947). Characterized by procedural narratives and stories often based on true events, the films derived much of their appeal to realism from extensive location shooting.[13] By drawing on techniques associated with documentaries, these films, according to *American Cinematographer*, employed a style that personified "the essence of reality."[14] In 1947 these stylistic changes provoked film critic James Agee to write, "One of the best things that is happening in Hollywood is the tendency to move out of the place—to base fictional pictures on fact, and, more importantly, to shoot them not in painted studio sets but in actual places."[15]

The story of *Runaway Hollywood* picks up once location shooting became an increasingly viable option for Hollywood filmmakers. During this period, the decision to shoot overseas rested on a set of geopolitical and financial conditions that were emerging in Europe. Because of financial volatility after the war, a number of Western European governments froze the earnings of Hollywood companies as a protectionist measure. By restricting the outflow of dollars, they hoped to force US movie studios to invest their earnings in local business activities. Viewing these maneuvers as highly unfavorable to its market access, the Hollywood film industry began negotiations with the United Kingdom, Italy, and France to create terms more advantageous to the United States. The ensuing pacts of the late 1940s eliminated import taxes, set more agreeable import quotas on the number of foreign films that could enter these European countries, remitted partial earnings, and—most important for the rise of runaway production—established the conditions to apply frozen funds toward Hollywood's foreign productions. Soon afterward, studios and independent film companies began using these frozen monies for their own productions, especially in Western Europe, where they could find skilled film workers, soundstages, and infrastructure to support this work. The desire to utilize these funds—along with the need for authentic foreign backdrops, cheap labor, tax incentives, foreign subsidies, and coproduction deals—laid the groundwork for Hollywood to make movies abroad in the postwar era.

We can consider the specific financial, industrial, and aesthetic reasons for shooting abroad as proximate causal forces that spurred filmmaking overseas.[16] Larger cultural events were factors, too. Observations from industry leaders about a changing postwar visual culture in the United States provide another context out of which international productions emerged. For many film companies, the authentic foreign locations of these productions became a way to differentiate their products and to entice US audiences who had been lured away by other leisure pastimes, especially television. Even though TV would eventually aim for realism through documentary techniques, with cinema—as promotional campaigns drove home—producers could more fully represent foreign locations through color and wide-screen technologies and deliver to audiences a vividness that TV could not yet approximate. In 1951, *Daily Variety* reported that Twentieth Century-Fox's production head Darryl F. Zanuck intended to shoot his company's movies in foreign locations whenever the subject matter called for it. For Zanuck, location shooting was one way for the film industry to successfully compete with TV.[17] Producer Irving Allen shared a similar view in suggesting that the future of Hollywood was in international production and that diverse location work would bring audiences back to the cinemas.[18]

Looking more broadly to cultural shifts, some filmmakers reflected on the increasing importance of shooting movies around the globe as a greater awareness of the wider world took hold among the public. For an industry trying to understand a changing filmgoing audience, the effects of World War II could help rationalize the notion that viewers' perceptions of the world were developing. The horizon-spanning experience of the war reported via radio, newspapers, and newsreels seemed to bring the US population a greater recognition of lands abroad. Through foreign-set stories staged in authentic overseas surroundings, filmmakers tried to exploit this knowledge while also capitalizing on the firsthand experience of the world that both foreign audiences and US military veterans had.[19] Cinematographer John Alton concluded in 1949, "During the war, millions of soldiers were sent to various locations to shoot, but not motion pictures. These men know a real London fog, were disappointed in the women of the jungle, and recognize Rio, Budapest, or Cairo when they see them on the screen. No more will they buy Hollywood-made Africa. Backgrounds now have to be authentic."[20] For Alton, the exploits of military duty made the studio-bound treatment of foreign characters and settings no longer acceptable. It's worth noting that the problem as it was perceived at the time lay not in exoticized portrayals of foreign places, but rather in the lack of authenticity of process photography and soundstage work. Producer William Perlberg appealed to more financial rationales. He argued that re-creating foreign backdrops in Hollywood studios was no longer practical due to the economic need to innovate: "Competition for the entertainment dollar has wedded us to big films and to global stories. Clarity of pictures and size of screen are increasingly taxing the abilities of our art directors to provide believable exterior settings. Our magic 'make-do' wand that has served us so well for almost fifty years is losing its power. When it comes to making Paris on the back lot, our trick bag is falling apart at the seams."[21] Filmmakers wanting to capture Paris and other foreign locales therefore had to go to the real places.

So, starting in the late 1940s, Hollywood film companies went abroad, and by the 1960s had undertaken hundreds of productions. These runaway films were a major concern for labor groups, who wanted to track the phenomenon to figure out the impact of foreign shoots on domestic job opportunities. In the mid-1950s the Hollywood Film Council of the American Federation of Labor (AFL) commissioned labor historian Irving Bernstein to produce a study examining changes in the industry and how these transformations affected employment. Published in 1957, *Hollywood at the Crossroads* attempted to explain the reasons for runaway productions, or what Bernstein called "American-interest films produced abroad."[22] He compiled data from the *Hollywood Reporter*'s production calendar to determine the number of foreign-shot productions from 1949 to 1957. His findings revealed that 314 features were shot abroad during this period. Broken down year by year, the number of such productions increased over time, representing 5 percent of total Hollywood productions in 1949 and 15 percent in 1956.[23] The numbers pointed to the growing trend, but they were also somewhat inexact. While trusted by the industry, the *Hollywood Reporter*'s production calendar was far from complete, since it listed films that didn't always go into production, and it overlooked other films that were actually in pro-

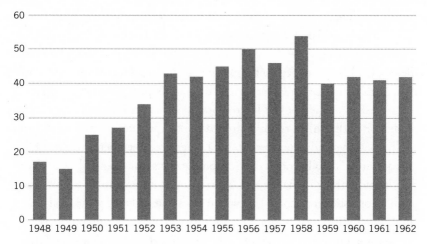

CHART 1. Hollywood's International Productions, 1948–1962.

duction. Nevertheless, future studies have replicated Bernstein's data in their analyses of Hollywood's runaway productions.[24]

In establishing a historical account of the runaway phenomenon, a retrospective view proves more fruitful. Examining the data on completed movies rather than features that were in the making can give us a better, if still provisional, sense of the frequency of runaway productions. The *American Film Institute Catalog* is a useful resource in this regard. Surveying the list of Hollywood productions from 1948 to 1962, roughly the period of this book, yields some telling results. During this time span, major Hollywood studios and other established US film companies released 563 films in which principal photography took place outside of the United States. Chart 1 reveals an upward trend in these kinds of productions from the late 1940s through the 1950s, with a peak in 1958. The numbers then plateau at around 40 pictures a year by the early 1960s. (See the appendix in this volume for a list of these films.) While this year-by-year data is difficult to compare to Bernstein's figures, the rate of productions abroad reveals that this phenomenon was robust, diverse in its shooting locations, and decidedly global.

Articulating what qualifies as an international production is central to understanding these numbers. The definition of "runaway production" was a contentious issue during this period, since the term took on different meanings based on what financial and geographic factors were being considered. Establishing what was a Hollywood production made abroad for the above data and the larger book project is more fixed. Borrowing from Irving

Bernstein's characterization of an "American-interest" film, this study delineates a Hollywood international production according to a series of identifiable financial, geographic, and labor conditions.[25] First, a Hollywood studio or a US-based independent film company financed these movies in whole or in part. Second, a significant piece of these films' principal photography was accomplished outside of the United States, either on location, in a foreign studio, or both. Third, the films relied on key production personnel from Hollywood, typically the director, and foreign crew members. This set of factors demarcates Hollywood's overseas productions from some adjacent examples, including movies that have foreign settings but were shot in a Hollywood studio (domestic productions) or foreign films that included some Hollywood financing (for instance, a coproduction that played as a foreign product).

Focusing on these international productions, *Runaway Hollywood* traces the development of production practices and location work up to the early 1960s, when Hollywood's foreign activities began to transform. By this time, Hollywood companies were modifying their involvement in global movie shoots. The much-publicized budget overruns of films such as *Mutiny on the Bounty* (1962) and *Cleopatra* (1963) were evidence that shooting abroad was not always cost-effective, especially with production expenses increasing overseas.[26] Concurrently, unions continued their campaigns against runaway production, eventually working with producers in 1962 to form the Hollywood Joint Labor-Management Committee on Foreign Film Production, which promoted policies toward reducing overseas filmmaking.[27]

In addition, some of the economic incentives that had previously spurred runaway productions, such as frozen funds and tax exemptions on foreign wages, no longer held sway. Over the course of the 1950s, as European economies strengthened, countries relaxed their remittance restrictions, which allowed Hollywood companies to repatriate more of their foreign earnings. President John F. Kennedy also signed into law a tax-revision bill that limited the income tax exemption for US citizens residing abroad, thereby undercutting a factor that had impelled some movie stars to take up residence and work in foreign countries.[28] In the California gubernatorial election year of 1962, incumbent governor Pat Brown and his Republican rival Richard Nixon took an intensified interest in fighting runaway productions and protecting domestic work.[29] By the mid-1960s, the press was reporting a noticeable increase in Los Angeles–based production.[30]

Indeed, motion pictures such as *The Greatest Story Ever Told* (1965) and parts of *Spartacus* (1960) proved that big-budget epics could be made domestically.[31] Billy Wilder's *Irma la Douce* (1963), which relied on some background footage shot in Paris but with a majority of the film executed on a Parisian set in Los Angeles, was touted for its ability to accurately reproduce foreign scenery on Hollywood back lots. "We're reversing runaway[s] by bringing Paris to Hollywood," declared the film's producer, Harold Mirisch, in 1962.[32] In fact, his company was reported to have conducted a study that suggested movies shot overseas could be produced more effectively and with greater technical skill in Hollywood.[33] Also, much to the approval of many in the industry, the Screen Actors Guild in 1962 decided to not raise wage rates, a move that was meant to serve as an incentive for Hollywood films to be shot domestically.[34]

As these changes were occurring in the United States, overseas film activities took a slightly different form through the proliferation of Hollywood's subsidiaries abroad and their investment in more distinctly foreign films. While US companies had created foreign subsidiaries throughout the postwar period for the production of "Hollywood" films, US dollars were increasingly financing the production of what were legally deemed British, Italian, and French films starting in the late 1950s. According to the British National Film Finance Corporation, US sources provided 75 percent of the funding for British films in 1965–66. In 1967–68, the percentage continued to rise.[35] The foreign subsidiaries of Hollywood studios similarly increased their investments in "local" films in France and Italy in the 1960s.[36]

Simultaneously, European industries were experiencing a creative surge in film production with the British and French New Waves and Italian films stimulated by Italy's "economic miracle." By the early 1960s, these motion pictures made Hollywood production seem "old fashioned and creaky," according to Carl Foreman, a blacklisted screenwriter and producer who set up a production company in London. He added, "There is nothing here to compare with the ferment in Great Britain, Italy, France or even Poland."[37] Paradoxically, by investing in rebuilding the filmic infrastructures in Western Europe to support runaway productions, Hollywood accelerated the resurgence of film industries that became its own competition.[38] Ever ready to adapt, though, Hollywood companies capitalized on this trend by financing some of these productions and distributing them on the art film market for a receptive domestic audience.[39] Transnational synergies emerged during the 1960s, too, as the US film industry invested in what Peter Lev calls "Euro-American art films" such as Jean-Luc Godard's *Contempt* (1963) and Michelangelo Antonioni's *Blow-Up* (1966). This work blended the commercial sensibilities and investment of Hollywood with the aesthetic practices and directors of European art cinema.[40] The convergence of the abovementioned factors, mostly driven by economics and industry changes, points to 1962 as a significant moment of transition for Hollywood's postwar international filmmaking efforts, which also marks the end of this study.

Surveying the late 1940s to the early 1960s, *Runaway Hollywood* demonstrates that the industry's international productions functioned as a global strategy to exploit the financial and industrial flux of the postwar era. Various studies have analyzed the economic reasons for postwar runaway productions.[41] However, the ways that Hollywood filmmakers executed these productions, and the influence of this work on film aesthetics, remain underresearched. This book details the methods that Hollywood movie companies utilized to carry out productions in foreign countries away from the Los Angeles–area infrastructure that had long supported them. These methods reflected an adaptability that was always present in the industry's moviemaking process but that became more pronounced abroad as filmmakers mixed Hollywood and foreign services, craft practices, and labor pools. The effect of this mode of international production on the visual style of the films is also a focus of the book. Mirroring the adaptability of overseas production, location shooting became equally versatile. Filmmakers made locations a more prominent component of a film's visual design while simultaneously bringing these locales in line with the conventions of Hollywood story and style. All of these operations reveal that Hollywood's global might rested on its ability to maintain its practices and styles so that it could continue with business as usual.

Addressing these concerns in the subsequent chapters and case studies requires reconstructing the conditions of international productions. To do this, the book relies on primary materials gathered and viewed in the United States and Europe: studio production records, the personal papers of filmmakers, US State Department files, the trade and popular press, film professional publications, interviews with veteran crew members, and the movies themselves. These materials are vital records for unraveling the runaway production trend from diverse and sometimes competing perspectives, from crew members to industry policy makers. Synthesizing this evidence offers insight into the continuities and changes of postwar international production and a more complete picture of postwar Hollywood history. To guide this inquiry, this study is built around three broad concepts: the globalization of Hollywood, transcultural production work, and the history of film style. Each of these concepts provides context for understanding the significance of postwar international production within the study of cinema and media history.

Hollywood's involvement in postwar international production was a development in the industry's process of globalization. By the mid-1910s, Hollywood had established a global distribution network by opening sales offices around the world.[42] In the ensuing decades, the industry became a dominant cultural force by taking over many international film markets. It even enlisted Hollywood's self-regulating body, the Production Code Administration, to reach as wide an audience as possible by constructing culturally acceptable films that avoided censorship restrictions around the world.[43] Although some markets were closed during World War II, this dominance continued after the war, prompting certain countries to strengthen protectionist measures, such as import and screen quotas that safeguarded the showing of local films and the freezing of foreign box-office earnings. With moviegoing attendance falling in the United States, foreign box-office revenue was critical to the success of Hollywood studios. Some statistics suggested that foreign markets made up 40 percent of studios' theatrical revenue for the early postwar period. So Eric Johnston, the head of the Motion Picture Association of America (MPAA) and its Export Association (MPEA), worked hard to negotiate with foreign governments to ease these protectionist maneuvers, often enlisting the help of the US Departments of Commerce, Justice, and State.[44] From the perspectives of both Hollywood and the US government, these film trade deals fell under the guise of "internationalism," an ideal that promoted cooperation among nations.[45] Such a notion, however, obscured Johnston's pro-free-trade tactics that attempted to advance the unfettered distribution of Hollywood films. Internationalism also shielded the imbalance of power between a forceful Hollywood and foreign industries still recovering from the war.

As *Runaway Hollywood* establishes, Hollywood's postwar productions abroad emerged out of the conditions of these trade deals. However, the process of making these films was distinct from the industry's aggressive distribution practices and market dominance, which have been characterized as instances of Hollywood's cultural imperialism.[46] The realities of postwar global filmmaking complicate this portrait of power. At the level of investment, labor, and production practices, the US film industry's involvement in productions abroad was an example of cross-industry exchange. Certainly, US companies and filmmakers often dictated the terms of this exchange, but foreign industries welcomed Hollywood production and financing at the same time that they resisted it. This assessment squares with a number of studies of post-war Hollywood's international film relations that portray not only the moments of domination but also the instances of foreign resistance and cooperation.[47] Building on these histories, this book argues that Hollywood's global power was an adaptive process that conformed to the needs of foreign industries even as Hollywood forcefully pursued its own financial objectives. In this way, Hollywood's overseas production operation both reshaped *and* adjusted to European filmmaking methods in order to continue generating films that adhered to Hollywood's stylistic conventions.

These international exchanges portended some of the processes of contemporary global film production, such as the use of cheaper foreign labor, the reliance on overseas production centers, and the steadfast pursuit of economic incentives. Despite certain parallels, postwar runaway productions did not operate within the intensified financial interdependencies of today's global markets, and they were not the products of massive media conglomerates.[48] Postwar runaways were the result of film companies attempting to internationalize a mode of production in an exploratory and initially piecemeal fashion, which over time coalesced into an industry strategy. *Runaway Hollywood* aims to fill in the historical background of global Hollywood today. To compose this history, this study takes a Hollywood perspective, asking how studio filmmakers undertook the shooting of films overseas. Nevertheless, in order to substantiate these productions as instances of global exchange, I draw on historical materials from Europe and interviews with foreign personnel to consider the experiences of overseas crews from the United Kingdom, Italy, and France in collaborating with Hollywood companies. To provide a fuller sense of the scope of Hollywood's international production activities, this study will at times consider location shooting around the world, including neighboring countries such as Mexico, where Hollywood had important ties to the Mexican industry, and more distant locales like Tahiti, which provided unparalleled backdrops. But the specifics of international production work will concentrate on the UK, Italy, and France for some key reasons.

While the postwar geopolitical situation in these countries varied, the three nations shared certain commonalities in their relationship to Hollywood. After a series of agreements in the late 1940s, the UK, Italy, and France attracted Hollywood production with a mixture of access to frozen currency, infrastructure, and the promise of authentic foreign locations. Throughout the postwar era, these countries drew the largest number of Hollywood productions in Europe. These nations were also vital overseas markets with large filmgoing audiences, which resulted in high frozen earnings that could be applied to Hollywood productions. Although some of these countries' soundstages fell into disuse or were damaged during the war, working production centers still existed in London, Rome, and Paris, all of which could provide a labor pool and studio space to support big-budget Hollywood filmmaking. Hollywood's international productions would eventually help fund these industries by renting out studios, updating them, and hiring foreign film workers. My assessment of this global exchange is carried out with an eye to how the foreign film industries both shaped Hollywood productions and were influenced by them.

TRANSCULTURAL PRODUCTION

In going abroad to shoot motion pictures in these countries, Hollywood filmmakers encountered some production practices that resonated with the US industry's way of making movies and other diverging methods. I contend that this encounter wasn't so much transnational as it was transcultural. The concept of transnationalism within cinema and media has generated rich insights into the migration of filmmakers, the distribution patterns of films, and the contested identity of national cinemas.[49] In terms of the geopolitics and the multi-country financing of postwar runaway productions, these films were indeed a transnational phenomenon. But in trying to understand exactly how Hollywood *filmmakers* made productions in other countries, the notion of transnationalism lacks a certain precision to explain the specific processes and practices. As Hollywood filmmakers—who were themselves diverse in nationality—went abroad, their work was less a reflection of national identity than of Hollywood's production culture: its division of labor, its routines, its on-set rituals, and its shared sense of a work community.

Within the subfield of cinema and media production studies, recent scholarship on production cultures has sparked new insights into the interactions of contemporary media practitioners and how production work is a meaningful cultural practice.[50] Expanding on these concerns through an approach that is historical and international, *Runaway Hollywood* argues that postwar runaway productions were transcultural in their mixing of labor, languages, and craft practices.[51] Treating runaway production as a transcultural activity helps explain how Hollywood personnel, who had long worked within the studio system, were able to produce films in substantially different working environments abroad. Over the decades, Hollywood studios had developed a way of making movies that supported the mass production of films. However, once Hollywood companies began to broaden their production operations globally, studio filmmakers working overseas had to adapt to different production cultures and become more versatile in their approach. This shift resulted in a more transcultural way of making movies, in which filmmakers continued to employ practices established in the studio system while complying with some of the methods and union rules of foreign industries.

Scholarship in production studies has also sparked interest in the lived experienced of film workers, especially "below-the-line" crew members as opposed to "above-the-line" creative and managerial personnel.[52] My own study is concerned with the experience of film workers of all ranks who went overseas and faced the challenges of working on foreign locations with international crews, often after decades of operating on studio lots. A handful of above-the-line directors and producers, such as John Huston, William Wyler, Vincente Minnelli, and John Houseman, have prominent roles in this book, though I do not intend to advance an auteurist agenda. This project engages with creative choices and craft practices, and consequently, directors and producers receive attention because they represent the forces that directly shaped aesthetic and managerial decisions. In addition, foreign union rules sometimes restricted the importation of Hollywood personnel to only directors and producers. Nonetheless, understanding the nature of production work requires that we investigate the contributions of below-the-line workers as well: production managers such as Henry Henigson and C. O. Erickson; cinematographers like Oswald Morris; and script supervisors such as Sylvette Baudrot. While these individuals are more often footnotes in cinema history, they were pivotal in impacting the logistics and techniques of postwar foreign filmmaking.

STYLISTIC HISTORY

Postwar Hollywood was a stylistically heterogeneous period, and foreign location shooting contributed to this variety. Much has been written about how Hollywood developed new color, wide-screen, and stereoscopic technologies as a response to the loss of audiences in the early 1950s.[53] Some scholars have examined how location shooting both in the United States and abroad added to this mix, contributing to the formation of new postwar film trends such as "cosmopolitan" films, "travelogue romances," and motion pictures influenced by the "journalistic authenticity" of wartime newsreels.[54] My own assessment of foreign location work amplifies these cultural histories to offer a detailed stylistic history that investigates how changes in the film industry, technologies, and production practices affected location shooting.

To inform this investigation, I look to other histories of Hollywood film style, which effectively synthesize the interactions of industry policy, production methods, and aesthetics to construct an account of continuity and change.[55] Like these studies, I examine how large-scale forces, such as a more international mode of production, impacted stylistic practices, namely location shooting. In my analysis of location work, I turn to the useful structuring concept of "norms" to show how filmmakers who went abroad could draw on a set menu of options to compose shots in real spaces and combine these shots with new technologies such as wide-screen.[56] Once again, a flexible dynamic of stability and change surfaces, in which filmmakers looked to enduring compositional conventions while at the same time finding inventive ways to highlight the visual appeal of real locales.

As a historical study of foreign location shooting, this book recounts the technical and aesthetic challenges that Hollywood filmmakers faced when they traveled to locations abroad, and the unique solutions they brought to their work. Ultimately, through an examination of Hollywood's overseas productions from the late 1940s to the early 1960s, *Runaway Hollywood* provides a historical account of how film companies exported production around the world, as well as the effect of this move on visual style. The sum of these efforts illuminates how Hollywood created a more global production operation at a time of industry transition.

FOUNDATIONS, PRODUCTION, AND STYLE

To conduct this historical inquiry, I move across various interrelated concepts: economics, geography, industry politics, craft practices, production cultures, and film style. Part I establishes some of the foundational contexts that informed Hollywood's international productions. Leading off this section, chapter 1 systematically categorizes Hollywood's runaway productions based on three distinct factors: financing (where the film's funding came from); geography (where the film was shot); and the relationship between the story's setting and the film's shooting location (whether the film was set and shot in the same place). These factors shaped the making of these films and the debates surrounding the runaway trend. They also show that a term like "runaway production" was debatable, and reveal considerable variation in how organizations defined the phenomenon from the late 1940s to the early 1960s.

Each section of the book incorporates a case study to provide a specific illustration of the general characteristics of international production in each chapter. In the first case study, I examine John Huston's *Moby Dick* (1956), a film that was coproduced by US independent company Moulin Productions and Britain's ABPC and cofinanced and distributed by Warner Bros. This case study considers how the conflicts surrounding runaway production played out on a film that was set partly in the United States but shot entirely abroad. This analysis also probes the economic and political dimensions of runaway production with a look at how director John Huston dealt with tax evasion and red-baiting Hollywood unions. The patterns in how international productions such as *Moby Dick* were financed, organized, and debated establish the basis for understanding how these films were executed, the main theme of part II.

Building on the foundation of economics and geography from the first part, chapters 2 and 3 pursue the question of how these productions were carried out once Hollywood filmmakers decided to make a motion picture abroad. This section delves into the continuities and changes in production practices as Hollywood moved its filmmaking activities from the greater Los Angeles area to the UK, Italy, and France—three countries that hosted the heaviest concentration of runaways in postwar Europe. I survey dozens of productions to identify a set of prominent characteristics that typify Hollywood's system of production overseas. These characteristics range from the organizational support that studio foreign offices offered to the growing significance of location production management, and from the collaboration of Hollywood and foreign personnel to the supervision of these productions by studio personnel back in Hollywood. Each of these features signals that Hollywood developed a more adaptable and transcultural mode of production that continued certain established studio practices while conforming to foreign film industries. In this way, Hollywood's global might was characterized by a process of bending to and refashioning foreign production cultures to continue turning out films that adhered to Hollywood's aesthetic regimes.

The second case study explores William Wyler's *Roman Holiday* (1953), a Paramount production that was shot entirely in Rome, both on location and at Cinecittà studios. This case study looks closer at the logistical challenges of overseas productions, examined in part II, while shedding light on the specific experiences of working in Italy. The making of the film demonstrates the importance of production management through the figure of Henry Henigson, and it reveals the ways that Paramount Studios supervised the film shoot from Hollywood. The production also shows how Hollywood personnel exported their ideas about filmmaking practices while simultaneously adjusting to certain Italian methods. Balancing the wide-ranging account of the previous chapters, the analysis of *Roman Holiday* details the procedures that shaped the creative decisions of filming on location, a topic investigated in the next section.

Part III analyzes how shooting overseas affected the style of these movies. Because Hollywood's international ventures relied on a more adaptable mode of production, filmmakers were able to continue making motion pictures that were stylistically similar to films made back in Hollywood studios. While certain genres such as adventure pictures and historical epics became more prominent, these films adhered to the stylistic norms that had shaped Hollywood moviemaking for decades. However, location shooting became more prominent in these movies. In an era when Hollywood studios needed to differentiate their films from one another and from television, foregrounding authentic foreign settings became a vital way to promote this work.

To illustrate the full sweep of off-the-lot filming, chapter 4 moves beyond productions shot just in Western Europe to illustrate how Hollywood filmmakers harnessed authentic foreign locations from around the globe. I examine the logistical and technical factors that shaped the aesthetics of location shooting, including the role of location scouting and the development of wide-screen technologies. Surveying a wide sampling of movies, I show how Hollywood filmmakers selected locations, filmed them using conventions of composition, and found expressive ways to represent authentic foreign scenery. This chapter refines the large-scale issues of economics, geography, and production practices from the earlier chapters to uncover the precise creative decisions of location shooting.

The final case study profiles Vincente Minnelli's *Lust for Life* (1956), a biopic of Vincent van Gogh produced by MGM. The CinemaScope color film combined studio shooting on MGM's Culver City soundstages with location work abroad. This study illuminates how authentic locales became bold decorative elements and a central feature of the film's narrative, in which the depiction of real places conformed to the conventions of Hollywood storytelling.

The book finishes with a brief reflection on MGM's mega-production of *Mutiny on the Bounty* (1962) and a major pitfall of location shooting: budget overruns. Even a handful of inspired location ideas, rendered in Ultra Panavision, couldn't remedy a barrage of production setbacks in the South Pacific. The spectacular failure of *Mutiny on the Bounty* became a cautionary tale for Hollywood, which would modify some of its international strategies beginning in the early 1960s. The study then puts forward some concluding thoughts about the legacy of postwar production abroad and its connection to today's globalized film and media industries.

By moving from the general to the specific, this book unpacks the phenomenon of Hollywood international filmmaking to reveal how financing, geography, and settings interacted with the international mode of production that typified overseas moviemaking. This mode's production practices and means of organization, in turn, commingled with the aesthetic decisions involved in location shooting. *Runaway Hollywood* tells the story of how filmmakers assumed a transcultural method of production and hit upon solutions to working on locations far from an industry that they were accustomed to. The work they undertook helped solidify Hollywood's global power, which was at once accommodating and assertive. In the end, this is a story that helps provide some perspective on the globalized world of today.

PART I

———

Foundations

CHAPTER I

All the World's a Studio

THE DESIGN AND DEBATES OF POSTWAR
"RUNAWAY" PRODUCTIONS

TOWARD THE END OF THE 1940S, articles on Hollywood's international production activities began to appear in US magazines and newspapers, which provided accounts of the growing phenomenon of Hollywood films shot overseas. Using impressive photo layouts, these reports represented stars and moviemakers working in a variety of foreign locales and relying on local film industries. In 1948, *Collier's* captured director Gregory Ratoff and Orson Welles shooting the US-Italian coproduction *Black Magic* (1949) on location in Rome: "The Americans have been delighted with Italian artistic perfection. Costumes, sets and wigs have cost a tenth to a hundredth of what they would in America. Italian technicians, despite time out for Chianti, have proved amiable and adaptable."[1] A year later, in 1949, the *New York Times Magazine* presented a photo spread on Hollywood talent working and relaxing in Italy and its capital, what was then being referred to as "Hollywood-on-the-Tiber" (fig. 4). The piece attempts to explain the reasons for the influx of Hollywood actors and filmmakers: "For producers, part of Italy's lure has been the unblocking of frozen Hollywood funds. But part, too, has been Italy's own resurgence in film production."[2]

By the early 1950s, as international production continued to flourish, the popular press followed Hollywood's foreign activities not just in Western Europe but all over the globe. The *Los Angeles Times* published a photo essay entitled "Hollywood Now Reigns over Vast International Domain" and depicted Hollywood personnel working in Rome, England, Nicaragua, India, Monaco, and Mexico.[3] In a similar news item, the *New York Times* printed images of Hollywood talent making films in Rome, England, Paris, Bavaria, Quebec, Israel, and the Fiji Islands, under the pithy title "Hollywood Studio—The World." "In its growing enthusiasm for making movies about

JENNIFER JONES—Italy's Aldo Fabrizzi, known to American film-goers for his work in "Open City" and "To Live in Peace," meets the vacationing Miss Jones during a dance in Rome.

JOAN FONTAINE—The star of "September," new American movie, chats with producer Hal Wallis during a lull in shooting of Italian scenes. The film will be completed in Hollywood.

INGRID BERGMAN—A scene from her new film, "Stromboli," with the star as a fisherman's wife. The film, directed by Roberto Rossellini, was shot mostly on Stromboli, off Italy's toe.

GRETA GARBO—The elusive actress, in Europe to appear in the projected "Lover and Friend," is caught on a sightseeing tour of Rome. The film would be her first in eight years.

FIGURE 4. Photo spread of Hollywood actors and filmmakers in Italy, *New York Times Magazine*, September 25, 1949.

faraway places," the commentary notes, "Hollywood, which in the past has recreated all known parts of the world in its studios, is now making one great studio of the world."[4]

As these articles suggest, postwar film production was moving from Hollywood soundstages and back lots to authentic locations around the globe. Film production was becoming unmoored from the Hollywood

ORSON WELLES, TYRONE POWER—Two of the stars of "The Prince of Foxes," Hollywood film drama about the infamous Borgias of Renaissance Italy, rehearse a scene on location. An adaptation of the Samuel Shellabarger novel, the movie was filmed entirely in Italy, against the authentic backgrounds of Venice, Ferrara and other stamping grounds of the Borgias.

MYRNA LOY—On the quayside of the isle of Capri, one of Hollywood's veteran performers goes over a scene with Richard Greene for the forthcoming British film production, "If This Be Sin." While not so numerous as the Americans, both British and French movie-makers are adding to Italy's growing importance as a world motion picture production center.

studio and from Hollywood the place. To be sure, the film industry's international moviemaking was an important part of this phenomenon of production decentralization. Even though these photo spreads touched on some of the factors that motivated Hollywood producers to relocate production operations overseas—factors such as frozen earnings and cheap, skilled labor—these popular press reports masked the intricacies of making these films and the hot-button debates surrounding what unions termed runaway productions.

Behind these popular accounts was a filmmaking trend that was highly contested, with individuals and organizations justifying runaway productions in different ways. The complex discussion involved different stances from unions, studios, independent producers, and industry leaders, whose positions and alignments transformed from the late 1940s to the early 1960s, a period when the industry was redefining itself. For example, shortly after studios such as MGM and Twentieth Century-Fox devised European production plans in 1948 to put frozen funds to use, the Hollywood Film Council of the American Federation of Labor (AFL), which represented the majority of film unions, voiced its complaint about the number of films that were being shot overseas.[5] Created in 1947 to unify the industry's various labor groups associated with the AFL, the Film Council would be a steady and vocal opponent of runaways. Similarly, the Screen Actors Guild (SAG) threatened to protest the use of foreign actors instead of hiring Hollywood talent for the studios' international productions. MGM's *Quo Vadis* (1951), in particular, rankled SAG because the Italy-based production intended to use so many foreign actors and extras.[6] Despite these protests, Fox production head Darryl Zanuck maintained that his studio would continue to produce films overseas whenever stories necessitated foreign locations.[7]

Even with these articulated positions, it was difficult to pinpoint how these individuals and groups defined runaway productions. Unions coined the term "runaway" to describe films that were shot overseas to avoid paying union wages, hiring cut-rate foreign labor instead. In trade-press articles from September 1949, however, the Hollywood AFL Film Council offered tactics for fighting runaway productions *except* in the case when a film required foreign locations.[8] From its earliest investigations into these films, unions attempted to distinguish between productions that were made abroad for legitimate reasons (that is, the use of authentic locations) and projects that could be targeted as runaway productions (meaning, those that went overseas for cheap labor). But with producers often backing up their financial motives for making movies abroad with the need for authentic foreign locations, the distinction became debatable. Furthermore, the various industry stakeholders offered different ways of framing international filmmaking. Unions endorsed the pejorative term "runaway production"; the Screen Producers Guild used the more neutral "overseas production"; while MPAA/MPEA president Eric Johnston subscribed to the pro-free-trade "supplemental international productions." As I will show, runaways did not represent one *type* of production but a *mode* of production diverse in its financial interests, geographic sites, and story settings.

To begin analyzing runaway productions in a systematic way, this chapter categorizes these films based on three distinct factors that shaped their making: funding sources, geographic configurations, and the relationship between where the movies were set and where they were shot. These were critical forces that influenced the design of runaway productions and the industry debates about the runaway trend. Hollywood's ability to capitalize on a diversity of economic and geopolitical ties, as well as foreign film industries that were still recovering from the war, lays bare the calculating ways that the industry justified and sustained global filmmaking. The factors examined in this chapter point to Hollywood's strategies of self-interest, which at times benefited foreign industries. These factors also establish the context that informed how international productions were organized and executed, a topic developed in part II of this book.

ECONOMICS: FINANCING RUNAWAY PRODUCTIONS

While producers, unions, and industry leaders debated various causes for runaway productions, financial reasons were the primary, initial inducements for shooting films overseas.[9] In fact, the origin of the term "runaway production" was predicated on economic changes in the United States. During World War II, at least one mention of runaway production in the automobile industry meant overproduction in connection to the potential risk of glutting postwar markets with cars in anticipation of consumer demands.[10] Other references to runaway production during the immediate postwar period derive from the notion of unchecked costs in the manufacturing sectors and the motion picture industry.[11] With the rise of postwar foreign filmmaking, the "runaway" designation evolved to reflect various unions' resistance to production work moving abroad for financial reasons. For the Hollywood AFL Film Council, "runaway" didn't mean profligate spending but evasive productions and attendant employment opportunities that were leaving the centers of filmmaking in the greater Los Angeles area for new sites that promised economic benefits.

Within about a year of Hollywood studios' push to embark on international production, the "runaway" label entered the lexicon of the film trade press. In February 1949, an early use of the term materializes in a *Hollywood Reporter* article about the Hollywood Film Council's attempt to persuade the US government to fight "discriminatory trade barriers" that were compelling Hollywood studios to make films abroad.[12] Then in September 1949, the term seems to first appear in the *Motion Picture Daily* and *Daily Variety* in news items covering efforts by a special subcommittee of the Film Council to curb "'runaway' foreign production."[13] What's unclear in these early reports is who exactly came up with the name and at what moment. What *is* clear is that the outsourcing of production work to cheaper labor pools abroad was creating enough anxiety among unions that they needed an expression to anchor a campaign to fight the phenomenon.

In the years to come, the "runaway" moniker gained traction in the industry, eventually defining any production that left the Los Angeles area for financial reasons, but these reasons were never fixed. Just as there wasn't one kind of runaway production, there wasn't one clear financial factor that spurred Hollywood to look for production opportunities abroad. Additionally, the economic factors changed over time and converged, meaning that any production might have been motivated by multiple financial incentives. Even if the economics of runaways are difficult to bring to light, since much of this information was confidential, an analysis of the runaway phenomenon must begin with economic factors. Examining the industry discourse points us to the most probable foreign funding sources beyond production financing that came directly from studios and independent production companies. The following sources of production capital acted as essential causal forces, determining where films were shot and shaping the debates among film industry players.

Frozen Funds

Above all, the chief initial motive for shooting abroad in the postwar era was Hollywood studios' desire to access frozen foreign box-office earnings. In an effort to control the outflow of US money from their fragile economies, European governments froze the studios' earnings. The hope was that Hollywood studios and production companies would reinvest those blocked funds into film industries and foreign markets that had suffered during the war. Typically, the theatrical profits of Hollywood studios were paid out in local currencies, but due to limits on how much of a studio's earnings could be remitted, portions of the takings were held in foreign bank accounts. To access the blocked money, the studios had to gain government permission. With Hollywood's domestic market suffering as a result of decreasing audience numbers, these studios could not afford to leave their foreign earnings locked up.

One strategy for freeing up frozen currency was to invest in non-filmic activities. The Motion Picture Export Association (MPEA), the trade organization representing the Hollywood major studios in foreign markets, attempted to use frozen funds to buy local commodities and import them to the United States, where they were sold for dollars. For example, the MPEA used frozen French francs to raise an old tanker in Marseilles, refurbish it, and sail it to the East Coast to be sold. The organization also bought whiskey in Chile and shipped it stateside.[14] In a roundabout deal, the MPEA reportedly used frozen yen to build a pair of ships in Japan, which were then sent to Java, where they were traded to the Dutch for Indian rupees. This currency was then converted to pounds and finally to dollars.[15] These business transactions were nothing if not enterprising. They were also "off the record," according to Eric Johnston. The MPEA president didn't want to openly disclose these dealings to Hollywood company stockholders, who might have been concerned that profits were being generated from activities that had nothing to do with motion pictures in countries where only a fraction of film earnings could be directly transferred to the studios.[16]

Separate from the efforts of the MPEA, studios carried out investments on their own. MGM bought up apartment complexes in Copenhagen and office buildings in Australia and China. The company also invested in gold nuggets and marble in Italy and wine in Chile.[17] Other US film companies were able to unfreeze a fair amount of their earnings through shipbuilding in Italy. They also invested in construction and real estate in the UK and stock and commercial businesses in France.[18] In some ways, Hollywood's non-filmic foreign investments anticipated the move toward conglomeration in the 1960s, when non–motion picture companies such as Gulf & Western, Transamerica, and Kinney bought up movie studios to diversify their risk across an array of unrelated business ventures.

However, since Hollywood companies were still principally involved in the movie business, they concentrated their investment of frozen funds in film-related activities. In Australia, RKO applied freed-up monies to the purchase of a film lab, and Fox invested in its local newsreel division.[19] Producer Sol Lesser used blocked funds to set up overseas offices to acquire foreign films for distribution in the United States.[20] Lesser's offices also focused on purchasing foreign story properties, a plan that other US film companies pursued to utilize their frozen funds. In England, Fox bought the novel *War in Heaven* (1930), while MGM picked up the thriller *The Case of the Journeying Boy* (1949).[21] All of these activities ensured that Hollywood companies operated globally by bolstering their presence overseas.

Hollywood studios also looked to invest frozen earnings in their own overseas production opportunities. One option was to apply this money to improving foreign infrastructure that could then support their filmmaking activities. In preparation for its mega-production of *Quo Vadis* in Rome, MGM used its reserve of frozen funds to rebuild Cinecittà studios. MGM actually exceeded its balance of frozen lire with this undertaking, but because the Italian government was so eager for Metro's investment and the employment of Italian technicians, the studio struck a deal to apply future frozen earnings to the production.[22] In addition, MGM took an indirect tactic to repatriating frozen currencies from other countries to finance *Quo Vadis*. With the help of the MPEA, the US studio used some of its blocked kronor in Sweden to purchase Swedish wood pulp and import it to Italy, where it was sold for lire. The studio could then apply this money to the production of *Quo Vadis*. "It was a general house cleaning of their foreign bank accounts," as one reporter described MGM's commodity maneuvers.[23] These complicated transactions reveal the lengths to which studios were willing to go in order to recoup their profits from around the world. Despite these schemes, much of the focus of studios operating in Western Europe was on applying their frozen funds directly toward production. The industry's regulating bodies were instrumental in facilitating these deals.

Throughout the late 1940s, MPAA/MPEA president Eric Johnston, a dedicated advocate of free trade, took a series of trips to Europe on behalf of the US film industry to confront various countries' foreign protectionist measures such as import taxes, film quotas, and the freezing of earnings. The bilateral agreements that emerged from these negotiations helped set in place the requirements for accessing blocked funds and their application toward production. One of Johnston's biggest diplomatic victories was resolving the conflict over the UK's 75 percent ad valorem tax.[24] As a response to Britain's financial crisis of 1947, this tax imposed a heavy duty on all films imported into the country. Since the UK was Hollywood's most important foreign market, the tax was a major setback for Hollywood, sparking outrage across all segments of the US film industry, from union leaders to movie stars. Independent producers were especially upset because of how reliant they were on the British market, and because they lacked the financial cushion major studios had. Walt Disney, Samuel Goldwyn, Mary Pickford, and other producers cabled President Harry S. Truman and the State Department with pleas for protection.[25] The US industry eventually retaliated by placing an embargo on film exports to the UK while also scaling back production operations in Hollywood studios in anticipation of a protracted fight.[26]

The conflict resulted in the Anglo-American Agreement, signed by Johnston, Society of Independent Motion Picture Producers (SIMPP) representative James A. Mulvey, and president of the British Board of Trade Harold Wilson. Pointing to the diplomatic weight of the deal, additional representatives from the British government and the US State Department took part in the negotiations. The agreement eliminated the ad valorem duty and remitted $17 million of British earnings per year to Hollywood companies instead of freezing that money. By distributing British films in the United States and its territories, US movie companies could also earn additional dollar remittances from the UK. The British Board of Trade stipulated that these payouts were based on the condition that these companies would invest their remaining frozen earnings in real estate, story properties, distribution rights, prints, advertising, and—most importantly for moviemaking implications—film production in England.[27]

A key component of this agreement was an addendum entitled "Schedule A," which outlined a series of filmmaking-related applications that frozen funds could be put toward in the UK. Frozen sterling could be used for the purchase and renovation of studios, which gave Hollywood companies the ability to invest in infrastructure that could sustain their own productions. These frozen monies could pay for equipment, costumes, and location expenses incurred by a company. Frozen funds could also cover the costs of freight and shipping, which helped a production company pay for the transportation of equipment and film stock in and out of the UK. In addition, frozen sterling could be used to hire British actors, directors, and film crews.[28]

From the British perspective, these provisions were intended to encourage Hollywood studios and independent producers to spend their earnings in the UK and strengthen the local industry. From the US perspective, many of these terms would establish the parameters that set in motion Hollywood's British production operation. Significantly, the US negotiators fought to not put any limits on the amount of frozen funds that could be invested in any of these areas, a move that ensured a robust production plan. Indeed, a day after the deal was struck, *Daily Variety* ran the headline, "Majors Due for Heavy

Production in England."[29] However, a British control commission attempted to monitor this spending to avoid damaging its own industry. As a product of the British and US governments and film industries, the agreement was a striking instance of bilateral negotiations that would have wide-ranging consequences for filmmaking. In this way, the political and economic ramifications of this deal would shape the particular mode of production that Hollywood companies would undertake as they exported filmmaking abroad.

Once the Anglo-American Agreement was negotiated, studios began to apply their frozen earnings toward a string of British productions that could potentially qualify as quota films. Some major studios and independents had to rent out shooting space to pursue filmmaking in the UK.[30] Other studios such as MGM and Warner Bros., who owned their own British facilities, were in a favorable position to ramp up productions across the pond. Using its studio outside of London, MGM aggressively pursued a slate of British productions, beginning with *Edward, My Son* (1949). The London area would become the center of Hollywood's foreign production efforts, but moviemaking spread to other countries where studios had their frozen funds tied up. Twentieth Century-Fox embarked on a steady production schedule in Europe by investing blocked earnings in the making of *I Was a Male War Bride* (1949) in Germany and England, *Prince of Foxes* (1949) in Italy, *The Big Lift* (1950) in Berlin, *Night and the City* (1950) in London, and *The Black Rose* (1950) in Morocco and England. Due to all this production activity, Fox reportedly depleted its frozen money in England, Italy, and France by the fall of 1949.[31]

The application of frozen sterling in the UK ushered in a new era of international production, as London and its surrounding studios formed an important filmmaking center for US companies. Around the same time, Hollywood studios began applying their frozen funds in Italy and France, where similar bilateral agreements encouraged them to utilize their blocked earnings for production. In Italy, a series of pacts in the late 1940s outlined the partial remittance of earnings and the various uses of frozen lira, which included investment in cinemas, studios, film processing, and production.[32] In France, the earnings of Hollywood studios accrued in part due to the Blum-Byrnes film accord of 1946, which allowed for the unlimited release of US movies. Access to the French market was only slightly lessened by screen and import quotas that attempted to safeguard French films in French cinemas. In addition, the accord came up against some attempts at protectionist measures by the French government. Overall, though, the agreement allowed for the release of a backlog of Hollywood motion pictures that were withheld during the war.[33] As with the UK and Italy, access to the revenue of these films was controlled by a treaty that set an annual remittance rate and the conditions for accessing blocked francs. The frozen funds could be applied to the purchase of story properties, the distribution of French films, and, of course, production in the country.[34]

Initially, independent film companies faced more challenges than their studio counterparts in using frozen earnings. Represented by SIMPP and its foreign distribution arm, the Independent Film Producers Export Corporation, independent producers were often jockeying to get a seat at the table alongside the MPEA during negotiations with foreign governments to ensure their fair share of import permits, remittances, and access to blocked funds.[35] These producers were also in the difficult position of not always having enough frozen funds to mount a full production. This situation at first affected United Artists in England, since its foreign revenue belonged to a dispersed group of independent producers, which meant that the company did not have enough frozen funds to finance its own British productions.[36] As a potential solution for independent companies, producer Stanley Kramer proposed that independents pool their frozen British earnings and set up a collective London production company to produce films in England.[37] In the end, Kramer's lawyers advised him against investing frozen funds in foreign production. Instead, Kramer used his blocked funds to purchase foreign story properties, such as the 1897 play *Cyrano de Bergerac*, in the face of the pound devaluation of 1949.[38]

At various points in 1949 and 1950, Hollywood labor groups lobbied industry management and the US government to negotiate the easing of blocked foreign earnings. Unions argued that frozen funds, especially in the UK, and the resulting foreign productions were leading to unemployment in Hollywood. Union leaders even met with President Truman and Secretary of State Dean Acheson to discuss the screen quota and frozen-fund situation in the UK.[39] However, little progress came from these lobbying efforts, leaving matters in the hands of industry leaders like Eric Johnston to negotiate directly with foreign governments. As head of the studio-backed MPAA, who had cordial relations with labor groups, Johnston was in the tricky position of having to represent the studios' free-trade interests on the one hand while trying to pacify unions' demands to fight runaway productions on the other. So in order to justify deals with countries that incentivized production abroad, Johnston appealed to labor groups' anti-communist views by advancing the idea that the industry could help spread democracy through its global reach.[40] By the time Johnston testified in a 1961 Congressional hearing on the impact of foreign trade on US employment, he had intensified his pro-free-trade stance by suggesting that runaway productions, or what he termed "supplemental international productions," would have never been shot in Hollywood. He insisted that these supplemental productions would "produce revenue that comes back to provide additional income and jobs in the United States."[41]

Despite these counterarguments, unions continued their campaign against frozen funds and runaway production through the 1950s. In 1953, Roy Brewer, president of the Hollywood AFL Film Council and international representative of the International Alliance of Theatrical Stage Employees (IATSE), criticized the way frozen funds became a de facto subsidy for foreign production. At the same time, he gave an allowance to "the reasonable utilization of frozen funds," ostensibly when blocked funds were applied to non-production efforts.[42] Once again, the unions' fight against the use of frozen funds was met with mixed results, so they turned their attention to other tactics such as mounting anti-communism campaigns and opposing directors and actors who went abroad for tax benefits. For unions, a major point of contention was the eighteen-month tax loophole, which a number of Hollywood above-the-line talent exploited so that taxes on earnings for seventeen of eighteen consecutive months of living overseas were exempt. By taking advantage of the loophole, these filmmakers and stars encouraged Hollywood production to move with them. Moreover, other financial sources eventually superseded the importance of blocked earnings once European markets stabilized thanks in part to Marshall Plan aid. The frozen-fund situation also improved to some extent due to the aforementioned bilateral agreements and Hollywood's wide-ranging strategies to access those funds.[43]

Foreign Subsidies

Political economist Thomas Guback writes, "While blocked earnings were responsible for the first wave of runaway production, the availability of subsidization was the cause of its perpetuation and development into a second wave."[44] In order to revitalize their weakened film industries, foreign governments looked to creating film subsidies. In the late 1940s, Italy and France created subsidies aimed at supporting local filmmakers, and shortly afterward the UK initiated its own.[45] Even though these subsidies were intended to back domestic industries, Hollywood productions qualified for this assistance through a variety of means. Hollywood studios could apply for subsidies by creating subsidiaries in Europe and by working through foreign coproducing partners. Or they could meet the requirements for government assistance by putting together the right configuration of investments, geographic locations, and cast and crew makeup in order to qualify as a "national" production. In Italy, if a film was eligible for Italian nationality, it could receive a subsidy of 10 percent of the film's gross through a rebate and an additional smaller subsidy if the film was deemed to have cultural value by the government's central film office.[46] Qualifying for Italian nationality, however, was no small feat. The majority of a film had to be developed, produced, and processed in Italy, and the better part of the cast and crew had to be Italian.[47] In France, Hollywood companies could apply for a subsidy from the government agency Centre national de la cinématographie on the condition that a film had a French-language version, relied on a majority of French funding, and used a largely French crew.[48]

For Hollywood, one of the biggest draws of making films in the United Kingdom was its production subsidy. Known as the Eady Levy, the British Film Production Fund generated a pool of funding from a cinema admissions tax. At first, exhibitors contributed to this pool on a voluntary basis, but by 1957, the measure became statutory. Hollywood producers could apply for this subsidy in the form of a rebate on the cost of films shot in the UK.[49] Although originally intended as a financial incentive to strengthen British production, the levy prompted a concerted push by Hollywood studios to shoot films in the UK. Even some independent US producers made the case that the Eady money was the only way to bring their films into existence. Horror-film producer Herman Cohen claimed that he was unable to find film financing in the United States and had to go to England, where he received support from the Eady Levy to make his movies.[50]

Even though Hollywood production was helping to keep British studios running, US companies' participation in the Eady Levy elicited objections from segments of the British industry. Some complained that Hollywood firms were taking advantage of funding originally intended to strengthen British productions. Others protested that it was unfair for Hollywood producers to sell these films as US products stateside and as British quota pictures elsewhere while simultaneously driving up production costs in the UK.[51] In 1956, John Davis, the head of the Rank Organization and president of the British Film Producers' Association (BFPA), attempted to convince the British film industry and government to take a harder line against supporting Hollywood production. Among many proposals, Davis attempted to create a distinction between "British-British" films and "British-American" films, so that Hollywood-backed productions would be denied many of the financial perks accorded to British films, including the privilege of Eady funding. However, the BFPA did not endorse Davis's measures.[52] A year later, filmmaker Charles Frank, writing in *Film and TV Technician*, the journal of Britain's film trade union, crystallized many of these concerns by highlighting the fact that Hollywood's foreign productions were reaping the benefits of money generated by British cinemagoers and intended for British filmmakers:

> Time and again in recent months we have witnessed the fantastic spectacle where some of the biggest productions (financed with frozen money, every penny of which had been paid by the people of this country) had an American producer, an American director, an American script and one or more American stars; and each of these films was given British Quota, and all of them are eligible for money from the Eady fund, a fund specially created to help British producers in their struggle against overwhelming odds![53]

Ultimately, the writer's blame fell not on Hollywood but on the British industry for not protecting itself. This sentiment reflected a fear across the British industry rooted in cultural protectionism and the risk that it was becoming too "American."[54]

In the United States, Hollywood's use of foreign subsidies met with resistance from labor unions, too. European governments had enacted film quotas and subsidies as measures of cultural promotion and preservation. However, Hollywood unions viewed foreign subsidies as an incentive that foreign governments were using to encourage Hollywood production abroad.[55] As a countermove, unions campaigned for the US government to create its own subsidy. *Hollywood at the Crossroads*, the 1957 report on the state of the US film industry commissioned by the AFL Film Council, attributed the rise in runaway productions partially to the availability of foreign subsidies. The Film Council subsequently demanded that the government create a national subsidy similar to the UK's Eady Levy to stimulate domestic production.[56] But state and federal support remained out of reach for an industry that had traditionally kept government involvement in the film business at arm's length. While the government made overtures to reducing runaway productions, it was resistant to subsidizing a private enterprise. When union representatives asked in 1962 if the government would lend a helping hand with a film subsidy, California Governor Pat Brown rejected the notion, declaring: "Count out subsidies, which you'll never get."[57]

Debates about foreign subsidies reached a critical point in the early 1960s when a House subcommittee investigated the effect of foreign trade policies on US labor in sectors such as agriculture, transportation, and motion pictures. After testimonies from various film industry leaders and union representatives, the subcommittee recognized that foreign subsidies were the main impetus for shooting overseas. A subsequent subcommittee report charged that foreign governments' subsidization of production was in violation of the General Agreement on Tariffs and Trade, which deemed subsidies a violation of fair competition.[58] Nevertheless, little came of these hearings and reports, as the government made no moves to offer the domestic film industry either protections or incentives. Instead, Congress focused its attention on unemployment in car manufacturing and agriculture.[59] Without countermeasures, subsidies in the UK, and to a lesser extent in France and Italy, encouraged Hollywood companies to continue making films overseas into the 1960s, sometimes through their own subsidiaries.[60]

Foreign Subsidiaries

To qualify for local subsidies and bypass quota restrictions, studios set up foreign subsidiaries to serve as producing companies for international productions. A studio or independent company from the United States could establish an overseas subsidiary that qualified as a legal foreign entity with a board of directors largely made up of foreign subjects. But the US parent company could direct its policies, which was key to Hollywood studios' ability to shape these entities.[61] In Britain, Hollywood studios had already set up a number of subsidiaries in the 1930s to turn out low-budget "quota quickies" that satisfied the requirement that a certain percentage of films shown in the UK had to be indigenous products. After the war, these studios used their established subsidiaries to make what were legally deemed British films and take advantage of Eady Levy funding. MGM, Paramount, Warner Bros., Twentieth Century-Fox, Columbia, United Artists, RKO, and Disney all had subsidiaries in the UK.[62] MGM and Warner Bros., in particular, could finance an aggressive production schedule because of their subsidiaries and close ties to studio facilities. In addition, independent producers from Hollywood set up British entities, which in effect functioned more like autonomous foreign production companies than subsidiaries. In 1952, the producing team the King Brothers reportedly founded organizations in England and Italy so that the films they shot in those countries could avoid quota constraints.[63] Other British firms established by independent producers included Irving Allen's Warwick Films, Sam Spiegel's Horizon Pictures, and blacklisted screenwriter-producer Carl Foreman's Open Road Films.[64] All of these companies produced legally British films that met the criteria for British subsidies and quota-film status.

While Britain was home to the most foreign subsidiaries, France saw its share of Hollywood studio offshoots. Paramount formed a French subsidiary under the name of Les Films Marianne, while MGM launched Cypra with French producer Jacques Bar to make French-language films.[65] In the 1960s, United Artists used its Paris-based subsidiary to produce wholly French films by directors such as François Truffaut, Claude Lelouch, and Philippe de Broca.[66] These French subsidiaries underscore the fact that by the 1960s, Hollywood's foreign activities included the funding of what would qualify as full-fledged European films. In Italy, the creation of studio subsidiaries as Italian corporations had drawbacks, since a film created by any Italian company had to pay income tax and be accountable to Italian currency control regulations.[67] Some studios, such as MGM and Fox, maintained subsidiaries, while other studios, like Warner Bros., opted to only operate a branch office in Italy.[68] For both France and Italy, a Hollywood company could do better entering into coproductions to get its films made overseas.

International Coproductions

Another option for Hollywood companies wanting to make a film overseas was to seek out a coproduction deal with a foreign company or individual that could provide partial financing and talent. Beginning in the late 1940s, European industries experienced a slowdown in national productions and looked to bilateral coproductions to compensate for this reduction.[69] Officially, US film companies could not participate in a coproduction with a European country, since the bilateral agreements among European nations were in part aimed at competing with Hollywood movies. Nevertheless, both Hollywood studios and independents could participate in one of these deals through their own foreign subsidiary or under the special authorization of a foreign government by ensuring that the production fulfilled the requirements of being a national film product.[70] In France in the late 1940s, a government-sanctioned agreement was approved between US production company

Benagoss and the state-run Union générale cinématographique.[71] This pact initiated a series of Franco-US coproductions, including Rudolph Maté's *The Green Glove* (1952), which was distributed by United Artists stateside. However, such incursions into the French production landscape elicited opposition from France's Communist film unions against the agreement's support of US-interest films rather than purely domestic productions.[72]

Coproduction deals benefited the invested partners in different ways. In aligning itself with a foreign company, the US partner profited from producing what was considered a domestic film in the country where it was made, thereby bypassing quota restrictions and qualifying for local subsidies. The foreign producing partner would, in turn, achieve Hollywood-style production values for a relatively moderate investment with a film that would be distributed internationally.[73] Important European coproducers included British-based Alexander Korda, who collaborated with David O. Selznick to produce British coproductions such as *The Third Man* (1950), directed by Carol Reed.[74] French-based producer Paul Graetz struck a coproduction deal with Twentieth Century-Fox, which viewed this move as a way to foster "good will in democratic France."[75] Italians Carlo Ponti and Dino De Laurentiis had a coproduction agreement with Paramount, in which the studio cofinanced the productions and then recouped its costs by distributing the films in Italy.[76] This pact produced big-budget movies such as *Ulysses* (1955) and *War and Peace* (1956). In some cases, these coproduction deals resulted in what would have been considered British, French, and Italian films directed by foreign directors. The arrangements with these producers prefigured the coproduction deals that would become more common in the 1960s, when Hollywood studios such as United Artists, Columbia, and Universal intensified their efforts of financing foreign films and coproducing films in the UK, Italy, and France. Eventually, the larger studios, such as MGM, Fox, Paramount, and Warner Bros., moved into funding foreign films as well.[77]

A Hollywood foreign production could have any combination of the aforementioned funding sources. Oftentimes, the financial configuration was complex, as was the case on Robert Siodmak's swashbuckler *The Crimson Pirate* (1952). Principal financing was divided between the Warner Bros. studio and the independent company Norma Productions, which was run by agent Harold Hecht and actor Burt Lancaster, who starred. Shot across multiple countries with an international crew, the film also relied on three different frozen currencies. For the studio work in England at Warner's Teddington Studios and ABPC's studios, the producers used frozen pounds. For the location work in Italy, the shoot applied frozen lire. To pay for the costs of the French crew and overhauling ships docked in France that were featured in the film, the production utilized frozen francs.[78] Despite all these international financial sources, the film qualified as a British quota film because the production spent enough money in the UK. Additionally, the film's producers hid from the British Board of Trade the cost of Italian and French labor by charging these expenses to Warner's Rome and Paris offices instead of Warner's British subsidiary.[79] To be sure, the bankrolling of international productions could come off like a cunning plot.

The mixture of financing signals how by the postwar era, the funding sources of a single film could be diversified, with money coming from studios, independent companies, and foreign entities, which all represented an array of influencing forces on the film. The foreign forces, especially in the form of frozen funds, had implications for how runaway productions were coordinated. The various funding sources also demonstrate that the financial configurations tended to change over time. At first, frozen funds were an important wellspring of film financing. As the 1950s progressed, though, frozen earnings were replaced by the availability of foreign subsidies and coproduction deals. Increasingly by the 1960s, Hollywood firms backed what were deemed "legal" foreign films. Ultimately, these configurations prove that the process of financing a film was a truly international affair, with funding resources spanning the globe, a situation that was mirrored by these films' diverse shooting sites.

GEOGRAPHY: LOCATING RUNAWAY PRODUCTIONS

While Hollywood unions' application of the term "runaway production" was rooted in the economic benefits that came with shooting overseas, the expression also had geographic connotations. The designation suggested that film shoots were fleeing far beyond what the industry would eventually sanction as the Thirty Mile Zone, a centralized production region in the greater Los Angeles area, to locations abroad.[80] Perhaps more than the term's economic connotations, the notion of running away gave the label a pejorative charge of cowardice. In devising the moniker, unions were also identifying the wider geographic shifts that were occurring in postwar Hollywood, as film units were no longer bound to Los Angeles–area studios and back lots. The promise of foreign funding, cheaper crews, and authentic locations spurred film productions to move to all reaches of the globe.

From an organizational standpoint, the geographic locations had decisive ramifications. Where a film was shot determined the flow of labor, equipment, and production materials from nation to nation. Working across multiple countries posed a technical challenge of matching different locales, interiors with exteriors, and location footage with rear-screen projection. Geography also affected the national character of the cast and crew. The features analyzed below reveal that the films in question were wide-ranging in their geographic configurations, with some shot in one foreign country, others shot in multiple foreign nations, and still others shot both in the United States and abroad.

A Single Foreign Country

Films shot entirely in one foreign country typically used real-world locations and the interiors of that nation's studios, since the majority of postwar Hollywood movies still relied on some soundstage work. For Hollywood producers, shooting in a single nation provided a number of benefits. This move allowed a production to maintain a consistent cast and crew, minimize travel expenses, and focus its organization within one region. Filming the entire production in one country could more likely lead to national subsidies and help that production qualify as a quota film. In sum, the one-nation option resulted in consistency and efficiency.

In the late 1940s, certain Hollywood studios shot productions entirely in the UK to access frozen sterling and take advantage of their own British facilities. MGM undertook British productions at its Borehamwood studio while also filming exteriors in Britain. Meanwhile, other companies looked to the support of foreign-owned studios for their productions. Since Warner Bros. had part ownership of Associated British Picture Corporation (ABPC), the Hollywood company used the ABPC studios to shoot its British productions.[81] For both MGM and Warner Bros., their investments in British studios put them in a good position to apply their frozen earnings toward productions that were filmed wholly in the UK. Walt Disney Productions also undertook a number of films shot entirely in Britain with frozen money, employing primarily British casts and crews. For its first British production and inaugural live-action feature, the studio hired Hollywood director Byron

Haskin to make *Treasure Island* (1950) at Denham Studios and on location around England. Shooting a film there was not without its problems, though. The production violated child labor laws by not securing a foreign work permit from the Ministry of Labour for the film's US star, twelve-year-old Bobby Driscoll. Disney managed to carry on filming Driscoll while the case was in the appeals court process. Despite "brazenly flouting the laws of the land," the production qualified as a quota film not only because of its geographic basis but also because Disney hired principally English talent and established a British corporation along with its distributor RKO.[82]

Though Italy and France had less filmmaking infrastructure than the UK after the war to support Hollywood productions, a number of films were still shot entirely in these countries. In Italy, MGM filmed the mega-production *Quo Vadis* at Cinecittà studios and on location in areas surrounding Rome. A few years later, Paramount made *Roman Holiday* (1953) on location in Rome and at Cinecittà, where the film's postproduction work was done. In France, Allied Artists executed all of *Love in the Afternoon* (1957) at the Studios de Boulogne, with a few authentic locations captured around Paris. Although director Billy Wilder reported that the movie could have been shot entirely in Hollywood since few exteriors were used, he felt that the atmosphere of Paris could be felt in the studios—a somewhat misleading notion that obscures the practical and economic reasons for shooting the film overseas.[83]

The practice of filming interiors on foreign soundstages drew criticism from the Hollywood AFL Film Council. The labor group decried producers' assertions that foreign production was motivated by authentic locations, since the interiors could have been shot in the United States, using domestic crews.[84] Indeed, the reasons for working entirely in a single foreign country belied the financial imperatives of runaway productions. For producers, filming in foreign studios in the same country where the exteriors were done increased the chances that a production was eligible for subsidies and quota status. The decision also mitigated shipping and travel expenses. Interestingly, at least one foreign studio was sensitive to the controversy of using foreign facilities in trying to attract Hollywood productions. Germany's Studio Hamburg advertised its soundstages in a July 1962 issue of *Daily Variety* and included the caveat: "We do not encourage 'runaway' productions, we just say: 'When in Europe, then at Studio Hamburg, Hamburg West Germany.'"[85] Even foreign studios understood the political risk that some producers took in making films overseas.

Multiple Foreign Countries

Instead of focusing a film shoot in just one foreign country, a production could spread its filming sites and studio work across multiple foreign nations. This method complicated the coordination of production, since the Hollywood company had to arrange the movement of personnel and equipment across various borders and submit to the requirements of each country's filming protocols. Sometimes shooting in different nations was dictated by a story that took place in multiple foreign locales. More often, the exteriors were shot in one country and the interiors were shot in a studio in another.

Many of Hollywood's African productions were filmed in diverse countries, with location work done in Africa and studio work accomplished in Europe. In these cases, the African nations lacked the soundstages to support the extensive studio shooting of big-budget filmmaking, so Hollywood producers turned to European facilities. John Ford shot the interiors of *Mogambo* (1953) in MGM's British studios and the exteriors in various African countries and colonial territories. Nicholas Ray's *Bitter Victory* (1958) was made in La Victorine Studios in Nice, France, and on location around Tripoli, Libya. Fred Zinnemann filmed the Warner Bros. production of *The Nun's Story* (1959) in the studios of Rome's Centro Sperimentale and Cinecittà, while locations were accomplished in Belgium and the Belgian Congo. Warner Bros. was able to exploit the ties between Belgium and its colony to secure locations and shooting permissions in the Congo.[86]

Working in multiple countries could risk diluting the nationality of a film and losing its attendant quota status. If enough time, money, and hiring effort were expended in one of the host countries, however, a multi-country production could still yield quota eligibility. Even though Fox's *The Black Rose* was shot in both French Morocco and at London's Shepperton Studios, the film fulfilled the UK's 40 percent quota because the company spent most of its production budget in England, principally relying on a British crew. As a quota picture, the film could play British theaters without restrictions, and all earnings were accessed through Fox's foreign subsidiary, Twentieth Century-Fox Ltd.[87] However, Columbia's *The Victors* (1963), which was partly shot at Shepperton, lost its British quota and Eady Levy qualification because of its extensive use of foreign locations in Sweden, Italy, and France and its reliance on US and continental actors. Producer-director Carl Foreman asserted that the benefits of an international cast and the realism that was achieved by shooting on location outweighed the quota standing and subsidy.[88]

The multi-country approach carried other complications, often requiring more complex logistical synchronization than just shooting in a single foreign country. The production of Richard Fleischer's *The Vikings* (1958) employed two script supervisors, who had to coordinate with each other through correspondence from two different locations. Lucie Lichtig, working in Norway, had to communicate with Sylvette Baudrot in France to ensure that the costumes and actions of the film's Viking leads embarking in Norway during first-unit shooting matched their doubles disembarking in France on the simultaneous second-unit shoot.[89] Another difficulty was that the shipment of filming materials forced companies to comply with international bureaucracy. On Orson Welles's *Othello* (1952 premiere, 1955 US release), the film's Moroccan footage was reportedly held up for three months in British customs when some rocks that were used as ballast in shipping crates were declared "unidentified mineral objects."[90]

As with films shot in a single foreign country, the Hollywood AFL Film Council criticized the practice of shooting interiors on foreign soundstages on multi-nation productions. The labor group argued that the interiors could have been just as easily replicated in Hollywood studios, using domestic labor.[91] If productions justified the move overseas because of the need for authentic foreign locations, unions repeatedly made the case that producers should agree to take a large crew from Hollywood.[92] The AFL voiced these grievances during periodic campaigns against runaway productions. In the early 1950s, the AFL attempted to publicly make known a film's geographical shooting locations by pushing for a federal law that required any film shot overseas to carry a label in the opening credits naming the countries where the film was shot.[93] The union hoped that audiences would stay away from films they knew were made in foreign countries. An AFL press release urged the enforcement of this law to ensure "that the American public no longer be hoodwinked by 'runaway' American motion picture producers."[94] This legal strategy failed to gain traction. In the late 1950s and early 1960s, unions renewed their efforts to require all Hollywood films to carry country-of-origin markers.[95] But once again, these lobbying efforts never picked up much momentum.[96] In actuality, a number of overseas productions identified foreign locations both in the opening credits and in their promotional campaigns, not so much to satisfy unions but as a way to acknowledge the support of foreign authorities and to emphasize the authenticity of place.

Whether working in a single foreign country or across multiple nations abroad, Hollywood producers risked aligning themselves with Communist labor groups, a particularly controversial subject during the postwar anti-"Red" fervor in Hollywood and across the United States. In countries like France, where the Communist influence on the film industry was deep, this alignment was a real possibility.[97] In response, the Hollywood AFL Film Council sharpened its attack on runaway productions by accusing the producers of these films of giving "aid and comfort to the Communist conspiracy against the free world." The organization charged that more than 50 percent of technicians working on Hollywood films shot overseas were Communists.[98] Other union groups, such as the Scenic Artists Local 816, rebuked studios for employing Communist unions in Italy and hiring blacklisted filmmakers who had moved to Europe.[99] One vehement faction of the film unions published a pamphlet titled "Awake, America!" that assailed runaway productions for their use of Communist workers: "Are you aware that hundreds of thousands of jobs have been taken away from Americans and given to foreign workers—including Communists?"[100] Despite these protest tactics, Hollywood unions failed to obtain widespread support in their anti-runaway-production campaigns by using anti-communist sentiments.[101] Nevertheless, these maneuvers contributed to the witch-hunt atmosphere of the postwar era both in Hollywood and abroad. As Rebecca Prime has demonstrated, the tactics of the AFL and right-wing groups helped ensure that the blacklist held sway over the lives of filmmakers exiled in Europe.[102]

Abroad and Stateside

More in line with union dictates were productions that combined location work abroad—either in a single nation or in multiple foreign countries—with work done in the United States. Technicians could match authentic foreign exteriors with Hollywood studio interiors and choreograph actors with the rear-screen projection of background plates shot overseas. Working in this way, productions could employ the expertise of Hollywood studio technicians while taking advantage of authentic foreign scenery. However, this approach still involved challenges. The productions had to coordinate the transportation of labor and equipment and, in some cases, navigate the bureaucracy of importing into the United States foreign talent who had been employed on the locations.[103]

In a letter to the *Hollywood Reporter*, AFL Film Council president Roy Brewer voiced his support for this production strategy. He acknowledged that while story content could merit shooting in foreign locales, many films could represent authentic locations abroad by working in Hollywood studios with rear projection or by having a US location stand in for a foreign setting. Brewer cited *The Snows of Kilimanjaro* (1952) as a production that successfully balanced background shots from multiple countries in Africa and Europe with work done in Fox studios and the Fox Hills of Culver City, where battle scenes from the Spanish Civil War were staged.[104] In IATSE's publication *International Photographer,* the still photographer Al St. Hilaire shared a similar recommendation. He asserted that runaway productions could be avoided when most of the film consisted of interiors that could be created in Hollywood. He had worked on the production of *Judgment at Nuremberg* (1961), which filmed six days of exteriors in West Germany and constructed its interiors at the Revue Studio in Hollywood, where the majority of the movie was shot. "An interior is an interior," St. Hilaire reasoned, "and interiors are better made, better lit, and better photographed here than anywhere else."[105] Following these prescriptions, a producer could therefore appease union demands by capturing authentic foreign locations while taking advantage of Hollywood studios, equipment, and labor.

Many productions mixed authentic foreign locations with interiors and rear-projection work done in Hollywood. For example, MGM's *King Solomon's Mines* (1950) was shot on location in the Belgian Congo and British East African countries while the interiors and rear-projection setups were filmed at the studio's Culver City lot.[106] In other instances, the principal photography was accomplished overseas, while retakes and additional footage were finished in Hollywood. On the independent production *Black Magic* (1949), which was shot on location in Italy and at Scalera studios in Rome, retakes were filmed at Hollywood's Motion Picture Center.[107] For these productions, additional shooting was easier to do in the United States rather than facing the expense of reassembling the international cast and crew in a foreign country for a short period of time. Restricting retakes and added scenes to the United States suggests that executing large-scale undertakings abroad yielded greater savings than filming small-scale operations. Exporting a minor production overseas cost more than was saved by using a cheaper foreign labor pool—a differential that partially explains the lower number of small and mid-budget pictures that were shot internationally.[108]

As the geographical configurations of runaway productions reveal, these films' shooting sites were as varied as their stories, spanning the United States and multiple countries abroad. This global sweep shaped the debates that surrounded runaway productions as producers and Los Angeles–based unions were coming to terms with progressively decentralized production work. Furthermore, geography had an important impact on a film's aesthetics, with foreign locations serving as dominant stylistic elements, a crucial feature related to a movie's setting.

SETTINGS VERSUS LOCATIONS: DEFINING RUNAWAY PRODUCTIONS

Considering that Hollywood cinema produces narrative-based products, the runaway-production phenomenon was never the same as outsourcing the manufacturing of cars, clothing, or technologies. Mass-produced standardized products do not carry clear traces of their place of assembly, whereas films do retain some visible traces of where they are created, especially when they're made on location. Moreover, as a storytelling medium, films are rooted in some setting, whether specific, ambiguous, or entirely invented. The relationship between where the film's story takes place and the real-world location where the film was shot is central to understanding runaway productions.

Along with the economic and geographic characteristics of runaway films, the setting-versus-location configuration had a major impact on the coordination and aesthetics of international productions. Often, the story setting determined where the motion picture was photographed, in which case a production unit went to the setting's actual locale to bring to the film a semblance of realism that could not have been replicated in Hollywood. Even if a film was not shot in the same location as the story's setting, the producers sometimes chose another locale that resembled the setting or conveyed an air of "foreignness." Regardless, whenever a film was not shot where its story was set, producers stood a chance of eliciting criticism from unions. Thus, the relationship of a film's setting to its shooting locations had wide-ranging implications for how the industry defined and debated runaway productions.

Authentic Foreign Locations

The clearest way that Hollywood producers could justify shooting overseas was when a film was set and shot in the same foreign place. Producers deemed these shooting sites "authentic foreign locations," since the locality served as the actual setting where the story occurred. This situation was a change from the standard of Hollywood studio-bound production, in which a story occurring in Paris would be shot on a set of Paris erected in a Hollywood studio. The US work of Ernst Lubitsch exemplifies the continental atmosphere created in Hollywood studios. In films such as *So This Is Paris* (1926), *Trouble in Paradise* (1932), and *Ninotchka* (1939), Lubitsch re-created European settings through a mixture of Paramount's set design and soundstage atmospherics. He famously said, "There is Paramount Paris and Metro Paris, and of course the real Paris. Paramount's is the most Parisian of all!"[109] In some cases, Hollywood films were set in make-believe foreign lands erected in studios. Ruth Vasey has shown that prior to World War II, Hollywood movies at times relied on "mythical kingdoms" to avoid causing offense to potential overseas markets with specific references to national characters and locales.[110] After World War II, however, the need to fill screens with authentic foreign locations in service of the story became a driving force to shoot the film in the place where it was set.

Even for a historical motion picture, Hollywood filmmakers promoted the idea that linking a setting to its original location imbued the movie with an air of realism. Producer Sam Zimbalist claimed that *Quo Vadis* attained more realism by shooting in Rome's historic locales.[111] When Joseph Mankiewicz took over directing duties on Twentieth Century-Fox's *Cleopatra* (1963), he said that the original plan to do the film entirely in England, including exteriors, was "idiotic." When Fox then arranged to shoot the film's interiors on its studio lot, the director made a strong plea to use authentic historical locations in Italy and Egypt. Mankiewicz insisted, "The barge we're going to use in 'Cleopatra' belongs on the Nile, not on the Los Angeles or Colorado Rivers. We can no longer build foreign places on the back lot." Alluding to shifts in postwar visual culture, he added, "The public no longer will tolerate what we used to give them."[112]

In many cases, the appeal to authenticity demanded filming in real locations if the setting could not be accurately re-created anywhere else. After about a dozen years of producing overseas shoots, Darryl Zanuck argued:

> The only excuse in my opinion for anyone to make a picture abroad is because it cannot be properly produced anywhere else except on the locale dictated by the story.... What do I gain by making another six thousand mile expedition and going into territory where I have to bring everything from stars to grips?

I gain only quality and realism and if I am successful, I bring to audiences a sense of honesty and show them something they have never seen before.... The locale must be the only barometer for production abroad.[113]

Zanuck, like many other producers, privileged the authentic location as a primary justification for shooting overseas. This stance helped counter the labor unions' argument that these films were unnecessarily being made overseas and taking away jobs from Hollywood workers. Such arguments also resonated with the industry at large. In 1953, the Motion Picture Industry Council, a joint labor-management committee, publicly approved the practice of shooting overseas when authentic locales added to story values that could spur foreign box-office profits.[114] Despite this support, unions contended that certain producers' choice of story material was a facade motivated by the financial benefit of shooting in foreign regions. One of the AFL Film Council's resolutions on runaway production asserted, "Some producers claim they are making their pictures in foreign countries because they need foreign locale for their scenes, while in fact in many cases the producer has a deliberate policy of seeking scripts calling for foreign locales."[115]

In truth, Hollywood companies had since the late 1940s actively sought foreign story properties that called for foreign settings. Twentieth Century-Fox placed a talent executive in England to hunt for story material for international productions while the studio also worked with a European story editor in Paris.[116] MGM sponsored story searches in Europe and created story departments in Paris and London.[117] From the late 1940s through the early 1950s, Billy Wilder and producers Hal Wallis, Sol Lesser, and Arthur Hornblow Jr. took European story-scouting trips.[118] All of these activities imply that there was a push to develop European story properties, so that Hollywood producers could reap the financial rewards of shooting on location abroad while also generating stories that appealed to international markets. The reasons for shooting abroad therefore had to be backed up by a story that demanded a foreign locale.

Approximate Foreign Locations

In another configuration of setting versus location, a film could be set in one foreign country but shot in another, typically when the latter could replicate the former. These locales can be regarded as "approximate foreign locations." In the case of historical epics, the original locations either no longer existed or were so altered by modernization that the actual story setting could not be captured. In its place, producers shot in an area that would resemble the historical backdrop to achieve verisimilitude. Producer Samuel Bronston specialized in these productions. In Spain, he shot the biblical epic *King of Kings* (1961) and the Boxer Rebellion tale *55 Days at Peking* (1963), letting the Spanish landscape substitute for historical settings. He was also able to take advantage of a cheap labor pool and support from Spain's Franco regime.[119]

For some productions, external pressures prevented a film company from shooting in an original location, forcing a unit to replicate the setting in another foreign locale. Fox's *The Inn of the Sixth Happiness* (1958), a tale of an English missionary in China, was unable to film in Taiwan, a stand-in for mainland China, due to bad publicity surrounding the movie's depiction of foot binding. Moreover, the exiled Nationalist Chinese government was concerned with the film's portrayal of China's poverty and lack of development. Hong Kong was another possibility, but Fox personnel were apparently dissuaded by the city's modernization. Shooting stateside was out of the question since the film's star, Ingrid Bergman, refused to work in the United States at the time. So the production moved to MGM's British studios and locations in England and Wales, which replicated Chinese scenery.[120] Controversy also shaped the shooting of the Warner Bros. film *The Roman Spring of Mrs. Stone* (1961). The production was forced to move from Rome to England after Italian officials refused to grant the studio a shooting permit, ostensibly over the racy story based on Tennessee Williams's novel about a widowed entertainer's affair with an Italian gigolo. While the finished film included some authentic backdrops in Rome, most of its Roman settings were re-created in British studios.[121] However, these kinds of approximate foreign locales ran up against Hollywood unions that argued that these settings could have been replicated in the United States, where a domestic cast and crew could have been hired.[122]

In time, unions had some success in convincing certain Hollywood filmmakers to shoot their historical epics back home. Actor-producer Kirk Douglas, who filmed much of the ancient Rome–set *Spartacus* (1960) in Los Angeles and the Southwest, supported this effort: "If you must start from scratch, if you must build your sets from the ground up, if you must create the streets and homes and shops—an entire image of something which no longer exists—then I think Hollywood is the place to do it."[123] Even though some of *Spartacus*'s battle sequences were filmed in Spain, where the Spanish army played Roman soldiers, the move won the endorsement of the AFL. The union even promoted the film in *Daily Variety* with a full-page letter of support and a plea that producers "stop looking across the sea for greener grass. It is greenest right here."[124] Holding a screening of the film for its constituents, the labor group used *Spartacus* as a centerpiece in its anti-runaway-production campaign.[125] Then in 1962, the high-profile domestic production of George Stevens's *The Greatest Story Ever Told* (1965) showed that a biblical epic could be made entirely in the United States using a large cast and crew. Stevens had earlier publicly proclaimed the savings in production spending by working abroad, so the decision to make the film in the United States was a coup for labor groups.[126] This situation arose through special arrangements between unions and the film's producers to keep costs down.[127] Both of these productions conveyed to the US film industry that major motion pictures set in foreign locales could be successfully shot domestically, without the extravagant spending of films such as *Mutiny on the Bounty* (1962) and *Cleopatra*.

Stand-in Foreign Locations

Another option was for a film to be set in the United States but shot in a foreign country. In effect, the foreign location became a "stand-in" for a US setting. By far the most contentious type of production with unions, it was also an exception in the postwar era. Most international productions were set and shot in the same location, but financial incentives could be attractive enough to motivate some producers to shoot in a foreign country even though their films took place in the United States. The few examples covered by the film trade press provoked swift and vocal protest from unions. W. R. Frank's production of *Sitting Bull* (1954), a biopic about the eponymous Sioux chief, was set in South Dakota but shot in Mexico. The film drew heavy criticism from an IATSE local, which mobilized a Sioux group in South Dakota to oppose the production. Ralph Peckham, a former South Dakotan and secretary-treasurer of the IATSE Motion Picture Set Painters Union, argued that the production was denying employment and money to both Hollywood technicians and residents of the Dakotas, who could benefit from the film shoot.[128] Similarly, Republic's *Daniel Boone, Trail Blazer* (1956) was shot in Mexico and set in the Southwest, a situation that the Hollywood AFL Film Council opposed.[129] For unions, these kinds of productions were barefaced attempts to cash in on the less expensive labor costs in neighboring Mexico.

However, the union outcries triggered counter-defenses by Hollywood producers. Al Gannaway, codirector and producer of *Daniel Boone, Trail Blazer,* criticized the AFL's objection to his production. He explained that he had decided to shoot the film in Mexico once locations in Tennessee and North Carolina proved inadequate. He also expressed resentment toward the AFL's charge of "un-Americanism."[130] In another case, producer Carl Krueger demanded that Film Council leader Ralph Clare apologize for including Krueger's production of *Comanche* (1956), set and shot in Durango, Mexico, in a list of runaway productions: "A casual reading of our screenplay will prove my production is not a runaway but a picture legitimately filmed in a foreign locale to assure authenticity. The picture opens with the Comanche sacking and destroying a Mexican pueblo on the outskirts of Durango."[131] Whether justified or not, these films' use of Mexico as a location sparked vocal disapproval from unions.

Films that were set in the United States and shot in Europe also prompted boycotts. For *John Paul Jones* (1959), producer Samuel Bronston aimed to film primarily in Spain, including scenes that occurred in the United States, such as the signing of the Declaration of Independence. With such patriotic subject matter, the AFL Film Council was particularly irate, even threatening to take their protest to President Dwight D. Eisenhower and Congress.[132] In response, Bronston dismissed the notion that he was re-creating Independence Hall in Spain and proclaimed that the Declaration of Independence scenes would actually be shot in Philadelphia and Williamsburg. This assertion contradicted an earlier Warner Bros. press release, which explained that Independence Hall would be constructed at Estudios CEA in Madrid, a detail that Bronston later admitted to. Further defending himself, the producer contended that he was employing thirty-eight US technicians on location and that the sole way to get the film made was to use frozen foreign currency only available upon shooting overseas.[133] In the end, under pressure from the AFL's boycott threat, Bronston agreed that in addition to the foreign locales of Spain, Versailles, and Scotland, he would film scenes in Virginia, Maryland, and Pennsylvania.[134]

The example of *John Paul Jones* underlines how important the connection between the setting and shooting location was in the discourse surrounding runaway production. Unions were sometimes able to influence decisions on where parts of films were shot, but their remonstrations were only effective when they could make a clear case that authenticity was not a viable justification for filming overseas. Interestingly, the AFL's dispute over Bronston's film led to rifts within the organization, which tried to expel its business agent, Herb Aller, for standing in the way of its boycott.[135] The internal upheaval was a sign that unions did not always present a united front in their campaigns against runaway productions.

HOLLYWOOD'S SHIFTING INTERNATIONAL STRATEGIES

The debates about runaway productions were reflected in a 1960 analysis of the situation from *Variety*'s Robert J. Landry, who charged both unions and producers with employing propagandistic efforts to justify their own positions. He claimed that the term "runaway production" was just as much a propaganda measure as the producers' "appeasement" tactics. While he accused studios of not doing enough to keep productions in Hollywood, such as lowering overhead, Landry suggested that the industry had changed, and that little could be done to return it to its previous circumstances. He concluded, "Trends rise and fall and the film medium grows constantly more 'international.' Hollywood must adjust to the new set of circumstances and survive in a new context. There is a good deal of evidence, despite all wailing, that it is doing precisely that. In any event, there is no turning back the calendar to the old, easy days."[136] While Landry explored both sides of the runaway debates, his sympathies seemed to rest with studio management. Certainly, Hollywood studios and producers underwent a major transition from the late 1940s through the early 1960s, as runaway production became a strategy to weather the difficulties of the postwar period. To the detriment of Los Angeles–based workers, these changes would alter the stability of local employment for decades and contribute to the decentering of Hollywood as a production hub.

Around the time when Landry made these comments, the financial and geographic configurations of international filmmaking were shifting, as the US film industry was beginning to retrench and restructure. Hollywood studios were already scaling back their foreign operations, a reflection of the general belt-tightening.[137] In the UK, Warner Bros. unloaded its Teddington Studios to ABPC for television production and closed its regional sales branches across England, Scotland, and Wales.[138] MGM sold its dubbing studios in London and Rome, and considered selling its Borehamwood studios, but the Hollywood firm had trouble finding a buyer.[139] RKO also began to cut its foreign distribution network as the studio itself began to downsize, handing over its administrative operations to Britain's Rank Organization.[140] Then in 1960, the British Board of Trade ended the Anglo-American Agreement, which lifted all remittance restrictions.[141] This move, in effect, reduced Hollywood's need to invest in the British industry, although years of interdependence would keep cooperation alive through the 1960s. In Italy, studios started cutting their distribution agencies, a move that prompted the Italian government's customs authorities to deny film import permits because of the layoffs of Italian staff members.[142] Even though many of these cutbacks came from the distribution sector, these moves indicate changes in a wider overseas strategy. Studios reduced their physical presence abroad, with fewer production operations and distribution offices, while increasing their financial position through the funding of coproductions and full-fledged foreign films.

Despite the cuts to foreign infrastructure, the number of runaway productions fluctuated in the early 1960s. In 1960 and 1962, *Daily Variety* announced that Hollywood was actually increasing the number of foreign-shot films, while elsewhere Paramount was supposedly scaling back its productions abroad.[143] In 1960, Fox planned to carry out an ambitious production plan in the UK.[144] However, the studio soon found itself enmeshed in the production mess of *Cleopatra*, which almost ruined it. By September 1962, Fox put a six-month suspension on its productions and laid off half of its studio staff.[145] That same year, Paramount, Columbia, Seven Arts, and Embassy Pictures all began to concentrate more heavily on making films in the United States.[146] By the end of 1962, the trade press reported that the downscaling of the US film industry resulted in the closing of foreign operations and an increased focus on domestic productions.[147] Still, Hollywood continued to undertake international productions, as indicated by the data in this book's introduction and appendix. Onward through the 1960s, the industry kept producing big-budget overseas extravaganzas such as *The Fall of the Roman Empire* (1964) and *The Sound of Music* (1965). By advertising these films through behind-the-scenes promotional featurettes that were broadcast on television, Hollywood found new ways to maintain its global image.[148]

Looking at the period from the late 1940s to the early 1960s, the financial and geographic configurations of international productions point to the fracturing of how films were financed and where they were shot. Film funding came from multiple international sources. The locations spanned the globe, often extending across a few continents. Setting and location became increasingly significant factors in the selection of story material and in the look of the movies. However, as this chapter has shown, there were trends in how these films were funded and coordinated.

Above all, the configurations denote that these films were the result of a true internationalization of production. While a large portion of Hollywood films were still made domestically, postwar runaway productions signal that the world and its film industries became a vast pool of resources from which US-based companies could assemble personnel, equipment, and locations to create more global films. It was partly through Hollywood producers' ability to export and reconfigure a mode of production that the industry was able to persist through the postwar era. Part II takes a closer look at what that production process was like for Hollywood filmmakers who went overseas.

Tax Evasion, Red-Baiting, and the White Whale

MOBY DICK (1956)

"If I have a trademark at all, it's that I prefer to make my movies where they happen."

JOHN HUSTON[1]

JOHN HUSTON WAS A SELF-AVOWED "LOCATION MAN" who valorized, as the epigraph suggests, shooting films in the actual locales where their stories were set.[2] More than any other Hollywood director in the postwar era, Huston specialized in producing decidedly international motion pictures that relied on foreign crews, infrastructures, and locations. In a 1963 issue of the *Journal of the Screen Producers Guild*, he justified his overseas production work: "Story needs and not economics should dictate where a picture should be filmed. I have never saved money by shooting on location. The cost is just as much in the long run. You take people to another country, support them, incur travel expenses and consume time."[3] Like many Hollywood producers, he appealed to notions of authenticity and creativity rather than finances to defend his reasons for making films overseas. But few other Hollywood figures would financially benefit so greatly by living and working abroad. Beneath Huston's veneer of artistic motivations were a range of economic ones.

Many of these came to a head on the complicated production of *Moby Dick* (1956). The film was coproduced by the independent company Moulin Productions and Britain's Associated British Picture Corporation (ABPC). It was cofinanced and distributed by Warner Bros., the studio that had previously adapted Herman Melville's classic with *The Sea Beast* (1926), *Moby Dick* (1930), and its German-language version, *Dämon des Meeres* (1931). Far more international in scope, Huston's *Moby Dick* was shot in Ireland, Wales, Portugal, Spain, and ABPC's studios in England. Working across multiple land locations and out at sea gave rise to shooting snags that swelled the negative cost of the film to more than $4 million.[4] No doubt, the hazards of runaway production led to runaway costs, reinforcing a pitfall of working abroad: budgets ballooned and shooting schedules elongated as a result of the unpredictability of location filming. The experience led Huston to eventually conclude, "*Moby Dick* was the most difficult picture I ever made. I lost so many battles during it that I even began to suspect that my assistant director was plotting against me. Then I realized that it was only God."[5]

Here I examine Huston's *Moby Dick* within the context of the director's international productions from the early to mid-1950s, which represented an important phase in his career as he established himself in Europe. This phase yielded an eclectic cycle of mostly independent productions that were shot abroad: the romantic adventure *The African Queen* (1952), the Technicolor biopic *Moulin Rouge* (1953), and the shaggy-dog yarn *Beat the Devil* (1954), culminating in the movie adaptation of *Moby Dick*. The logistical complications of that last film reflect the different financial and geographic configurations explored in the previous chapter, while exhibiting a relationship between story settings and shooting locations that stood a chance of being labeled a runaway production by Hollywood unions. This risk was heightened by the controversial figure of Huston himself, whose tax evasion and political positions made him a target of the red-baiting union groups that were protesting runaways. The case of Huston and *Moby Dick* helps elucidate the financial and political stakes of expanding production around the world.

FINANCIAL AND GEOGRAPHIC CONFIGURATIONS

Huston's work on *Moby Dick* coincided with the continuing expansion of independent productions that began with his early forays into international filmmaking. Previously he had made movies for a variety of studios, including Universal, MGM, and Warner Bros., first as a contracted writer and then as a writer-director. His penchant for working autonomously, though, incentivized him to break from the studios and eventually work outside of the United States. His partnership with independent producer Sam Spiegel's Horizon Pictures proved an auspicious opportunity to pursue this autonomy.[6] Their first outing was *We Were Strangers* (1949), a coproduction with Columbia that was partially shot in Cuba. But not until *The African Queen* did Huston make a decisive move abroad, motivated by a mixture of the tax benefits of working overseas and political disillusionment with Congress's anti-communist investigations into the Hollywood community.

After the international independent productions of *The African Queen*, *Moulin Rouge*, and *Beat the Devil*, which were all distributed by United Artists, *Moby Dick* was something of a return to Warner Bros. At Warner, the director had made some of his highest-profile films, including *The Maltese Falcon* (1941) and *The Treasure of the Sierra Madre* (1948). Unlike Huston's previous work with Warner, the studio had limited control over *Moby Dick*, providing only distribution and partial financing. At one point, studio head Jack Warner tried to convince Huston to shoot the film in CinemaScope, since the firm was promoting the anamorphic system with both domestic films and international productions. Nonetheless, the director and his trusted cinematographer Oswald Morris decided to shoot in a "flatter," non-anamorphic format, which resulted in a somewhat narrower aspect ratio.[7] The primary producing entity became Moulin Productions, which supervised the film and contributed additional funding, including coverage for the budget overruns.[8] Due to its ties to Warner Bros., ABPC was the third coproduction partner, which furnished studio space and technical support.[9]

With the financing set, the *Moby Dick* production took place in a variety of locations, balanced by studio work in England (fig. 5).[10] While most multi-country productions might use authentic locations in one country and the studio of another, Huston's film stretched across a range of locales. This geographic configuration was partly due to the logistical complications of the film shoot rather than the dictates of the story settings—a fact that would have consequences for the debates surrounding the work. In the spring of 1954, the shooting phase of *Moby Dick* commenced with second-unit photography around the Portuguese archipelagos of Azores and Madeira, where hunters who still harpooned their kill were filmed during the seasonal whale migration. In July, first-unit filming began in Youghal, Ireland, for a four-week shoot with a one-day excursion to Powerscourt Estate in Wicklow to capture the film's prologue.

"There's nothing that compares with the fury of a real storm at sea," asserted Huston in a justification for authentic oceanic locations.[11] So in August, ocean sequences were shot off the coast of Fishguard, Wales. However, one of the drawbacks of aiming for realism, especially on the high seas, was exposure to the unpredictable elements. An accumulation of inclement weather, injury, and mechanical whales that sank in the ocean

FIGURE 5. John Huston (facing the camera) and crew film a scene from *Moby Dick* (1956) out at sea. Cinematographer Oswald Morris is to the right of the camera splash bag. (Courtesy of the Margaret Herrick Library, Academy of Motion Picture Arts and Sciences)

dragged the production behind schedule and over budget. As a result, Moulin Productions did not have the money to carry on paying the film's star, Gregory Peck, beyond the period that his contract dictated.[12] In fall 1954 the production moved into ABPC's Elstree studios for interiors and tank work with models of the *Pequod* ship and the white whale.[13] But in order to finish sea footage, additional filming was required in the warmer waters around the Canary Island of Las Palmas in December 1954. But even here, more troubles ensued when the latex-and-steel whales were lost at sea.[14]

Working in so many locations ran the risk of diluting the nationality of *Moby Dick*. Previously, Huston and his independent producers had made concerted efforts to have the films with ties to the UK be eligible for the British quota. Starting with *The African Queen*, a production pattern was set to film locations outside of the UK, followed by work in British studios. *The African Queen* was shot on location in the Belgian Congo and Uganda and matched with footage made in Isleworth Studios in Outer London. Subsequently, Huston filmed the exteriors of *Moulin Rouge* in Paris and re-created interiors at Shepperton Studios. *Beat the Devil* was made on location in Ravello, Italy, and again at Shepperton. For all of these, the producing companies spent sufficient time and money at British studios to qualify them as quota pictures and have them seen in the UK as British movies.[15]

With *Moby Dick*, Huston and producer Harold Mirisch sought the participation of ABPC, which could provide studio space, technical support, and the ability to ensure that the production followed the necessary mandates of the British quota laws.[16] One of those dictates imposed limits on the use of non-British personnel in the cast and crew, but even so, there were a handful of notable exceptions. Huston, his secretary Lorraine Sherwood, and associate producer Lee Katz were all US citizens; production manager Cecil Ford and second assistant director Kevin McClory were Irish; and makeup artist Charles Parker was Canadian, though he regularly worked for MGM's British studios. Away from ABPC's studio, the strictures on the national makeup of the crew loosened, so the location unit in Ireland was able to rely on nonunion locals as extras and below-the-line workers.[17] In Las Palmas, the production had to hire a group of Spanish crew members from the Sindicato Nacional del Espectáculo.[18]

While the film eventually qualified as a British quota picture, Huston wanted *Moby Dick* to be seen as a local production within the UK and a US production outside of the UK: "I would hate to see MOBY presented anywhere else than in England as anything but an American picture."[19] However, on certain international stages, the film's nationality became more complicated. The possibility arose of screening *Moby Dick* at the Cannes Film Festival in France, where competitors had to represent particular nations. If it had been shown as a US production, it would have sacrificed the benefits of being considered a British quota film and being eligible for Eady funding.[20] The director argued against showing the film at Cannes, instead opting for a premiere in New Bedford, Massachusetts, where it was set but not shot.

Despite the work's slippery national origins, some British film critics proudly considered it a British product. Writing for the *Evening News*, a reviewer affirmed, "Apart from the American director and two other American stars, Orson Welles and Richard Basehart, 'Moby Dick' is very much a triumph for British acting and British studio technicians."[21] The film's ability to be equivocal about matters of national cinema points to the contested nature of international productions. In this burgeoning landscape of global moviemaking, a film's financing, geography, and the nationalities of the cast and crew traversed multiple countries, allowing divergent industries and critics to lay claim on what they deemed theirs. The question of nationality was also complicated by the residential and political status of Huston, an always-peripatetic filmmaker.

HUSTON AND TAXES

John Huston's global ventures spanned much of his life. He bookended his twenties with stints abroad, first riding with the cavalry in Mexico, subsequently working as a screenwriter for Gaumont Studios in London, then becoming an amateur painter in Paris. With the United States' entry into World War II, he served in the Army Signal Corps, filming military campaigns in the Aleutians and Italy.[22] Huston's postwar overseas experiences were different, however, connected as they were to both personal and economic motivations. He spent the 1950s dividing his time between his home in Ireland and film projects in Africa, East Asia, the Caribbean, Europe, and Mexico. Working away from the studio's supervision suited not only Huston's swashbuckling ways but also his sometimes undisciplined, dilatory shooting methods. A number of biographers have cited wanderlust as an explanation for the director's adventurous character. "Like Hemingway," Axel Madsen wrote, "he has made Europe his movable feast."[23] But invoking personal biography only goes so far in explaining the realities of production work. We need to take into account the financial benefits that Huston reaped by making films in foreign countries.

Due to Huston's luxurious lifestyle, profligate spending, and need to support various ex-wives and children, the director sought an advantageous tax situation, which he found overseas. From 1951 through 1952, roughly covering the period of the making of *The African Queen* and *Moulin Rouge*, he gave up his residence in the United States and lived and worked abroad, partly to take advantage of the eighteen-month tax rule.[24] Hollywood AFL Film Council head Roy Brewer identified and blasted Huston—along with Humphrey Bogart, Ava Gardner, Gene Kelly, Gregory Peck, Gene Tierney, and William Wyler, among others—for exploiting the tax scheme.[25] Congress would rein in the exemption on foreign earnings after 1953, thanks to the lobbying efforts of the AFL Film Council and the Motion Picture Industry Council.[26] In anticipation of this change, Huston's business manager advised him to earn as much money as possible during the tax-free period. As a result, Huston was one of the few Hollywood filmmakers to benefit fully from the entire tax exemption.[27]

The director, with the help of his business manager and lawyer, also looked into the possibility of becoming an official resident of Ireland, which would further improve his tax standing beyond the new limits of the eighteen-month tax clause. To help establish his Irish residency, Huston leased a house in Kilcock, County Kildare, in 1952, and a year later he purchased a manor house called St. Clerans near Galway.[28] By November 1953, the film trade press was calling Huston an Irish resident.[29] Although he did not become an Irish citizen until 1964, the director lived in St. Clerans until 1972 in between location-shooting sprees.

As Eric Hoyt has shown, Huston's foreign residence left him in an uneasy professional position: he had to steer clear of film projects with any "modern day American setting" to avoid making plain his reasons for staying abroad. Huston openly expressed this fact to his agent, Paul Kohner:

> Whenever I am interviewed, one of the question [sic] is why have I chosen to make pictures away from the United States. And I am able to answer that it is simply because my recent pictures—yes, including *Moby Dick*—were more easily made away from home. Either foreign scenes were their background or, as in the case of *Moby*, the little Irish town, which served as the location for the only dry land sequence, is more like old New Bedford than anything in New England today. If, however, I were asked that question having made a picture about New York kids in Mexico or Canada, I would have to confess that it was only to avoid paying taxes, as there isn't a single other reason that would hold water.[30]

For Huston, the use of an Irish town as a backdrop for *Moby Dick*'s setting could be seen as a legitimate creative decision, since the shooting location better evoked the times of Melville than anything in the United States. From another view, the disjunction of story setting and location belies a convenient ploy, since Huston's turn to approximating the past served as a believable cover for his tax benefits.

Time and again, the justification for not shooting *Moby Dick* in its original setting or other similar US port towns, such as Nantucket, was that those places were too modern. Press releases circulated by Warner Bros. and the production's unit publicist repeated Huston's reasoning like a refrain: "Too many neon signs, too highly industrialized."[31] Certainly, some economic considerations were in play, such as the fact that converting an Irish seaport town like Youghal into New Bedford was cheaper than doing it in the United States.[32] But much of the argument behind the all-too-modern US small town deflected attention from Huston's need to maintain his foreign residence in order to avoid paying US taxes. His tax dodge would have further upset Hollywood unions and jeopardized the public's perception of the director. In actuality, Youghal was not an easy stand-in for Melville's New England and required much reworking. The production's art department transformed the town by outfitting building facades with mid-nineteenth-century false fronts and rebuilding some of the original New Bedford settings from the days of Melville. Moreover, to allow for safe passage of the *Pequod* rigger, the town's harbor bottom had to be dredged.[33]

For other tax reasons, Huston had to limit his time in England in 1955. A law required that anyone who spent three or more months for four successive years in England be regarded as a resident of the country, which would have led to taxation on Huston's worldwide income for the time he spent there.[34] So to avoid returning there for postproduction, the director, along with editor Russell Lloyd, cut *Moby Dick* in Ireland in Huston's Kildare mansion. One newspaper reported that Huston had built the first Irish film studio to support the film's postproduction. Obscuring the economic reason why the film was edited in Ireland, the article describes how working away from Elstree Studios allowed "for greater concentration and to be free from noise and bustle."[35]

Adventure, locations, and creative freedom—all of these reasons veiled the financial benefits that Huston stood to gain by having an international film career. At a time when the politics of runaway production drew attention to the finances of filmmakers and the geography of film shoots, Huston needed to deflect potential controversy. However, avoiding it would be difficult in the anti-communist climate of the postwar era.

HUSTON AND RED-BAITING

Already in a precarious position with Hollywood unions because of his tax situation, Huston intensified this standing with the more conservative wings of Hollywood labor groups with his political views. The director's first major move into the realm of US politics occurred in 1947 when he, along with William Wyler and screenwriter Philip Dunne, formed the Committee for the First Amendment (CFA), which spoke out against the Communist witch-hunt trials of the House Un-American Activities Committee (HUAC). In the fall of 1947, a delegation of the CFA traveled to Washington, DC, on a highly publicized trip in support of the "unfriendly" witnesses from Hollywood called before HUAC.[36] In some segments of the press, specifically the Hearst newspapers, Huston's name became associated with the Communist Party, although HUAC never subpoenaed him. Additionally, the CFA was pegged as a front for Hollywood Communists, even though it eventually dissolved after its estrangement from blacklisted filmmakers and writers. Rumors of Huston's association with Communism were further fueled when he made *We Were Strangers*, a film about a group of Cuban revolutionaries who try to assassinate the country's dictator, partially shot on location in Cuba. Upon the film's release in 1949, the *Hollywood Reporter* charged, "It is the heaviest dish of Red theory ever served to an audience outside the Soviet." Adding to the attack, the reviewer called it "a shameful handbook of Marxian dialectic."[37]

Huston's move overseas for *The African Queen* in 1951 created some temporary distance from the political turmoil back home. In his memoir, the director recalled his relocation to Europe and insisted, "I felt no great desire to return to the United States. It had—temporarily at least—stopped being my country, and I was just as happy to stay clear of it. The anti-communist hysteria certainly played a role in my move to Ireland shortly afterward."[38] But unlike the blacklisted Hollywood filmmakers who exiled themselves to Europe to find work and sanctuary, Huston chose to openly continue making films for studios. Despite his public pronouncements, his decision to stay abroad was ultimately more about finances than political contempt or refuge. Nevertheless, the director would find himself drawn back into the anti-communist fervor in the United States.

By 1952, the Hollywood AFL Film Council escalated its campaign against runaway films by attacking overseas productions that used any "unfriendly" witnesses from the HUAC hearings or Communist foreign unions.[39] The US release of *Moulin Rouge* coincided with this period of intensified red-baiting. Both Huston and the film's star, the politically liberal José Ferrer, became targets of anti-communist protests by members of the conservative political organization the American Legion. A small group of Legionnaires picketed the premiere of *Moulin Rouge* with signs reading "Communist Press Praises John Huston" and "American Legion Bans Jose Ferrer."[40] The Legion also attempted to leverage its boycott of the film's release in exchange for a denouncement of Communism by the actor and director.[41] Ferrer's political leanings were especially at issue, and many newspapers refused to write about the actor. This kind of journalistic blacklisting forced *Moulin Rouge*'s publicity efforts to deemphasize Ferrer's performance and play up "the gaiety of Paris, the can-can dancers, the *Moulin Rouge* sex angles."[42] In the end, Ferrer wrote a letter to the national commander of the Legion to decry Communism. Then, in a joint statement, the actor, Huston, and producing firm Moulin Productions expressed their willingness to cooperate with the Legion "to eliminate Communist influences throughout America."[43]

Huston's difficulties with Hollywood unions persisted into 1953, however, with the production of *Beat the Devil* in Italy. His name landed on Roy Brewer's list of Hollywood talent accused of working overseas to take advantage of the eighteen-month tax clause.[44] At the same time, further anti-run-away-production campaigns and anti-communist efforts took place. The American Legion joined forces with the AFL to promote legislation that would block the import of films from heavily Communist countries and movies made with blacklisted Hollywood talent and Communist sympathizers.[45] Within this politically treacherous atmosphere, Huston and his *Beat the Devil* unit found themselves in the tricky situation of working in Italy, where the most skilled technicians were aligned with Communist unions.

When Hollywood labor got wind of Huston's work in Italy, the AFL's European representative, Irving Brown, pressured Huston to avoid employing Communist crew members.[46] In January 1953, as Huston was preparing *Beat the Devil* in Rome, the director met with Brown, whose Brussels office was attempting to stem the tide of Communist unions in Europe.[47] What was discussed at these two meetings, first over drinks and then lunch, remains unclear. But it's likely that they were devising a strategy to avoid hiring Communists for the film shoot, a notion supported by the film's star, Humphrey Bogart, who later explained to a reporter that Brown had helped the production secure non-Communist workers.[48] *Daily Variety* reported that the employment of non-Communists in Italy forced many of the "Red" union members to switch to the "free" unions.[49] Around the same time, Huston was engaged in a protracted negotiation with his agent Paul Kohner, Roy Brewer, and actor and prominent anti-communist Ward Bond to craft a letter of recantation that openly rejected Communist ideology. In the letter, Huston also dissociated himself from Communist front groups and the

Hollywood Ten, who had refused to testify before HUAC. The letter wound up in Huston's FBI file.[50]

Interestingly, the AFL may have used *Moby Dick* as a bargaining chip with Huston during these discussions. Correspondence suggests that the plans for moving forward on *Moby Dick* had to be put on hold until controversies surrounding runaway productions were settled.[51] Huston's desire to make *Moby Dick* with foreign locations standing in for US settings likely raised eyebrows among Hollywood unions, who were intensifying their anti-runaway-film crusade. In its place, Huston began to consider other foreign production projects, such as a Spanish-set film entitled *Matador*, which didn't require stand-in locations.[52] Following Huston's demonstration that he would avoid using Italian Communist unions on *Beat the Devil*, Huston's agent, Paul Kohner, notified the director, "I am to inform you, *in strictest confidence*, that Brewer will release you from your promise and that they guarantee that you can go ahead with MOBY DICK with Brewer's and the unions' complete blessings."[53] At a time when Hollywood unions began targeting the supposed threat of foreign Communist crews to fight runaway productions, Huston's appeasement likely prompted Brewer and the AFL to offer their own concessions. They seemed willing to overlook the fact that *Moby Dick* was using stand-in foreign locales rather than authentic US-based locations. Any claims of inconsistency could be countered by the director's own public declarations of "Too many neon signs, too highly industrialized."

As a diplomatic gesture, Huston spoke at one of the AFL's meetings when he returned briefly to Hollywood after shooting *Beat the Devil*. *Variety*'s coverage of the event suggests that the bond between the AFL and Huston was sealed, as the director proclaimed that the Communists were losing control of European film unions. Huston also asserted that Irving Brown "has done as much if not more than any politician in Europe to fight communism." For his part, Roy Brewer praised Huston for his contribution to weakening Communism's grip on Italian unions by not hiring Communists on *Beat the Devil*.[54]

Once a target of anti-communist attention, Huston ultimately cooperated with the AFL, an organization known for its red-baiting tactics. In the process he won a diplomatic victory that probably helped garner the labor group's approval of *Moby Dick*, a stand-in location film that fit the unions' very definition of a runaway production. While these negotiations may have undermined the director's outspoken political progressivism, they also reflect the strength of the anti-communist fervor sweeping Hollywood, which forced even Huston to recant. In the end, although he received the AFL's blessing to make *Moby Dick*, he still had to maintain that it was impossible to shoot in the United States so that he could obscure his tax situation. Huston's navigation of these issues sheds light on the economics and politics of runaway production and the growing complexity of international filmmaking at this time. It is to that complexity that we turn next.

PART II

—————

Production

CHAPTER 2

London, Rome, Paris

THE INFRASTRUCTURE OF HOLLYWOOD'S
MODE OF INTERNATIONAL PRODUCTION

IN 1947, DIRECTOR DELMER DAVES AND PRODUCER Jerry Wald convinced Warner Bros. executives to shoot their new production, *To the Victor* (1948), partly on location in France. The film, which follows an ex-patriot US soldier turned black marketeer who falls for the wife of a Nazi collaborator, called for a French setting. Daves and Wald wanted to shoot exteriors on location in Paris and Normandy and interiors at the Warner Bros. studio in Burbank. Initially, the front office was reluctant to approve the location trek because of the uncertainties of shooting far away from the studio. But at Warner Bros., which had transitioned to a producer-driven unit system of production, Wald had a powerful voice with the authority to nurture and oversee projects.[1] So, the producer and director were able to convince studio executives to sanction the location work by invoking familiar reasons: the lure of authenticity and the savings of filming the real Paris rather than trying to build it at the Burbank studio. A location shoot offered other economic incentives, such as low wage scales in France and the studio's frozen francs that could be applied to the production.[2] Warner Bros. executives eventually endorsed the journey, but even when filming commenced in Paris, personnel back home relished the location unit's setbacks. Wald, who remained at the studio to supervise his other projects, kept in contact with Daves while the latter was in France. Wald relayed, "Certain individuals around here are delighted to hear that things aren't going too well.... This kind of sabotaging burns me up."[3]

For Daves and Wald, a lot was riding on the success of the location trip. They had to prove to Warner Bros. that the unit in France could generate footage that couldn't be reproduced in a studio. The high stakes were heightened by a crisis that was gripping Hollywood. Because of the market uncertainty from the UK's ad valorem tax, all movies in production at Warner had ground to a halt. The shoot for *To the Victor*, however, carried on; with the off-the-lot project already in motion, Warner Bros. opted to let the production continue. "We are carrying the load for the entire studio," Wald conveyed to Daves.[4] Adding to the expectations, the producer and director hoped to use *To the Victor* as a test run that could validate the viability of going on location in the future. Wald wrote, "There are many here who have been scoffing at this trip, but I know that in the long run, it will be well worth all the time and trouble you are going through. The more production you are able to get on the screen—the kind of stuff I mean that is just impossible to reproduce here—the easier it makes things for any other projected production trips we contemplate."[5] In spite of all the lack of support, *To the Victor* would be a proving ground for Hollywood's move toward international productions.

Coming ahead of the wave of Hollywood productions in Western Europe, *To the Victor* had no clear models for working on French locations. The film was one of the first postwar Hollywood movies to conduct extensive first-unit photography in France, although other companies were venturing into the country. Just as *To the Victor* was rolling in France in summer 1947, RKO filmed *Berlin Express* (1948) in Paris and Germany. But working in France was still an untested experience, and required a pioneering effort. In ways that anticipated the tactics of future international productions, which will be explored below, Wald and Daves cultivated overseas contacts. They looked to Warner's Paris distribution office to organize a local camera crew to assist the bare-bones unit sent from Burbank, and French filmmaker René Clair consulted on local shooting challenges.[6] In the meantime, Warner Bros. followed the filming progress through protocols that would become typical of productions abroad. The frequent exchange of letters and cables and the viewing of dailies allowed the studio to track the location unit. Wald wrote to Daves with an appraisal of the footage from France: "Everything we have seen up to date has been just great, and it certainly has proved that locations are still the best way to make pictures."[7] In the end, the outcome of this early postwar global venture was mixed. From a commercial point of view, the film failed at the box office and received mostly negative reviews.[8] But from a logistical perspective, the production legitimized the feasibility of international moviemaking.

This mode of international production is the focus of this section, as it considers how Hollywood filmmakers executed production specifically in the United Kingdom, Italy, and France, which attracted a substantial concentration of runaway productions in Europe from the late 1940s to the early 1960s. In this process, Hollywood reshaped European filmmaking practices, while European production and labor protocols correspondingly refashioned Hollywood methods. This exchange was not always mutually beneficial or equal. Hollywood reaped the rewards of European financial incentives and cheap labor, but European unions and infrastructures influenced Hollywood production in a manner that benefited foreign industries. After all, it was the dictates of protectionist film policies in the UK, Italy, and France that impelled Hollywood companies to invest their frozen foreign earnings in these countries.

Identifying patterns in how these movies were planned and carried out reveals that international production work was standardized to a degree, in that it adhered to proven methods developed in Hollywood. Furthermore, overseas filmmaking achieved a form of standardization as Hollywood crews adapted to the new circumstances of working in Europe, which in turn coalesced into practices and trade knowledge that subsequent productions relied on. These adjustments to the organization of large-scale commercial films point to a development in the Hollywood mode of production specifically related to the interplay of industrial standardization and differentiation, as persuasively advanced by Janet Staiger.[9] Rather than a static conception of the industry, this notion uses continuity to throw change into relief. Staiger in fact suggests that variations emerged in the prevailing mode of production when shooting abroad became a significant trend in the 1950s.[10] Part II of this book illuminates those variations in collective production work as Hollywood filmmakers went overseas.

Using the Hollywood mode of production as a baseline, this section details a series of prominent characteristics that came to typify Hollywood's system of international filmmaking. Before analyzing the personnel and practices of overseas production in the following chapter, this chapter concentrates on the infrastructure provided by foreign studio offices, studio lots, laboratories, and equipment suppliers. For Hollywood companies that wanted to engage in international productions away from the infrastructure of the Los Angeles area, they had to find these resources in new centers. The areas in and around London, Rome, and Paris afforded this support. Hollywood's ability to simultaneously contribute to these filmmaking centers, which were still recovering from the war, and take advantage of them sheds light on what the globalization of production looked like on the ground in the postwar era. These exchanges resulted in an adaptable and transcultural filmmaking process that was key to Hollywood's assertion of influence worldwide.

As the case of *To the Victor* reveals, Hollywood studios faced the challenge of how to prepare the groundwork for mounting productions in cities and countries where their production management had little experience. Traditionally, a Hollywood company, whether working within the walls of a studio lot or on location in Southern California, would run its filmmaking operations from studio production offices. On European shoots, a studio's geographical distance from the satellite film sites limited the role of these offices. Instead, certain studios looked to their networks of overseas offices, which housed distribution and exhibition operations, subsidiaries, and, in some cases, personnel in charge of scouting foreign story properties. The studio foreign office was vital to preparatory work in regions that studios were largely unfamiliar with before a Hollywood unit arrived to do principal photography. The foreign office was especially important to Hollywood studios such as Paramount and Fox, which did not have control of foreign production facilities, as MGM and Warner Bros. did in England.[11]

In London, Paramount split its operations between two locations. Under the banner of Paramount British Productions Ltd., a production office that handled story properties and casting was situated near Piccadilly Circus. Additional production organization came out of the company's distribution office, Paramount Film Service Ltd., in Soho, where many of Hollywood's British branches were clustered.[12] In Paris, Paramount productions were coordinated from the company's distribution branch in the 9th Arrondissement, while in Rome, the studio relied on its distribution office in the Via Veneto area.[13] Twentieth Century-Fox also had offices in London and Rome. In Paris, the Fox setup was divided between a distribution office on the Champs-Élysées and a nearby production office that would eventually become a base for Darryl Zanuck's DFZ Productions when the studio production chief relocated to Europe as an independent producer.[14]

Once a studio authorized a production to shoot overseas, these foreign offices received directives from Hollywood to scout locations, contract foreign labor, and negotiate with local unions and authorities to secure shooting permits. For *September Affair* (1951), one of Paramount's early postwar foreign productions, the studio's Rome office was charged with securing import and export licenses for equipment as well as entry permits for the crew coming from Hollywood.[15] Paramount also put to use its network of smaller distribution offices throughout Italy to aid with location surveys in Florence and Naples, where the film was shot.[16] On Alfred Hitchcock's remake of *The Man Who Knew Too Much* (1956), Paramount's London office scouted locations by taking photos of various locales and sending them to personnel in Hollywood.[17] Because the film was shot on location in Marrakech as well, the studio benefited from France's colonial ties to French Morocco by working through its Paris office to organize permits, crews, and equipment. Acting as a cultural point of contact, the studio foreign office could educate Hollywood on cross-cultural sensitivities and commonsense practices on overseas locations. Hitchcock, who wanted to work in Morocco as discreetly as possible, wrote to the office, "I certainly got a feeling when I was taking pictures there myself that some of the people resented being photographed."[18] After making some inquiries, the office wrote back explaining the practice of veils on women and that locals "sometimes resent being snapshot by tourists as if they were a curiosity."[19]

In each of these offices, a multilingual staff member worked with the studio to help initiate productions by hiring local cast and crew and working with local authorities, from police to government officials. "They were not only useful," production manager C. O. "Doc" Erickson recalled, "they were essential."[20] For much of the 1950s at Paramount, Richard Mealand, a former studio story editor, was the production representative in the London office, while Luigi Zaccardi looked after productions in the Rome office. The representative in Paramount's Paris office was Edouard de Segonzac, a central figure in organizing preproduction for *Little Boy Lost* (1953), *To Catch a Thief* (1955), *Funny Face* (1957), and the Moroccan phase of *The Man Who Knew Too Much*. While preparing *Little Boy Lost*, producer William Perlberg praised Segonzac, claiming, "He is a wonderful guy and has been a tremendous help to us. We are together all the time and his grasp of our needs is amazing."[21] Correspondence in later years, however, reveals that some Paramount personnel became frustrated with Segonzac's "sloppy methods."[22] He also had to be "pushed along."[23] Certainly one of the risks of working away from a studio was the lack of employee supervision needed to meet the expectations of production efficiency. But whatever shortcomings a foreign office representative might have had, these in-the-field liaisons were indispensable to laying the groundwork for a studio unit to carry out production.

When Twentieth Century-Fox began applying its frozen earnings toward European productions, it likewise looked to its foreign offices. In 1948, Fox turned its London branch into an active production center not only for British projects but also to supervise filmmaking units around Europe.[24] As

Fox expanded its production activities in France, its Paris office provided the studio with production support, too. On *A Certain Smile* (1958), Edward Leggewie of the Paris office was charged with lining up a French crew, performing location surveys, and securing access to shooting sites.[25] While Fox gave him a great deal of responsibility, the studio closely monitored his activities, especially the foreign office's spending. After the Fox home office learned that Leggewie had prematurely put a French unit manager on salary and hired an office assistant, production executive Sid Rogell admonished him for needless spending.[26] About a year and a half later, Fox's dependence on Leggewie and Fox's Paris office persisted. Leggewie was entrusted with coordinating *Seven Thieves* (1960) in the south of France by securing locations, equipment, and crew members.[27] Impressively, shooting commenced three weeks after the initial request was submitted to the Paris office.[28] As with Paramount, Fox had to balance giving its foreign office the authority to organize a production and supervising that work from a great distance.

The staff at the various foreign offices were also an asset, since they were often familiar with the politics of local filmmaking. To avoid trouble back home with HUAC and red-baiting labor groups, US companies could not align themselves too closely with Communist film unions in Europe. While US foreign embassies could advise Hollywood filmmakers on the political affiliations of foreign film interests, the studios' overseas offices used their more specialized knowledge of the local production landscape to help Hollywood studios operate within the tricky labor situation in Europe.[29] This guidance was especially beneficial in France, where the Communist Party had a strong presence in national politics and the film industry. When Paramount undertook the production of *Little Boy Lost* and needed to hire French crew members, the studio sought help from its London and Paris offices to navigate a conflict between Communist and non-Communist unions.[30] During the preparations for *To Catch a Thief*, the Paris and London offices built on their experiences from *Little Boy Lost* to once again help Paramount. They advised that by shooting outside of Paris, the production would have an easier time securing non-Communist workers rather than hiring members of the Confédération générale du travail (CGT), a Communist-led union that endorsed wholly homegrown productions and thus objected to Franco-US coproductions.[31]

When a film company did not have a foreign office to assist with a production, other possibilities existed. Both studio and independent companies involved in coproductions could count on the office of the foreign producer to meet some of their preproduction needs.[32] Opening temporary offices in foreign cities was another alternative for independent producers, such as Otto Preminger, who set up an office in London for the production of *Saint Joan* (1957).[33] A Hollywood production could also use a foreign studio as a base of operations, especially when a unit was shooting interiors at that studio. *Quo Vadis* (1951), *Roman Holiday* (1953), and *Ben-Hur* (1959) all used Cinecittà as a production headquarters. A piecemeal approach was a further option for a company like MGM, which could take advantage of the resources available at its British studios while also looking to its offices in Paris and Rome for additional production support. Even before *Quo Vadis* established its operation at Cinecittà, personnel from MGM's British studios worked with MGM's Rome office for the film's early preparations.[34]

By the early 1960s, some foreign companies supplied production-service support to Hollywood units in Europe, in effect supplanting the role of the foreign studio office. In Italy, a group of Italians who had worked on a number of Fox pictures formed a company called International Film Service. Employing the motto "With I.F.S. you will be at home anywhere this side of the world," the organization offered its assistance in handling many of the responsibilities that studio foreign offices had dealt with, including obtaining permits and hiring local crews, throughout much of Europe, Africa, and the Middle East.[35] Jean Negulesco used IFS for *Jessica* (1962), and later Warner Bros. engaged the firm for *Rome Adventure* (1962).[36] A mix of Italian and Hollywood personnel based in Rome started another company, the General Film Production Service, which provided similar help to foreign producers working in Italy and Europe.[37] These services in many ways heralded the foreign film commissions that became more common in cities and regions around the world in the 1970s and 1980s to attract and facilitate international coproductions.[38]

In sum, foreign offices and their representatives functioned as intermediaries that paved the way for a studio unit to carry out production. Back in the mid-1910s, Hollywood studios had in part achieved global dominance by switching from sales agents in London to their own distribution offices worldwide.[39] In the postwar era, these offices took on a crucial added role in providing the needed support base to initiate a film operation at a distance from the traditional spaces of Hollywood production.

Hollywood companies faced another challenge in the postwar era as they mounted productions away from Los Angeles, where an infrastructure of studios, filmmaking services, and workers had supported production work for over three decades. More than just a symbolic space, Hollywood was the geographic nexus of film companies in the Los Angeles region. Economic geographer Allen J. Scott attributes the growth and stabilization of this phenomenon in Southern California to industrial agglomeration, in which a dense cluster of individual production firms arose in one area. A more dispersed collection of laboratories and equipment houses eventually surrounded the concentration of film studios, thereby reinforcing the physical and economic accumulation.[40] But what happened to this clustering pattern when Hollywood films went on location to far-flung, foreign countries?

On one hand, the agglomeration structure in Los Angeles became some-what de-territorialized as certain Hollywood studios looked beyond the local support system to foreign regions. On the other hand, these productions moved to new filmmaking agglomerations in the metropolitan areas of London, Rome, and Paris, where studios, associated firms, and skilled crews could support Hollywood projects. While the production hubs in European cities may not have been as dense as their counterpart in Los Angeles, the clustering was significant enough to maintain both Hollywood and local production during the 1950s and into the 1960s. In effect, runaway produc-tions contributed to a shift in the geographic structure of film industries: Hollywood functioned as a center where studios developed projects, supplied interior sets, and often carried out postproduction work, and this center interacted with foreign nodes rooted in the infrastructures of studios in London, Rome, and Paris.

British Studios

The area outside of London offered the greatest concentration of film studios in Western Europe. In 1950, sixteen British studios could handle large-scale production on a total of sixty soundstages.[41] While this was a significant number, these studios could not always produce enough British films to meet the country's own quota of indigenous motion pictures. So they looked to

Hollywood companies as coproducers to help meet this demand and to keep their stages operational and their technicians employed.[42] Hollywood studios that already owned local facilities launched into British production after World War II, especially when the British Board of Trade threatened to ban the further purchases of British studios using frozen foreign earnings of Hollywood companies.[43] Instead of solely relying on their foreign offices in London to help organize film shoots, the Hollywood majors that owned British studios could use these movie plants as production headquarters and places to film interiors.

In the late 1940s MGM led Hollywood's push into British production by converting its recently purchased Amalgamated Studios in Borehamwood, north of London, into one of the most modern studios in the country. Managing director Ben Goetz headed the British plant and worked with the home studio in Culver City to devise an MGM-style plan for British productions.[44] Rivaling the scope of some Hollywood studios, the facilities included a full production staff, five stages, a water tank, a special effects department, dubbing and scoring theaters, and camera, lighting, and sound recording equipment.[45] Its first British production, *Edward, My Son* (1949), wrapped nine days ahead of schedule, a testament to the efficiency of the Borehamwood plant, according to the film's producer.[46]

Film historians Sue Harper and Vincent Porter have demonstrated that MGM's British studio re-created the organization of the company's Culver City lot by enlisting a mix of prominent British technicians and imported Hollywood talent.[47] MGM immersed many of the British film personnel in Hollywood production culture in a deliberate effort to cultivate their skills. British cinematographer Oswald Morris, who shot a number of films at Borehamwood, remembered, "Everybody was very envious of the MGM pictures because MGM basically took the cream of the technicians and put them under contract. They were a cut above everybody else."[48] However, Britain's Association of Cine-Technicians (ACT) criticized MGM for having one of the biggest studios in the UK but employing one of the smallest staffs and making only one film at a time, when the British film industry was undergoing increasing unemployment.[49] According to some estimates, the number of British studio workers dropped from about 7,700 in 1948 to 4,000 in 1950.[50]

By the early 1950s, production picked up and MGM's British studio could balance three major shoots with careful coordination, as was the case with the overlapping filming of *Crest of the Wave, Flame and the Flesh*, and *Knights of the Round Table* (all released in 1954).[51] Shortly afterward, though, the studio reduced its workforce significantly and moved from maintaining a staff who carried over from one film to another to hiring workers on a film-by-film basis, a realignment that received additional criticism from ACT.[52] Nevertheless, the studio was still capable of handling mega-productions and employing large crews for MGM films and other companies that rented out portions of the lot. For Fox's production of *The Inn of the Sixth Happiness* (1958), the Borehamwood studio constructed a replica of a Chinese city, covering half a million square feet on the back lot, reportedly the largest outdoor set constructed in Europe at that time.[53]

In 1931 Warner Bros. acquired its own British facilities to produce quota quickies when it purchased Teddington Studios, located in a southwest London borough. Production came to a halt during World War II when a German plane blitzed the site, but after the war, Warner rebuilt the studio into a modern, well-equipped space, hoping to rent it out to independent productions. Shortly after its reopening in 1948, however, Teddington shut down because not enough companies were renting its two soundstages.[54] So instead of using its own Teddington facilities, Warner Bros. focused its film-making efforts at the studio of the Associated British Picture Corporation (ABPC), which was partly owned by Warner. This partnership gave the Hollywood studio access to a British facility and theater chain. Originally the home of British International Pictures, ABPC's Elstree studio, down the road from MGM's Borehamwood operation, was rebuilt and modernized after a period of inactivity during the war, when it was used as an army depot.[55]

Once ABPC's studio became operational, Warner Bros. began making films there. This alliance sheds some light on the benefits and limitations of foreign studios for Hollywood companies. On *The Hasty Heart* (1950), the first Warner production at ABPC, director Vincent Sherman had to construct both the interior and the exterior sets for the movie's Burmese setting on the studio's small soundstages, an approach that probably would have been avoided in Hollywood at the time. "In America we would have built the exterior somewhere on the ranch," Sherman explained in a letter to Warner production executive Steve Trilling, "but it is ridiculous to consider shooting any exteriors here at the moment, because of the weather."[56] The director later recalled that England experienced an unusually harsh winter that year.[57] As a solution, ABPC's British art director, Terence Verity, introduced a "turntable technique" that used a revolving stage and "flying backgrounds" that came down from the ceiling to allow for rapid set changes.[58] Sherman also noted that because of the difficulty of filming exteriors in English weather, the ABPC staff had developed excellent miniature work for less than half of what it would cost in Hollywood.[59] The *Hasty Heart* production clearly benefited from the ingenuity of British personnel habituated to working in limited studio space and difficult weather conditions.

Overall, though, working at ABPC was a challenge to a director like Sherman, who was accustomed to Hollywood studios and organization. He complained about the ABPC's technical problems and shooting a tropical-set motion picture on a cold British soundstage in the winter. He also remarked that he could have worked much faster at Warner's Burbank studio, and with that extra time, he could have devoted more attention to the actors.[60] He summed up his involvement at ABPC:

> They have a good organization here but they are still young in picture making. This is a new studio with new people and while I think they are the healthiest and best group they still have to go some in order to have the same efficiency that we have at Warner Bros. This is natural of course, because we have an organization which has been functioning for many years and they need an equal amount of time to reach the same degree of experience.[61]

A couple of years later, director Robert Siodmak, who shot a portion of *The Crimson Pirate* (1952) at ABPC, complained to Warner Bros. about the British studio's continuing problems. Its management and labor were often in conflict because the crews were paid only minimum wage and banned from working overtime. Also, since the crews had no guarantee of future employment, they had little incentive to work quickly.[62]

From the British side, ABPC was eager to coproduce with Warner Bros. so that it could showcase the potential of its new studio and gain access to Warner's international distribution network. British producer Alex Boyd expressed to Steve Trilling the pleasure of working on *The Hasty Heart*: "Everyone connected with the picture here is very happy to know that their efforts appear to have been successful. As you know this was our first big picture in our new Studios and we were naturally keen to show the world that our plant and the technicians in it were capable of turning out an article of which anyone, anywhere, could be proud."[63] As the British industry slowly began to recover after the war, its cooperation with Hollywood companies helped bring in investment and talent to boost the prospects of its own film output. Despite the different working conditions and production practices, ABPC provided Warner Bros. with a base to bring forth a small but steady stream of British-made productions.[64]

While MGM and Warner Bros. had the closest ties to the film infrastructure of the London area, Twentieth Century-Fox had a connection to the British industry through its ownership of Wembley Studios, located in northwest London. Fox first leased the studios in 1932 to produce quota quickies, but once World War II commenced, it became a base for the production of military training films.[65] Following the studio's bombing during the war, Fox renovated Wembley, which was then mostly rented out to independent companies for commercials and short films.[66] For its own productions, Fox signed a deal with producer Alexander Korda to shoot several films at his Shepperton Studios. Then, after signing an agreement with producer J. Arthur Rank, Fox shifted some of its production to Rank's Denham and Pinewood Studios.[67] Independent companies, meanwhile, rented out foreign-owned, London-area studios such as Shepperton, where the interiors of *Moulin Rouge* (1953) and *Beat the Devil* (1954) were shot. Walt Disney filmed the interiors of his British productions at a number of studios, including Denham, Pinewood, and ABPC. Without its own British studios, Paramount tended to carry out only location shooting in the UK, reserving soundstage work for its facilities in Hollywood.

Despite the relatively favorable working conditions in England, British studios faced challenges throughout the 1950s. In 1956, the Film Industry Employees' Council, which represented the various British film trade unions, presented a postmortem on the industry after the sale of Ealing Studios. Since the war, several studios had closed, including Islington, Teddington, Welwyn, Isleworth, and Denham, while others converted to TV production, leaving only four major studios in operation. Along with these closures came greater film production unemployment and a downturn in the number of films made in the UK.[68] But for those Hollywood studios and filmmakers with links to the British industry, the production infrastructure in and around London offered modern studios, a skilled pool of crew members and actors, and a filmmaking system that generally meshed well with Hollywood practices. More than any other production center, the British studio system allowed Hollywood to invest its un-remittable sterling and launch a more international filmmaking operation.

Italian Studios

In Italy, Hollywood production concentrated around film facilities scattered throughout southern Rome, though studios also existed in Venice, Milan, and Turin. Due to wartime ruin and the fact that much equipment had been stolen, hidden, or destroyed during the German occupation, many of the studios in Rome were unable to sustain a large number of productions in the early postwar era. Moreover, electricity needed for movie-set lighting was in short supply because of damage to power stations and limited coal reserves. In 1947, an MGM producer surveyed the Italian studios and wrote, "Compared to the standards of U.S. Studios the Italians are to be considered most modest."[69] Hollywood companies had to find a way to work within these constraints and help rebuild the Italian infrastructure so that they could mount big-budget productions using their frozen lire.

In the south of Rome, Scalera studios had six stages, a carpentry shop for building sets, and equipment for lighting, cameras, and sound.[70] Scalera supported the independent production *Black Magic* (1949) as a coproducer and studio space. It also served as a base of operations for Roman location shooting on MGM's *The Red Danube* (1949) and provided the interiors for Orson Welles's *Othello* (1952 premiere, 1955 US release). In the southeastern part of Rome was the smaller Centro Sperimentale di Cinematografia, which the Fascist government started in 1935 as both a studio and a training ground for actors and technicians. Then, the German army ransacked the studio's equipment during the war. The Italian company Universalia eventually rented out the facility and replenished it with new gear. Another revived studio was Titanus, which expanded after the war to include new stages and US-brand film equipment.[71] In the early 1960s, the Dino De Laurentiis Studios were established in the southern outskirts of the city.

Cinecittà, situated in southeastern Rome, was by far the most important studio to Italian filmmaking and eventually Hollywood's Italian-based productions. Opened in 1937 by Benito Mussolini, it became one of the largest studios in Europe, but during World War II it was a shelter for the German army and a target of Allied bombardment. After the war it served as a munitions depot, and then a camp for displaced persons.[72] Film production resumed in 1947, and a year later Fox's *Prince of Foxes* (1949) was shot there against a backdrop of disarray. In order for MGM to gauge the possibility of making films in Italy, its British studio staff were charged with surveying Italian infrastructure. They produced reports on the state of the country's

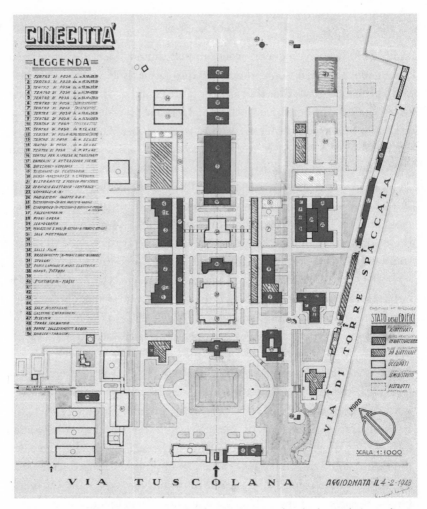

FIGURE 6. A map of Cinecittà dated February 4, 1948, details the studio's condition. Buildings are labeled as destroyed, semi-destroyed, reactivated, or in the process of being reactivated. A number of structures are listed as occupied, probably by displaced persons. (Courtesy of the Margaret Herrick Library, Academy of Motion Picture Arts and Sciences. Licensed by Warner Bros. Entertainment Inc. All Rights Reserved.)

studios and supplied a detailed plan of the Cinecittà lot that identified the condition of its facilities (fig. 6). In one of these reports from early 1948, MGM's British production manager, Dora Wright, shared her impressions of Cinecittà:

> Lines of laundry, large groups of people, soup kitchens, dogs etc. seem to be everywhere. Despite this confusion, a limited amount of production and

reconstruction is in progress. The latter, however, is considerably handicapped by lack of funds. A vicious circle is created by the fact that the only real hope of making headway on reconstruction appears to be through revenue from production, and production cannot really increase until the place is put into some semblance of order. At a rough guess, it would take perhaps twelve months to get the Studio properly working again, assuming that the D.P. camp could be dispersed—of which there is no sign at the moment. We therefore suggest eliminating this Studio from our calculations.[73]

MGM had already been considering building its own studio in Rome, but when the costs proved prohibitive, MGM began investing blocked lire in modernizing Cinecittà to support its epic film *Quo Vadis*.[74] Once principal photography commenced in 1950, however, much of the studio was still in disrepair, and even some refugees remained.[75] *Quo Vadis* cinematographer Robert Surtees remarked that the stage walls and ceilings were in such bad shape, they couldn't support the weight of heavy arc lights. In another stage, the construction of a roof had been interrupted by the war, but the MGM production used that drawback to its advantage by constructing a massive banquet set in the open air, using the sun to light the set.[76]

In his correspondence with MGM in 1949, *Quo Vadis* business manager Henry Henigson portrayed Cinecittà as a large and serviceable studio. In addition to nine working stages, it had a machine shop, a construction department, and space for a production office. The studio also housed a wardrobe manufacturing department, staffed plumbing division, tin shop, blacksmith shop, and upholstery workshop.[77] Cinematographer Surtees reported that because *Quo Vadis* was such a large undertaking, a number of departments had to occupy several soundstages.[78] Tying it all together, Henigson organized the entire studio to fall in line with Hollywood departmental organization and practices.

A few years later, during the production of *The Barefoot Contessa* (1954) at Cinecittà, producer-director Joseph Mankiewicz encountered a studio still hamstrung by organizational problems. After the first day of shooting, the Hollywood and Italian production personnel met to take stock of all the issues that had impacted the start of filming. A livid Mankiewicz delivered a list of grievances, including the late arrival of extras, an overcrowded set, a disorganized wardrobe department, and unheated dressing rooms that made it difficult for the extras to apply their makeup. Meeting notes underscored the importance of the last point: "This is a perfect example of false economy— heating only the stars' dressing rooms—but if you have 120 freezing extras unable to get their make-up on and you lose 1/4 of a day, where is the economy?"[79] Cinecittà consequently hired a worker to spend the night in the studios and wake up at five in the morning to turn on the heat and prepare hot water for the morning call times. The Hollywood production covered the costs of the hired help and extra heat.

Italian studios had additional disadvantages; for instance many sound-stages were not fully soundproofed because Italian films primarily dubbed dialogue instead of recording sound directly. The underwhelming quality of sound equipment and re-recording facilities prompted MGM's studio office representative to proclaim, "This is the worst handicap of Italian studios."[80] Furthermore, while Cinecittà was one of the biggest studios in Europe, the demand for soundstage space by large-scale productions created competition. According to Fred Zinnemann, his film *Teresa* (1951) had to be shot in a small studio in Rome since *Quo Vadis* monopolized Cinecittà.[81] About a decade later, because the immense production of *Cleopatra* (1963) was dominating Cinecittà and spilling over to the nearby Centro Sperimentale, Jerry Wald's production of *Hemingway's Adventures of a Young Man* (1962) was denied space and had to move studio work back to Hollywood.[82]

Despite these shortcomings, Italian studios provided infrastructure to support enough US productions to earn the name "Hollywood on the Tiber" and to transform Rome into an energetic center of motion picture production. Cinecittà played a particularly significant role in Hollywood moviemaking; by the late 1950s, films shooting in the Italian studio wanted to become associated with its brand. In 1959, advertisements promoting the release of *Ben-Hur* highlighted the fact that the film was shot at Cinecittà. One ad in *Daily Variety* reads, "Filmed at Cinecitta . . . the studios of spectacular productions . . . Rome-Italy." It then lists off previous Hollywood productions shot there, including *Quo Vadis, Roman Holiday, The Barefoot Contessa, Helen of Troy* (1956), *A Farewell to Arms* (1957), *Boy on a Dolphin* (1957), and *The Nun's Story* (1959).[83] The studio's services to some of Hollywood's biggest international productions helped transform the name Cinecittà into a mark of excellence.

French Studios

French studios were concentrated in Paris. In the postwar era, the principal Parisian plants included Studios de Billancourt, Studios de Boulogne, Studios de Neuilly, Studios Éclair, Studios des Butte-Chaumont, and Franstudios, which encompassed the consortium of Studios Joinville, Saint-

Maurice, Francoeur, and Clichy.[84] Studios outside of Paris included Studios La Victorine in Nice and Studios de Marseille in Marseille.[85] Despite the variety of shooting options, Hollywood restrained its use of these studios in the late 1940s and early 1950s, to some extent owing to soaring production costs in France at the time.[86] Additionally, limited filmmaking resources within these studios discouraged Hollywood companies from shooting on French soundstages.

Like some Italian studios, French facilities had been gutted by German occupiers, leaving them undersupplied or with outdated equipment. The studios were also understaffed in order to maintain low overhead.[87] The banking credit restrictions of the late 1940s and French studios' inability to maintain year-round staffs and a consistent production output all contributed to problems. Instead, the studios were often rented out empty to short-lived production companies, either without a set staff or with a very small workforce.[88] Several US film personnel working in France noted the limited infrastructure. In a 1947 *American Cinematographer* report, a representative of a US equipment company visited studios around Paris and described "antiquated equipment," small layouts, and "practically no activity."[89] From his experience of shooting *The Ambassador's Daughter* (1956) in Parisian studios, producer-director Norman Krasna praised the work of French technicians, but then explained that Parisian studios were not equipped with the necessary set materials and props to handle "American action."[90] Some of these comments come off as ethnocentric on the part of Hollywood personnel, but it is true that the French studios played a secondary role in attracting Hollywood production; authentic French locations were a more important lure. However, a handful of Hollywood productions were shot in French studios with sometimes-mixed results.

With a great deal of attention focused on the prospect of early Franco-US collaboration, Irving Allen and Franchot Tone's production of *The Man on the Eiffel Tower* (1950) began interior work at the Studios de Billancourt in 1948. Because of space constraints, the production was eventually expanded to the Joinville studios about ten miles across the city, only to encounter a labor strike there, which delayed the filming. More serious was a coal shortage in France that led to electricity rationing at both studios, a problem that was compounded by the need for specialized lighting brought over from England that could produce enough light for the film's Ansco color cinematography. Electricity was cut two days a week at both Billancourt and Joinville on alternate days, forcing the production to shuttle equipment and materials back and forth. When further power limitations threatened to send the shoot to Hollywood, the US Embassy in Paris stepped in and convinced French authorities to provide enough electrical current to finish filming. The diplomatic intervention not only ensured that a Hollywood company could shoot a film entirely in France, it also preserved the promise of future Franco-US collaborations.[91]

Subsequent productions in French studios encountered fewer problems. Billy Wilder's *Love in the Afternoon* (1957) was shot at Studios de Boulogne, where the interiors of several Parisian locales, such as the Ritz Hotel and the Paris Opera house, were replicated. Darryl Zanuck balanced location work on his D-Day epic *The Longest Day* (1962) with numerous indoor and outdoor sets at Boulogne. Despite the increase in Hollywood companies' use of French studios in the early 1960s, the number of facilities dwindled as location shooting became more common and the popularity of television cut into the rate of French film production. Some studios also disappeared as urban expansion took hold of the area surrounding Paris, where apartment buildings supplanted studio space.[92] Regardless of their flaws, Paris studios, along with facilities in London and Rome, formed significant clusters of production spaces that were bolstered by a loose network of support services.

FOREIGN LABS

Productions undertaken far from laboratories in the Los Angeles area proved a challenge for processing film footage, as the home studio generally wanted a first look at the footage the foreign unit was generating. Some studios opted to fly footage shot on location to New York and Hollywood, which delayed developing and viewing dailies. In order to send exposed footage from Nairobi to Los Angeles during production of *King Solomon's Mines* (1950), re-icing stations were placed along a stopover route at Johannesburg, Leopoldville, Dakar, the Azores, and New York to keep the film cool.[93] Even with productions in Europe, from which air service was quicker, shipping time still resulted in a holdup in processing and viewing dailies. In the case of the Italian shoot for *Prince of Foxes*, processing the dailies in Los Angeles allowed Darryl Zanuck to study the rushes before they were returned to director Henry King in Italy.[94]

When dailies had to be processed in Los Angeles, the foreign location unit had to shoot "blindly" without knowing the results of its filming work. Such waiting and lengthy shipments caused anxiety. "There is no better road to nervous prostration," remarked writer-producer Carl Foreman, "than to await the return of rushes which have to be air-expressed to a laboratory three or four thousand miles away—the usual lot of the distantly-based producer."[95] For the production of *Little Boy Lost*, footage was shipped from French locations to Los Angeles for development, where Paramount studio personnel viewed the rushes and reported their assessment to the unit in France. However, because of unpredictable weather conditions on location, the production unit needed to shoot daily tests, which were developed closer at GTC Labs in Paris, providing the crew with more immediate photographic results.[96]

The establishment of US-owned laboratories in Europe was a boon to Hollywood's foreign activities, giving the film units sent abroad the security of familiar processing procedures. In 1949, the US Cinecolor Corporation opened a lab in London, where Hollywood companies could expend frozen funds to develop dailies and release prints.[97] Probably the most important facilities were the Technicolor labs in Europe. Technicolor Ltd. was established in 1935 in London, and other labs were set up in Paris and Rome in the 1950s.[98] While Technicolor installed these plants to generate European film prints, they also supplied Hollywood's European shoots with equipment and developed dailies closer to the filming sites of international productions. Before the Technicolor lab in Rome was built, the footage for *Quo Vadis* was flown to the Technicolor plant in London, where two prints of the dailies were made. One was flown to MGM in Culver City and the other back to Rome, allowing the unit in Italy to figure out more quickly if it needed to do retakes or add scenes.[99] With the introduction of Eastman Color in the early 1950s, Technicolor lost its grip, as the newer, single-strip, multilayered color film could be processed in nearly any lab. In time, Technicolor Ltd. in London began processing Eastman Color film.[100] The spread of Eastman Color spurred the production and manufacturing of color films in Europe's motion picture industries.[101]

Hollywood productions also made use of foreign labs near the filming location, some of which looked at the Technicolor facilities as a threat to their business.[102] For *Roman Holiday*, director William Wyler and his editing staff worked with the Luce laboratory in Rome. Despite the fact that it ruined a couple of scenes as well as the retakes of those scenes, Wyler characterized the lab as "modern and well-equipped."[103] During the Paris shoot of Vincente Minnelli's *Gigi* (1958), MGM wanted to fly the exposed footage to the United States for developing. To avoid delays, however, the location unit insisted that the film be processed closer to the shooting site, so it was done at the LTC lab outside of Paris. According to Minnelli, the results were so impressive that MGM copied the processing technique at their Culver City lab.[104]

Instead of shipping unexposed film stock from the United States, some productions used foreign-made film stock. While shooting in France, Billy Wilder's *Love in the Afternoon* used French-manufactured Eastman Plus-X black-and-white negative film, which was faster than US-made Plus-X. The French-made stock allowed director of photography William Mellor to engineer dramatic shots that used unusually low-key lighting setups.[105] However, foreign-made stock was not always praised. During the London production of Stanley Donen's *The Grass Is Greener* (1961), the director complained about the poor quality of the Eastman Color film stock that was manufactured in Britain, which produced grainy and bluish images.[106] Conversely, for the shooting of Richard Fleischer's international production *The Big Gamble* (1961), the same stock was commended. Producer Darryl Zanuck attributed the quality results to tests performed by MGM and Fox and the close collaboration with Paris's LTC laboratory, where the movie was processed.[107] Ultimately, since most of the postproduction of Hollywood's continental films was done in Los Angeles, US companies usually used European labs to process dailies and Hollywood labs to develop prints for postproduction work. While the results of European labs could be mixed, they were an integral component of the foreign infrastructure that Hollywood units relied on.

EQUIPMENT

A challenge of Hollywood's big-budget filmmaking abroad was supplying far-flung units with enough production equipment to support their ventures. One solution was to export these materials from the home studios. At the beginning of 1950, *Daily Variety* reported that Hollywood companies had shipped more than one million dollars of sound and electrical equipment to locations around the world over the course of a few months.[108] For *Quo Vadis* alone, MGM dispatched more than two hundred tons of equipment from its Culver City lot to Cinecittà, despite the pressures Italian equipment interests applied to the Italian government to deny import permits to Hollywood companies. Much of the exported material included generators and the electrical and lighting equipment needed to produce enough power and light to

FIGURE 7. Lighting units shipped from MGM's Culver City studios illuminate the *Quo Vadis* (1951) set of Emperor Nero's throne room for the Technicolor camera at Cinecittà. (Courtesy of the Margaret Herrick Library, Academy of Motion Picture Arts and Sciences. Licensed by Warner Bros. Entertainment Inc. All Rights Reserved.)

shoot in Technicolor, since Cinecittà was only suited to meet the electrical requirements of black-and-white filmmaking (fig. 7).[109] One MGM official reported that any saving accrued from Italian set building and cheaper local labor was offset by the expense of transporting staff and equipment.[110]

Over time, though, transferring equipment from the United States was discouraged due to shipping costs, import and export taxes, and the risk of delays in clearing customs. To secure the required resources, Hollywood companies formulated a global assemblage approach, shipping essential equipment from Hollywood and obtaining the rest from European studios, rental houses, and other Hollywood productions shooting on the continent. On *Little Boy Lost*, Paramount used a Parisian company for electrical equipment, generators, and trucks, while the Mitchell cameras came from

Hollywood.[111] To facilitate transporting equipment, Paramount used the shipping agency Frank P. Dow Company, which coordinated the exportation of filming materials from the United States. Once the materials arrived in Europe, the studio employed foreign shipping brokers, such as Italy's Cipolli & Zannetti and France's Michaux & Co. and Paul Donot, to clear the equipment through customs and send materials back to the States once production wrapped.[112] Hollywood's complex international operations benefited from transoceanic shipping that was modernizing in the postwar era.[113]

Another way to reduce the costs of moving equipment in and out of Europe was to look to other Hollywood productions already shooting on the continent. With quality equipment at a premium overseas, Hollywood foreign units could become valuable supply sources, engaging in a kind of production piggybacking. The key was exploiting consecutive and nearby productions. For studios that were scheduling multiple foreign shoots, productions had to be coordinated so that equipment could be transferred from one working film unit to another. For example, after the location shooting of Paramount's *Funny Face* completed in Paris, the camera and accessories were sent to Madrid for the Paramount-financed production of *Spanish Affair* (1958).[114] Even rival studios shared production materials. For *Roman Holiday*, Paramount arranged with MGM to use office equipment from *Quo Vadis* and camera dollies that had been left behind in Italy by the shoot for *When in Rome* (1952).[115] Anatole Litvak's independent production *Act of Love* (1953) hired Paramount's transparency cameraman and rented the studio's transparency equipment that had been brought over for *Little Boy Lost*.[116] In these new frontiers of production, competing film studios and units exhibited much cooperation to help ensure the availability of high-quality equipment. This form of what David Bordwell calls "cooperative competition" had long been part of the business of Hollywood, in which studios loaned out stars and filmmakers to one another and colluded to dominate first-run theatrical markets.[117]

Just as US labs had branches in Europe, US equipment firms also operated on the continent. Hollywood lighting company Mole-Richardson had a production plant in London and supply shops in Rome and Paris. In 1949, Italian-born company head Peter Mole (né Pietro Mule) spent three and a half months traveling through Europe to establish business ties and lay the foundations for supplying equipment to various foreign film industries.[118] Mole-Richardson's London firm was particularly effective at profiting from British-Italian exchange benefits to make equipment available to Italian studios that had been looted during the war.[119] By the early 1960s Mole-

Richardson had established branch offices throughout Europe; the company advertised in *American Cinematographer*, proclaiming, "Production worries in Europe solved by Mole Richardson."[120] In addition to generating dailies, Technicolor's European branches supplied Paramount's foreign productions with VistaVision cameras (the Technicolor labs processed most of the format's films). On *The Man Who Knew Too Much*, Technicolor London furnished the production with two Technicolor-converted VistaVision cameras and a sound blimp that helped reduce camera motor noise for filming in Morocco and England.[121] With US equipment manufacturers having secured a foothold in Europe, Hollywood productions could rely on the technologies they were accustomed to using in the United States.

As Hollywood production internationalized in the postwar era, US labs and equipment companies had been establishing outposts in Europe to export Hollywood-based technologies and methods to foreign industries. This equipment contributed to the European film industries' use of new wide-screen systems and sound and grip gear. On the Warner Bros. production of *The Hasty Heart*, a unidirectional microphone, already in use at Warner's Burbank lot, was employed for the first time in England.[122] British cinematographer Christopher Challis recalled that in the postwar era, Technicolor London imported a dolly from the United States, which the supplier customized with a hydraulic mechanism that functioned like a crane.[123] British director of photography Jack Cardiff penned an article in *American Cinematographer* about the English production of *Under Capricorn* (1949) and acknowledged his debt to US-made lighting equipment, such as Mazda photospots and photofloods.[124] Through these exchanges, Hollywood's international productions helped to promote Hollywood technologies and styles in Europe.

The exchange of equipment worked both ways, with some Hollywood productions relying on foreign-made equipment, which in certain instances proved more advantageous than US equipment. To help supply international productions, the French publication *La Technique Cinématographique* ran an English- and Spanish-language equipment advertising section that targeted foreign readers who would have been interested in using local equipment while shooting in France.[125] On one of these productions, *The Man on the Eiffel Tower*, Hollywood director of photography Stanley Cortez used a French-made Debrie Super Parvo camera that he reported was "mechanically superior" to many 35mm cameras that he had used before.[126] For *Gigi*, cinematographer Joseph Ruttenberg employed a dolly system developed in France that assisted in executing dynamic camera movements in a variety of locations.[127] The swapping of equipment formed an important piece of the overall international infrastructure, in which filmmakers shared materials across different industries to complete their productions. As I will illustrate in the next chapter, a transcultural flow of labor and craft practices accompanied this exchange.

NETWORKS OF INFRASTRUCTURE, PERSONNEL, PRACTICES

Hollywood's productions in the UK, Italy, and France contributed to an expanding network of infrastructure. This global growth reflected a larger industry trend that analysts have described as a post-Fordist period of flexible specialization that began in postwar Hollywood and intensified through the last quarter of the twentieth century. The evolving industrial system was characterized by the vertical disintegration of the studios, an increase in the number of subcontractor companies, and a "package-unit" system of production in which the whole industry, instead of a single studio, provided labor and equipment on a project-by-project basis.[128] Hollywood's international productions were simultaneously a result of and an influence on these industrial transformations. Hollywood's ability to take advantage of foreign studios and its own connections to overseas support services became an important strategy for navigating these postwar changes and wielding its global power.

As the opening discussion of *To the Victor* demonstrates, however, filmmakers who went overseas in the early postwar era did not have this vast network of services in place to facilitate working in new industries and locations. Director Delmer Daves and his small crew functioned with limited equipment and no support from a French studio. Despite these obstacles, Warner Bros. and its location unit managed to pull off filming in a foreign country where they had little experience working. In the years to come, this feat would become easier as Hollywood companies strengthened their ties to foreign offices, studios, labs, and equipment suppliers in London, Rome, and Paris. Still, as Hollywood filmmakers went abroad to these production centers, they encountered not only different production environments but also foreign personnel and methods, and the interchange of people and practices was itself a new production challenge. The importance of human agents in this process is the subject of the next chapter.

CHAPTER 3

Lumière, Camera, Azione!

THE PERSONNEL AND PRACTICES OF HOLLYWOOD'S MODE OF INTERNATIONAL PRODUCTION

AS HOLLYWOOD FILMMAKERS GAINED MORE EXPERIENCE ABROAD over the years, they devised various production strategies that could be shared with one another. A case in point: in May 1961, Vincente Minnelli was preparing the production of *Two Weeks in Another Town* (1962), part of which he planned to shoot in Rome. Hollywood filmmaker Jean Negulesco communicated with Minnelli, offering some advice on working in Italy, where Negulesco had directed portions of *Three Coins in the Fountain* (1954) and *Boy on a Dolphin* (1957) and at the time was producing his next film, *Jessica* (1962):

> I would say that the most difficult and the most important condition of making a picture in Italy is *to adapt yourself to their spirit, to their way of life, to their way of working.* A small example: This happened to me on location. As I arrive on the set and everything is ready to be done at 9 o'clock—the people are having coffee. Now, your assistant also is having coffee—and if you are foolish enough to start to shout and saying you want to work, right away you'll have an unhappy crew and not the cooperation needed for the picture. But if you have coffee with them, they will work for you with no time limit or no extra expense.[1]

Negulesco's letter underscores a key lesson that Hollywood moviemakers learned overseas when confronted with different working hours, production practices, and cultural customs. Rather than resisting these differences, the director recommends a modicum of adaptability to elicit the hard work and unregulated, long hours certain Hollywood filmmakers expected overseas.

The practice of adaptability was crucial to making Hollywood-style movies abroad and a development on the mass production of films in the studio system. In Hollywood, studios had created a specific division of labor and a set of craft practices that had governed filmmaking for decades. However, reflecting Negulesco's advice to adapt to local circumstances, Hollywood's postwar international productions operated in a more versatile mode, as filmmakers continued established studio-system practices while adjusting to foreign industries and locations. The Hollywood mode of production, which balanced standardization and differentiation, had always allowed for a degree of adaptability to respond to changes in technology and the need to innovate. Overseas, though, working in a more adjustable manner was not only an overarching method but also exemplified Hollywood's global production strategy, which simultaneously reshaped foreign practices and complied with them. One goal of this process was to continue making films that adhered to Hollywood's aesthetic conventions while also exploiting the appeal of foreign locations.

Building on the analysis of Hollywood's use of film infrastructure in the United Kingdom, Italy, and France, this chapter considers the impact of human agency by exploring the personnel and craft practices that typified production in these countries. These characteristics of international production included the increased importance of location production management; the cooperation of Hollywood and foreign personnel; the need to facilitate effective communication among multilingual crews; the intermixing of Hollywood and foreign production practices; the sharing of production knowledge as overseas experience accumulated; and a degree of supervision of runaway productions by studio management based in Los Angeles. In analyzing these features, this chapter takes the perspective of Hollywood filmmakers to show how they navigated new working environments. A key tactic that emerges is the kind of adaptability that Negulesco was advocating. Reflecting the transcultural nature of an international mode of production, this viewpoint is balanced by considering the contributions of foreign crews and their film practices. The goal is to explain how these crews both determined and were affected by what Hollywood filmmakers were doing, a dynamic that was simultaneously reciprocal and a consequence of how Hollywood exerted its production power.

LOCATION PRODUCTION MANAGEMENT

In the Hollywood studio system, the organization of individual film shoots was overseen by a production manager, who took care of preproduction arrangements, and an assistant director, who supported the director during shooting.[2] For foreign work, a unit production manager (UPM) with enhanced authority was sent to the filmmaking site to begin preplanning with the assistance of a foreign office or studio. The UPM stayed in frequent contact with studio production supervisors in Hollywood via telegraph messages and letters to update them on matters such as frozen funds, foreign labor, and the coordination of locations. Once shooting commenced, the unit manager was responsible for ensuring that all of these preparations functioned smoothly.

As production managers accrued enough experience overseas, they became highly valuable to studios, moving from one international production to another. One key Hollywood production manager upon whom Paramount Studios relied was C. O. "Doc" Erickson (fig. 8). He had risen through the ranks of Paramount's production department in the late 1940s, and by the mid-1950s had reached the level of UPM. He developed a specialization in location work after serving as production manager on a series of off-the-lot shoots, including *Shane* (1953), filmed in Wyoming, and *Secret of the Incas* (1954), shot in Peru. These productions initiated him to the challenges of working in remote locales and prepared him to organize the French location work on Alfred Hitchcock's *To Catch a Thief* (1955). With a great deal of responsibility, the up-and-coming production manager recalled that the shoot on the French Riviera "was a huge jump forward for *me*, working in a foreign country and a distant location, and all the good and bad points of doing that."[3]

Erickson's organizational skills, steady temperament, and commitment to both studio and director proved critical to the operation of *To Catch a Thief*. In February 1954, Erickson began preparations in Hollywood for organizing the French unit. He conferred with Bill Mull, the production manager on *Little Boy Lost* (1953), and studied correspondence from that earlier film to determine the procedures for shooting on French locations.[4] Then in France, he worked with Paramount's Paris office and French production managers to hire local labor, secure equipment, and negotiate with authorities. As preproduction got under way, Erickson's diligence extended to keeping the studio informed of logistical developments. Without a doubt, he remained a dedicated company man. He apprised Paramount, "I hope we are keeping you sufficiently informed of our operational plans and progress and that you are getting all the information you desire. If not, please let me know and we'll try to do better."[5] Paramount subsequently asked Erickson to wire the studio with updates every other day once shooting commenced.[6] His regular

FIGURE 8. Production manager C. O. "Doc" Erickson (in a suit) surveys the location in Tourrettes, France, during the filming of *To Catch a Thief* (1955). (Courtesy of Dawn Erickson)

communication continued when the first unit returned to Hollywood, and he remained in the south of France to manage the second unit. As a key force in organizing Paramount's overseas productions, Erickson was essential to mounting foreign location shoots while keeping the studio's interests in mind.

While Hollywood often dispatched abroad studio production managers like Erickson, certain film units also recruited foreign personnel to organize filmmaking matters. For shoots in the UK, the production manager was often British, since labor restrictions dictated that only a small percentage of the crew could be foreign. On *Little Boy Lost*, in accordance with French union regulations, the Hollywood unit manager, Bill Mull, was balanced by a French unit manager named Michel Rittener. Both were in charge of securing equipment, locations, and permits.[7] As Hollywood producers became more familiar with local crews, they began to depend increasingly on foreign production managers, such as Julien Derode, who worked on Warner's *The Nun's Story* (1959) and Fox's *Crack in the Mirror* (1960). Darryl Zanuck considered Derode one of the best European production managers, in part because Derode brought with him a crew accustomed to working together from film to film.[8] Whether they were relying on UPMs from the United States or abroad, Hollywood companies needed these individuals to help get production off the ground and facilitate cooperation between Hollywood and foreign workers.

THE MIXING OF HOLLYWOOD AND FOREIGN PERSONNEL

Debates over how many Hollywood personnel to employ on international productions arose in the United States and overseas. Some filmmakers, such as Charles Vidor, made a case for importing a high number of Hollywood crew members to ensure better production efficiency, even if it cost more.[9] As cinematographer Robert Surtees, who worked on numerous international productions, put it, "One American crew member is worth more to a production than all the inexperienced help recruited in the country where the picture is made."[10] Likewise, US film unions lobbied producers to take large Hollywood crews on foreign location treks.[11] Initially some studios adhered to this Hollywood-centric approach, much to the approval of the unions. In IATSE's official publication, *International Photographer*, several reports on large-scale epics such as *Helen of Troy* (1956), *Land of the Pharaohs* (1955), and *The Ten Commandments* (1956) highlighted the reliance on Hollywood crews for overseas shoots despite the sometimes-high transportation costs.[12] For Fox's early slate of postwar foreign productions, the quantity of studio personnel sent overseas resulted in a temporary depletion of the Fox lot's staff.[13]

Nonetheless, Hollywood companies capped the number of employees they brought to Europe, not only because they planned to hire cheaper, local skilled labor but also because European unions limited the importation of workers from the United States. In Britain, the Association of Cine-Technicians (ACT) union was disconcerted by the potential influx of Hollywood technicians.[14] Jonathan Stubbs has shown that ACT president Anthony Asquith voiced a nationalist concern over Hollywood's incursions into British filmmaking and the resulting production of decidedly British subject matter such as *Captain Horatio Hornblower* (1951).[15] Despite fears about the loss of work to Hollywood personnel, certain British workers profited from the presence of Hollywood in the UK at a time when film-sector unemployment was growing. Cinematographer Oswald Morris recollected that some British technicians welcomed companies such as MGM, since they were pouring money into big-budget productions and giving them an opportunity to learn.[16]

At first, US and British labor groups attempted reciprocity agreements, in which Hollywood workers could go overseas in exchange for British personnel coming to Hollywood.[17] The agreements aimed to support swapping Hollywood and British art directors and cinematographers for studio visits and filmmaking assignments on productions such as Fox's *The Mudlark* (1950).[18] The trading of talent also extended to acting, as the British Film Producers Association (BFPA) encouraged Hollywood actors working in England to join the British Equity union and British actors in Hollywood to similarly enlist in the Screen Actors Guild.[19] To many British personnel, the ability to work in Hollywood was very attractive. In addressing the British Society of Cinematographers, president Freddie Young promoted these agreements by appealing to notions of internationalism: "I think it a splendid idea that the creators of Motion Pictures, such as directors, writers, art directors, directors of photography, and others should be allowed to circulate freely and not be confined within the limits of their own countries."[20] Despite Young's call for a swapping of workers, the agreements were never fully realized, as they encountered labor protectionist measures on both sides of the Atlantic.

To safeguard the employment of British citizens in the motion picture industry, Britain's Ministry of Labour enacted some of the strictest regulations in Europe. In 1948, during the upsurge in British production by Hollywood companies, the BFPA limited the importation of Hollywood personnel to only a handful of producers and directors.[21] The British Actors Equity Association also restricted the number of actors brought over from the United States, especially to play British roles.[22] Hollywood technicians faced even greater impediments. On *The Miniver Story* (1950), made at MGM's Borehamwood studio, Hollywood director of photography Joseph Ruttenberg was able to work on the film only after the British-born and Hollywood-based actress Greer Garson threatened to walk off the film if he was not hired. In addition, a standby British cinematographer had to be employed.[23]

Over the course of the 1950s, Hollywood studios and British unions engaged in frequent negotiations over the importation of Hollywood talent.

Finally, a 1957 agreement between Hollywood's MPEA and Britain's ACT stipulated that US companies could export up to twelve Hollywood producers or directors a year for films that qualified for the British quota. However, the regulation did not apply to films that cost more than $840,000 if a British producer, associate producer, or director was involved.[24] In theory, the British Ministry of Labour in consultation with British unions aimed to grant foreign work permits to one or two lead actors and the producer or director. In practice, Hollywood firms and British unions arbitrated on a case-by-case basis.[25]

Despite the British industry's reliance on Hollywood production to keep studios open and workers employed, Hollywood companies encountered some resistance from local labor groups. During MGM's concurrent British productions of *Crest of the Wave*, *Flame and the Flesh*, and *Knights of the Round Table* in 1953, about two hundred individuals from the extras' union walked off all three films in protest over MGM's unwillingness to increase wages beyond an initial scale agreement after a group of extras on *Knights of the Round Table* complained about having to work long hours in heavy armored suits. The BFPA supported MGM by refusing to hire the hundreds of extras who boycotted the films until the situation was resolved. The walkout soon spread to other British studios when the Film Artistes Association, which represented the extras, retaliated by calling on more extras to strike. After a monthlong standoff, MGM finally capitulated and agreed to meet the extras' call for a pay raise.[26]

In France, segments of the film industry objected to the potential influx of Hollywood productions due to the strong influence of Communism in French film unions and a strain of anti-US sentiment that surfaced in the late 1940s. This stance arose in reaction to the threat of cultural domination prompted by the North Atlantic Treaty Organization, the Marshall Plan, and the Blum-Byrnes film accord, which enabled the free flow of US films into France.[27] Moreover, the Benagoss–Union générale cinématographique pact of 1949 aided the production of Franco-US films in France, much to the discontent of the Communist-controlled Confédération générale du travail (CGT) union, which favored supporting purely domestic work.[28] To regulate the possible flood of US film labor into France, French unions pressured the Centre national de la cinématographie to refuse filming permits to foreign productions unless a high number of French workers were used. The unions also required that any crew member brought from Hollywood be matched with a local worker of the same position, a procedure known

as featherbedding.[29] In practice, the French unions were open to nego-
tiating the balance of Hollywood and French personnel, although they were
more sensitive to protecting the employment of French cameramen.[30] As
Hollywood firms began to recognize the strengths of French technicians,
these companies reduced the number of US crew members to avoid featherbedding costs.[31]

The production situation was also tricky in Italy, where Hollywood was
mounting some of its largest foreign operations. The reliance on local infrastructure and the importation of Hollywood crews were therefore heavy. In
1949, an alliance of cinematographers at first threatened to ban technicians
coming from Hollywood for fear of being inundated with US workers.[32]
Over time, though, the Italian foreign labor restrictions were nominal.[33]
Italian cinematographer Sergio Salvati explained that Hollywood personnel
were welcome in Italy given the epic size of the productions and the opportunities for Italian workers.[34]

Nevertheless, relations with Italian film labor could be tense. On some of
the larger Italian productions, Hollywood companies had to navigate the
requirements of large labor pools. For *Quo Vadis* (1951), MGM had to work
with two labor unions. A committee charged with hiring Italian workers at
Cinecittà was made up of representatives from both the Federazione Italiana
Lavoratori dello Spettacolo (FILS), the Communist-controlled union, and
the Federazione Unitaria Lavoratori dello Spettacolo (FULS), the non-
Communist union. The US Embassy in Rome encouraged the production to
use the non-Communist option for fear of generating bad publicity in the
United States and Italy.[35] Screenwriter Hugh Gray recalled that once filming
commenced, the unions carried out "lightning strikes" (short-lived stretches
of inactivity) to protest the production's working conditions.[36] Years later, on
Fox's *Cleopatra* (1963), the FULS labor union called for a halt to all of the
studio's productions in Italy because of the many contract-violation suits filed
against the Fox operation and because more than one hundred Hollywood
technicians were apparently brought to work on the film.[37] The FULS-led
protest was likely spurred on because Fox hired most of its Italian crew from
the Communist FILS union, much to the consternation of the US Embassy
in Rome and the outcry of the American Federation of Labor's Hollywood
Film Council.[38]

Due to the convergence of foreign union demands and the need for
cheaper labor costs, the below-the-line crew on continental shoots was mostly
European. However, Hollywood studios could exert their influence logisti-

cally by working within this labor structure and assigning Hollywood personnel to the roles of department heads to bring the ranks of each department in line with Hollywood production practices.[39] European union dictates could balance this hierarchy by matching a department head—say, a key grip—with a bilingual foreign counterpart—another key grip—who could communicate with the foreign crew. The technical requirements of Hollywood production, however, required film companies to bring US crew members with specialized skills that could not be found in Europe. To execute specific cinematographic techniques, Hollywood sent over camera technicians. For example, the VistaVision shooting of *To Catch a Thief*, *The Man Who Knew Too Much* (1956), and *Funny Face* (1957) all called for largely Hollywood camera crews. In time, though, the specialization in Hollywood technology and style spread through European crews. As wide-screen filmmaking grew in Europe during the 1950s, studios could look to European technicians who had training in shooting wide-screen formats. Additionally, as studios became more familiar with European talent over time, established cinematographers such as Giuseppe Rotunno and Jack Cardiff, and art directors such as Alexandre Trauner, served as department heads.

For other specialized roles, Hollywood productions relied on certain bilingual foreign individuals, reemploying some of the most reputed from film to film. Multilingual script supervisor Sylvette Baudrot was one of those French workers who was able to move among Hollywood's overseas shoots (fig. 9). While training to be a "script girl" in the French film industry, she met French production managers Christian Ferry, Julien Derode, and Paul Feyder, who would all go on to serve on many Hollywood productions and help her obtain employment. "It was a sort of a network that brought me a tremendous amount of work between the 1950s and the 1970s," Baudrot recalled.[40] On her first Hollywood project, *To Catch a Thief*, Baudrot's job was one of the positions that the film shoot doubled up on. While the first unit filmed, she shadowed Claire Behnke, the script supervisor brought over from Hollywood. Baudrot studied how Behnke maintained continuity and filled out production reports. When Behnke and much of the Hollywood crew returned to Los Angeles to film interiors, Baudrot took over the role of script supervisor for the second-unit work. Her ability to navigate multiple languages and production methods contributed in important ways to Hollywood's capacity to film in France. After working on *To Catch a Thief*, she went on to assist many Hollywood directors, including Richard Fleischer, Vincente Minnelli, Stanley Donen, Gene Kelly, George Stevens, and Jean

FIGURE 9. Script supervisor Sylvette Baudrot on the set of Richard Fleischer's *The Vikings* (1958). (Courtesy of l'Iconothèque, La Cinémathèque française)

Negulesco, on locations throughout Europe. Baudrot's career demonstrates that the sharing of talent became an integral way for units shooting overseas to preserve some stability from one film to the next.

One of the attractions for Hollywood companies to operate out of London, Paris, and Rome was that in general a film production's division of labor in those industries was similar to Hollywood's labor organization, though in Italy the demarcation lines of responsibilities could be looser.[41] However, a notable exception was the gaffer, who was in charge of placing and rigging the lights on a set.[42] In European craft traditions, the gaffer did not always exist, which meant that the director of photography had to light the set. French production manager Christian Ferry pointed out that the absence of gaffers was not just a matter of altered duties for the cinematographer, but also resulted in a loss of efficiency. Precious time was lost since a set could not be pre-lit before the cinematographer and cast arrived, which according to postwar French union regulations typically occurred at noon.[43]

This change in work routine prompted Hollywood cinematographer Joseph Ruttenberg, who had shot MGM's British production of *The Miniver Story*, to write in the pages of *American Cinematographer*, "Certain technicians in Hollywood would blush to see me swinging a lamp in place or moving cables, gobos and barn doors, as I frequently did on this picture." Ruttenberg tried to offset this supposed demotion by reasserting his authority when he explained that he reorganized British "working procedures to more nearly conform with those followed in Hollywood."[44] Here, the cinematographer confirmed that when faced with altered work duties or a foreign crew unfamiliar with US methods, Hollywood technicians retrained below-the-line workers for increased production efficiency. By adapting to the specificity of foreign work duties while also training local crews, Hollywood personnel could exert their leverage and versatility.

Some Hollywood technicians acknowledged that one drawback of collaborating with foreign personnel who were not on long-term contracts was the lack of professional bonds that typically developed among crew members who worked together repeatedly. The time put into orienting new unit members potentially reduced efficiency.[45] Ruttenberg assessed the British film industry along these lines:

> Perhaps the greatest single factor that retards development of the technical side of the industry is [using] a different camera crew each time. In Hollywood, most directors of photography have the same camera and grip crews on every picture. In the British studios, the cinematographer invariably is given a new and strange crew of men, all of whom must acquaint themselves with the general working conditions and with the habits of the cinematographer to whom they are assigned. Working with Hollywood technicians, I think, has had tremendous influence on these men and the "team" idea seems to be catching on.[46]

For decades, the culture of the Hollywood studio system was shaped by the cohesion that came with stable contracted labor. In time, though, Hollywood faced the situation Ruttenberg describes, as technicians lost their long-term studio contracts, resulting in a pool of freelance workers who moved from one project to another. Certainly, the employment of Hollywood and European workers reflected the 1950s move toward a package-unit system of production, in which producers assembled crews from this industry-wide reserve for each motion picture. But on foreign shoots, instead of the entire US industry serving as a source for labor, the world's film industries served as one giant pool to pick from. The evidence of Hollywood's growing international clout was exhibited in the industry's ability to turn its mode of production into a more adjustable mechanism to take advantage of this global labor supply. One of the challenges was figuring out how to foster communication between Hollywood filmmakers and foreign crew members.

COMMUNICATION

Director Edward Dmytryk once remarked, "In his own homeland, a director must only put up with the inconsistencies of his own tongue. On alien ground, he must deal with the alien language."[47] With film workers of different nationalities working together and facing potential language barriers, how did Hollywood personnel and foreign crews communicate in order to execute the heavy demands of international production work?[48] After all, language lies at the heart of the filmmaking process, shaping the countless decisions made on a film set. Language informs creative options, like a director's ability to convey how to stage an action. It influences logistics, for example an assistant director's command of a set. Language informs technical matters, such as the discussion of lenses among the camera team. Any breakdown in communication risks shooting delays, mistakes, and even accidents—all potential pitfalls in the technically complicated work of filmmaking.

Anecdotes about the polyglot nature of Hollywood's international productions tend to treat language barriers as disturbances in the filmmaking operation. Discussing the obstacles of working overseas, producer William Perlberg explained, "One of our biggest headaches was the language barrier. Even in English (and this can happen in Hollywood), instructions passed along through three or four channels are apt to wind up with distortion. But, with a babel of tongues they can wind up in chaos."[49] Language differences also resulted in simple misunderstandings. Director Joshua Logan relates how on the French location shoot of *Fanny* (1961), during a silent scene, he called out to actress Leslie Caron to "look up!" Immediately, the French "clapper boy," thinking the director had called out *le clap* (the French word for the slate) ran into the shot, ruining the take.[50] Given that the profession relies on thousands of specialized terms, linguistic confusions unsurprisingly arose on international productions. As a sign of the need to foster effective communication among multilingual crews, the *Journal of the Society of Motion Picture and Television Engineers* in 1956 produced a list of technical terms in English, Spanish, French, Italian, and German.[51] A few years later, a French-English motion picture technical dictionary was published.[52]

Language barriers could also interrupt the production workflow. During the Italian location shoot for *September Affair* (1951), miscommunication prevented certain Hollywood technicians from distributing the workload to the Italian crew members. An assistant to the film's producer observed, "A great deal of the work cannot be allocated to others, as it continually means interpreters and interpretation, which never get the results. . . . The explanation is seemingly understood, but somehow and somewhere the operation is not successfully concluded or in some cases not even done."[53] In this case, the communication breakdown hindered a core organizing principle in Hollywood filmmaking: production efficiency. Language differences therefore posed a major hurdle to the smooth operation of overseas productions, as spoken directions either went through an interpreter, underwent a slow process of gesture and mimicry, or became lost in translation. While the Hollywood division of labor had always aimed to ease the flow of communications, the different languages on international productions complicated this process. There were three possible solutions: hire interpreters, employ multilingual foreign workers, or import Hollywood personnel familiar with the local language.

Using interpreters met with mixed results. Interpreters did ease communication among crew members, as was the case on the Paris location shoot for *The Man on the Eiffel Tower* (1950), where director of photography Stanley Cortez relied on an interpreter to work with his largely French crew.[54] For Hollywood's East Asian productions, language barriers were stronger and interpreters were in greater demand, but their insertion into the chain of communication could result in mistakes.[55] On *Soldier of Fortune* (1955), which was shot in Hong Kong and Macao, Edward Dmytryk discovered that much of what an interpreter had translated was incorrect. The director reasoned, "Blame it on the ambiguity of the language, or on the fact that almost everyone knows how to do it better than you do . . . this problem is universal. Whether the language was Italian, Hungarian, or Hebrew, local interpreters were frequently inexact."[56] In addition to these hazards of mistranslation and the resulting slowdowns in production, hiring interpreters also inflated the foreign unit budget.

Hiring multilingual foreign workers proved more efficient and cost-effective. Bilingual technicians were thus much sought after. In Italy, two US producers took advantage of this need by setting up a talent agency in Rome to scout English-speaking actors and crew members for Hollywood productions.[57] More often, in order to find bilingual talent, film companies relied on studios' network of foreign offices and reliable local organizers who knew the industry well. For the French locations of *Little Boy Lost*, Edouard de Segonzac of Paramount's Paris office recommended looking for key English-speaking French personnel rather than using interpreters.[58] In hiring international workers, language ability therefore became a new commodity alongside technical know-how. Amid the correspondence for *Little Boy Lost*, a list of French personnel identifies individuals and their language skills. Assistant director Michel J. Boisrond is described as an "excellent fellow—speaks English well and knows picture problems." Assistant cameraman Jean Benezech is characterized as a "jolly good worker—understands English—lots of fun." Transportation worker Hamlet Barbadoro "has own trucks—gets your equipment there on time—very dependable, which is something—all he can say is 'Let's go.'"[59]

Even though Hollywood companies hoped for as many multilingual foreign workers as possible, some roles, such as assistant directors, warranted English-language proficiency more than others, since these positions could serve as liaisons between the above-the-line Hollywood personnel and the below-the-line foreign staff. Positions involved with dialogue required a strong grasp of the language, too. As one of the few English-speaking script supervisors in France, Sylvette Baudrot was guaranteed steady work on Hollywood productions. She grew up in the cosmopolitan city of Alexandria, Egypt, and had learned to speak Arabic, French, Italian, and English—all languages that served her well during the growth of postwar international moviemaking.

Foreign production heads, such as cinematographers and art directors, often required some knowledge of English since they collaborated directly with Hollywood filmmakers. However, Italian cinematographer Giuseppe

Rotunno recounted that having only worked with Italian directors such as Luchino Visconti, he had just a smattering of English when he started working with Hollywood filmmakers like Samuel Taylor on *The Monte Carlo Story* (1957) and Henry Koster on *The Naked Maja* (1959). While he remembered some interpreters facilitating communication on set, the common ground was always the script and the story.[60]

Multilingual production materials were vital to international crews. To enable individuals of different nationalities to work together, production reports and script breakdowns were often printed in both English and the local language on the same pages, while shooting scripts were translated into different language versions.[61] Based on his experience with foreign crews, business manager Henry Henigson made a strong case to William Wyler in preparation for *Roman Holiday* (1953): "Scripts intended for foreign production should be much more fully written than they usually are when intended for production at home. The translation should be so detailed that even the foreigner who is forced to work by it will have in his mind a very clear picture of our intentions."[62] In this era of transcultural productions, paperwork, which had long made the Hollywood production process more efficient, now in translated form contributed to uniting crews divided by language.

Though not the norm, overseas productions sometimes relied on multilingual personnel from Hollywood. In response to the increasing internationalization of production work, language schools targeted the Hollywood community. In the mid-1950s, advertisements for the Berlitz Schools of Languages, which had various locations throughout Los Angeles County, began to appear in the pages of *Daily Variety*, aimed at Hollywood filmmakers planning to work abroad (fig. 10). Using a dapper-looking cartoon character in a pith helmet with a rifle in a vaguely exotic scene, the ads pitched language acquisition as a skill necessary to surviving the perils of working overseas.[63] Another school, the Polyglot Institute in Los Angeles, aimed to teach languages to filmmakers using a rather dubious technique. The head of the institute, Michel Thomas, a Frenchman who had studied psychology in Paris and Vienna, maintained that he could instill in his students conversational and reading knowledge in any language in just twenty hours of class time by using therapeutic techniques that tapped into the subconscious. According to Thomas, director Daniel Mann was able to discuss one of his films with a French person in French after only five hours of language learning.[64]

Just as foreign crew members used English-speaking skills to gain employment, Hollywood workers could tout a knack for language to secure

FIGURE 10. This advertisement for the Berlitz Schools of Languages from April 29, 1955, was one of many that appeared in *Daily Variety* targeting Hollywood filmmakers headed abroad.

work abroad. During the early hiring process for MGM's *Quo Vadis*, workers in the Los Angeles area who knew Italian wrote to John Huston, who was then assigned to direct the film. The Puerto Rican actor Alberto Morin, who had lived in Italy and taken part in the Italian campaign during World War II, spoke fluent Italian and offered his general services to the director. Morin had previously worked at Twentieth Century-Fox teaching Italian to the crew of *Prince of Foxes* (1949) in preparation for its shoot in Italy.[65] Query letters like Morin's are indicative of the transitional phase that Hollywood was undergoing in the late 1940s and into the 1950s as studio employees lost the stability of long-term contracts and moved into freelance status, which meant they had to find work through solicitation and networking.

When discussing the language abilities of Hollywood personnel, we should remember that the US film industry was filled with foreign émigrés and exiles. These filmmakers' move into postwar international production was something of a return to their roots, though they did not always work in their countries of birth or in their heritage languages. Although fluent in German and French, the German-born William Wyler went to Italy for *Roman Holiday* and *Ben-Hur* (1959), while the German-born Billy Wilder returned to his native country for parts of *A Foreign Affair* (1948) and *One, Two, Three* (1961). The Ukrainian-born Anatole Litvak, who had directed films in Germany, France, and England before moving to the United States, made Paris his headquarters in the 1950s as he shot Hollywood productions across Europe. For the Franco-US production of *Act of Love* (1953), the multilingual director shot English and French versions of the film.[66] Many technicians also emigrated to the United States and then returned to Europe for foreign location shoots. For Anatole Litvak's European-set war film *Decision before Dawn* (1952), shot in Germany, German cinematographer Franz Planer was able to communicate with the crew in his native language.[67]

While difficult, language differences were never insurmountable impediments, as Hollywood and foreign personnel adapted to each other's methods and customs. Production manager "Doc" Erickson worked on many international productions, but he never mastered a foreign language. He indicated that with a couple of gestures and a few foreign words, production workers could understand one another.[68] Whether a film relied on interpreters, English-speaking foreign personnel, or multilingual Hollywood workers—and some used all three—there was no clear standard for how an international production staff communicated. It varied not only from film to film but also from individual to individual. Just as the Hollywood mode of production became more fluid overseas by adapting to the features of foreign industries, communication among workers also became more variable. The role of languages on these sets was less about an intermixing of national identities than it was a transcultural mixing of film practices, in which foreign methods interacted with Hollywood techniques.

PRODUCTION PRACTICES

Another major hurdle of going abroad and working with foreign crews was that Hollywood filmmakers often found themselves confronting different working methods. Within this altered filmmaking context, they had to maintain certain Hollywood practices in order to sustain large-scale production and ensure efficiency. At the same time, Hollywood filmmakers had to adapt to local circumstances based on foreign union regulations and the skills of local technicians. So, how were Hollywood production practices exported to overseas industries? What happened when these practices interacted with foreign methods?

Within the first few years of Hollywood's move into European production, labor groups on both sides of the Atlantic made overtures to formalize an exchange of working methods through a number of measures. After a two-month European tour of foreign industries in 1950, Joseph Mankiewicz, then president of the Screen Directors Guild, sought to foster an interchange of directors and techniques between Europe and Hollywood.[69] Although short-lived, the proposed reciprocity schemes between Hollywood and the UK served to facilitate sharing practices. In a 1948 issue of the British publication *The Cine-Technician*, various ACT members, under the aegis of the schemes, reported on their visits to Hollywood. They studied RKO Studios and remarked on the "speed and efficiency" of various film units and the distribution of script "breakdowns" across departments.[70] In a similar vein, practices spread through articles printed in foreign industry publications about Hollywood methods and technologies, some written by Hollywood technicians.[71] Correspondingly, in *American Cinematographer* and *International Photographer*, Hollywood technicians reported on their experiences of working overseas. However, an industry-sanctified trading of ideas was limited by each nation's labor protectionist measures and a largely one-way flow of cooperation, as Hollywood gained a strong foothold in European industries while most European filmmakers and technicians remained in Europe.[72]

The exchange of methods therefore happened on the ground during the production of Hollywood films in foreign lands. For instance, US producers sought to train foreign workers in accordance with Hollywood shooting procedures. While local unions frequently dictated the working day's schedule, Hollywood filmmakers in the UK found that English workers fell in line with the pace of Hollywood production. After shooting *Under Capricorn* (1949) in England, Alfred Hitchcock, who was well established in both Hollywood and British industries, portrayed the increasing productivity of the British technicians: "They're learning that they have to prepare for shooting more carefully than they have been. . . . They are anticipating difficulties now, rather than waiting until they come up on the sound stage. They told me they were impressed with the way I rehearsed the cast on one stage while the technicians lit up another."[73] As an English-born-and-bred director, Hitchcock emerged as a booster of the methods of his adopted industry in the United States, now helping to spread Hollywood techniques back in Britain.

In Italy, Hollywood companies took advantage of a relatively inexpensive workforce who excelled in quality set and costume construction while also training the local crews. The training process became a primary means of promoting Hollywood's ways. During the shooting phase of *Quo Vadis*, problems with organization and communication delayed filming progress until the MGM staff taught Italian technicians at Cinecittà to work in teams and the thousands of Italian extras to take directions in English.[74] Reporting on the film's production in the pages of *American Cinematographer*, director of photography Robert Surtees remarked, "Adapting the Italian worker to our methods and integrating him with our own studio-trained men was greatly a matter of education." So a "school for electricians" was set up by the production's Hollywood gaffer to train Italian crew members in Hollywood lighting methods. Once the staff from Hollywood upskilled the Italians, Surtees said that the Italian crew grew rapidly in efficiency.[75] While remolding foreign crews was a necessary part of working abroad, Surtees's depiction of collaborating with local labor as a matter of reeducation reflected an ethnocentric stance common in the culture of Hollywood abroad and in the self-aggrandizing discourse of *American Cinematographer*. For foreign shoots outside of Europe, this rhetoric sometimes reflected a troubling colonialist attitude, in which Hollywood department heads expressed their need to train "native" casts and crews.[76]

In France, the Paramount staff working on *Little Boy Lost* found that the French crew operated in a more relaxed manner, eliciting an adaptive approach to collaboration from the Hollywood personnel. Unit production manager Bill Mull assessed the French crew, declaring, "We are fairly well organized for shooting, but sometimes they frighten me with their two hours for lunch and the business establishment's 'don't worry about anything' attitude." A week later, Mull's attitude had shifted: "We are pretty well organized and when we get some good light we move fast. The French staff and crew have been hand picked, and once [they] understand what we want they are very efficient." In due time, though, Mull admitted that the Hollywood workers "had to fall into their methods because they cannot change to ours."[77]

Minor differences in production practices also reflected European craft traditions that arose out of local filmmaking conditions, and Hollywood units learned to put to use these localized skills. During the second-unit photography in London on Paramount's *Knock on Wood* (1954), Hollywood cinematographer William Williams looked to British technicians who had developed techniques for shooting in rain and fog and the ensuing dramatic shifts in light.[78] Hollywood and foreign techniques could also intermix, resulting in a transcultural interchange of film practices. *Quo Vadis* art director Edward Carfagno claimed that he helped introduce the Italian set designers to the use of plastic in set construction. Conversely, the Italians showcased their own distinct methods. In creating a Roman arena for the film, the Italian set builders used a support structure called "sostacina" dating back to ancient Roman times, a procedure that impressed the Hollywood crew.[79]

Some practices, namely working hours, were ingrained in foreign production cultures, which attempted to make Hollywood units conform to union-controlled regulations. But Hollywood producers sometimes managed to negotiate different work schedules.[80] One practice that seemed nonnegotiable was the union-sanctioned tea break in Britain. For Hollywood filmmakers, this twice-a-day cultural custom broke up the momentum of a day's schedule in the morning and the afternoon. During the filming of *The Hasty Heart* (1950) at the Associated British Picture Corporation (ABPC) studios, director Vincent Sherman was baffled by this interruption. He wrote to studio head Jack Warner in Burbank: "Just as we were ready to shoot—came a tea break. This meant that everybody, from electricians way up high on down—had to stop to get tea!! From the time that the tea break was called until the men got back, a half hour was consumed. Then the actors had to be warmed up again, and we finally got our first shot around 11 o'clock."[81] Bertram Tuttle, a Warner Bros. art director who later worked on *Captain Horatio Hornblower*, also at ABPC, described the ritual in more detail:

A waggon is wheeled in which is known as the tea-trolley and which has an entire crew devoted to its maintenance and manufacture of tea. Even though the cameras are perfectly set-up, the lighting is just right, the entire crew queue up at the tea-trolley, at which time, tea is served with rolls with sometimes an occasional Frankfurter managing to get in. After tea is served of course the entire crew goes back in a procession, but with the cup still in their hand. Now here is the big problem, you must be sure that your set is clear of empty tea cups before you get your shot. . . . The same entire manouevre [*sic*] occurs in the afternoon at 3 o'clock, the only big difference being in the afternoon—it is pastry.[82]

The comments by Sherman and Tuttle point to an important aspect of working overseas: the interaction of Hollywood and foreign personnel and their respective working methods stood as a mixing of not just production practices but also cultural customs that could spur creativity, such as the methods of Italian set designers, or spark irritation, such as the British tea breaks. As Roger Corman, who shot a number of films overseas, put it, "The meeting of different cultures can be stimulating and exciting, but it can also lead to the most intense form of frustration."[83] Hollywood companies learned to cope with the meeting of cultures by exporting filmmaking methods and incorporating foreign working procedures. This process of adaptation and reconfiguration suggests that at the level of day-to-day work, international productions were a striking instance of the transcultural flow of filmmaking customs.

PRODUCTION KNOWLEDGE

As John Caldwell has pointed out, in the Hollywood studio system "trade knowledge" circulated through craft training and apprenticeships down a "vertical hierarchy" of rank.[84] In contrast, for postwar international work, vital production knowledge reflected the ecosystem of new filmmaking environments. Rather than moving in regulated ways down work hierarchies, Hollywood's units abroad obtained experience in a piecemeal fashion. These experiences over time consolidated into wisdom to be shared with production departments in Hollywood and with competing units overseas. This distribution of production knowledge worked in a two-way, transcultural pattern. In order to acquire experience abroad, Hollywood companies learned through trial and error and by soliciting information from on-the-ground contacts. The transmission of knowledge also functioned the other way, as Hollywood filmmakers applied studio craft practices to international productions by exporting Hollywood department heads and training foreign workers. This exchange of trade knowledge reaffirmed the importance of an adaptable mode of production, in which Hollywood filmmakers gathered information about the film landscape abroad and then adjusted to this landscape while promoting their own craft practices.

As the phenomenon of international production grew in the late 1940s, Hollywood studios had to figure out how to initiate film shoots in areas that were new to production management. The foreign studio office could certainly help organize preproduction on behalf of its home studio. But for some of the earliest postwar overseas productions, such as *To the Victor* (1948), film firms did not have the luxury of relying on their own previous experiences. Therefore, some studios turned to other production personnel working in Europe. For *The Hasty Heart* in England, Warner Bros. needed to figure out if the company was paying for costs at ABPC's studio at the correct rates. So Warner sought feedback on a budget item list from the general manager of Teddington Studios and the production manager of Hitchcock's *Under Capricorn*, which was then shooting at MGM's British studios.[85] The steep learning curve on *The Hasty Heart* caused Jack Warner to comment that the film "is sort of a proving ground and what we learn in this production is bound to help all those following—to their great benefit."[86]

Over the years, certain Hollywood production organizers who specialized in international filmmaking or lived abroad became important contacts. These production organizers—MGM production manager William Kaplan (*When in Rome* [1952], *The Last Time I Saw Paris* [1954]), Fox production manager Robert Snody (*Kangaroo* [1952], *The Snows of Kilimanjaro* [1952]), and freelance production manager Lee Katz (*Moby Dick* [1956], *The Longest Day* [1962])—functioned as go-to people for guidance on working abroad. "Doc" Erickson recollected that for location surveys, he solicited production personnel who had worked abroad for information on potential shooting sites.[87] By the late 1950s, the Unit Production Managers Guild formalized the distribution of overseas trade knowledge by compiling data on production resources in various regions around the globe. This information was made available to guild members and producers preparing to work overseas.[88]

Hollywood companies also relied on foreign contacts familiar with the customs and practices of each country or region. In the late 1940s, MGM looked to its Italian head of dubbing and sound in Rome to survey the local production landscape to determine the possibility of staging a major film like *Quo Vadis* in Italy.[89] In preparing for location work in Marrakech for *The Man Who Knew Too Much*, the Paramount Paris office consulted with French director Jacques Becker, who had earlier made the film *Ali Baba et les quarante voleurs* (1954) in Morocco. He offered advice on shooting in the country and recommended reliable Moroccan assistants.[90]

In time, producers and studios learned to depend on their own past experiences of working overseas to organize their films. While each new international production encountered unique challenges that demanded new solutions, filmmaking abroad did not result in a total breakdown of standardized procedure. In many cases, producers appealed to solutions that had worked in the past. Paramount assistant director Richard McWhorter, who helped organize Italian location shooting on *September Affair*, anticipated this point when he wrote to the studio: "[I] am sure that by the time we have finished shooting the picture, I will be able to help the next Company that goes to Italy, by discussing with them a few of the short cuts that I have found."[91] This kind of trade knowledge became integrated in each Hollywood crew member's craft practice, to be shared and replicated on future productions.

The circulation of production knowledge, however, was not just about collecting information on methods discovered overseas; knowledge moved in the other direction by applying Hollywood know-how to international production work. Promoting Hollywood practices became especially important with the introduction of new technologies. One way for Hollywood studios to export their technology and style was to invite foreign production supervisors and technicians to Hollywood. With the unveiling of CinemaScope in 1953, Twentieth Century-Fox halted all of its British productions, since none of the studio's British personnel were familiar with the new wide-screen format, so Fred Fox, the studio's production chief in the UK, traveled to Hollywood to study the process.[92] By 1955 Fox began to roll out the production of CinemaScope films in England with *The Deep Blue Sea* (1955).[93] Before shooting his first VistaVision film in Rome, *War and Peace* (1956), British cinematographer Jack Cardiff spent several weeks in Hollywood researching the new format and running tests.[94] As wide-screen filmmaking grew in Europe over the course of the 1950s, studios could turn to foreign cinematographers and crews who had been trained in these Hollywood methods. By training foreign labor, Hollywood's international influence rested on its ability to maintain production efficiencies while meeting the needs of foreign industries that wanted to innovate.

To facilitate the distribution of production knowledge, communication via letter and telegram helped Hollywood learn about working conditions abroad and helped Hollywood filmmakers apply studio practices to foreign work. Even if communication by telephone was an option, transoceanic connections were unreliable, as MGM discovered while trying to set up a production base at Cinecittà for *Quo Vadis*.[95] Telephone communication from locations outside metropolises was even more troublesome.[96] Airmail, on the other hand, proved reliable, even when it took anywhere from five to nine days from Western Europe to Los Angeles. By some accounts, the duration of mail delivery from the West Coast to Europe was faster.[97] The speed of messages sent via telegraph cables was still better. The very act of written communication ensured that Hollywood studios could collect information about foreign settings while also promoting Hollywood practices. For David O. Selznick's *A Farewell to Arms* (1957), the camera crew was having difficulty with achieving a range of technical issues, including shooting close-ups and performing camera movements with the new CinemaScope format. Twentieth Century-Fox then communicated by telegraph with Selznick, who was on location in Italy, on how to work through the shooting problems.[98]

With all of these acts of sharing information by correspondence, Hollywood studios were generating important written records of production knowledge that future personnel could consult. When location work on *Little Boy Lost* wrapped in France, production manager Bill Mull wrote a lengthy summary of the strategies for operating in Paris.[99] Subsequently, in preparing to shoot *To Catch a Thief* in France, "Doc" Erickson studied the correspondence to gain insights into the process of acquiring shooting permits and dealing with French unions.[100] In fact, Erickson made the case that *Little Boy Lost* functioned as a test run to orient future Paramount staff members who managed foreign shoots in subsequent years.[101] The communication between Hollywood studios and their location units thus became both a medium for the conveyance of trade knowledge and a running record of how to mount these productions. The flow of production knowledge through written correspondence also became a valuable way for studios to supervise their international film units.

STUDIO SUPERVISION

For some Hollywood filmmakers who craved independence, the freedom from studio interference was certainly a viable inducement for working on overseas productions. On the film *Jessica*, a Franco-Italian coproduction with United Artists, director Jean Negulesco expressed that he had almost complete organizational autonomy, handling many aspects of the film, from location scouting to production management. In the abovementioned letter to Vincente Minnelli, Negulesco goes on to explain, "It is a difficult and arduous job. I have never had so much to do, so much to think and so much to check, recheck, but the satisfaction of being able to make immediate decisions without waiting for an okay and even being in the 'in' of everything, it has excited me."[102] For both independent filmmakers like Negulesco and studio-contract directors like Minnelli, working abroad seemed to promise escape from studio suits, who back home usually supervised the details of production, from budgeting matters to the number of takes a director shot.[103] But exactly how much freedom did Hollywood filmmakers working overseas have from studio supervision?

Whether in production centers in London, Rome, Paris, or other locations around the globe, film units could avoid the watchful eyes of studio executives and managers. Because of the distance from the Hollywood studio, the film unit working on a foreign location not only had more responsibilities but also operated with more autonomy. Production manager "Doc" Erickson explained:

> You didn't have to answer to anybody. If you're in Hollywood, you've got to pay attention to the production office hourly, daily. They expected it and you responded accordingly. But once you get out of their clutches, you're pretty much on your own. You can make your own decisions. You don't have to run to the phone immediately and say what do you think about this? What do you think about that? So that's the difference. And you were accorded that respect from the locals, the people you're working with, because they know you're the boss. They're not going to have to worry about somebody else countermanding your orders.[104]

Erickson described that while filmmakers had a certain amount of leeway working on domestic locations, those units were still "handcuffed to the studio" through frequent updates via telephone and the presence of studio personnel.[105]

In a best-case scenario, Hollywood personnel working abroad could have access to Hollywood-size budgets and organizational might while trying out technical experiments that were easier to attain overseas. On *Moulin Rouge* (1953), John Huston harnessed the talents of Oswald Morris to come up with an unconventional use of Technicolor. Morris experimented with smoke, filters, and temperature at Shepperton Studios to achieve a bold play of colors associated with Toulouse-Lautrec's artwork in a way that the cinematographer said would have not been possible in Hollywood.[106] The results so startled the British staff of Technicolor that they first wanted their firm's name disassociated from the film until it met with success.[107]

In the worst case, shooting off the lot and without the careful supervision of budget-minded executives could result in production costs spiraling out of control, as was the case with *Mutiny on the Bounty* (1962) and *Cleopatra* (1963). On the production of *The Inn of the Sixth Happiness* (1958), which was renting out MGM-British Studios, producer-director Mark Robson wrote to Fox executive Buddy Adler to complain that the British production department had significantly added to the budget because of accounting carelessness and cost increases. Angrily, Robson blamed Fox's British production operation for its negligence. By shooting far away from Hollywood, such inattention could happen, and it took a reliable journeyman like Robson to alert the studio and call for an audit of all spending. Robson summed up, "I cannot tell you how I miss the efficiency and planning of our Hollywood production and budgeting department, because here this is a NIGHTMARE."[108]

For some scholars, notions of freedom explain Hollywood filmmakers' desire to shoot overseas in the postwar era. In *Hollyworld: Space, Power, and Fantasy in the American Economy* (2001), Aida Hozic argues that postwar location shooting brought filmmakers greater creative freedom, especially foreign location shoots, where the sheer physical distance from Hollywood diminished the power of the studio-based executive and producer to shape the production process: "The spatial expansion of production reduced the ability of Hollywood producers to both monitor the flow of production and control expenditures incurred on location."[109] In their study on global film production in *The Film Studio* (2005), Ben Goldsmith and Tom O'Regan similarly maintain, "In the 1950s and 1960s, 'going on location' (or location thinking) offered the promise of creative and financial freedom afforded by distance from Hollywood."[110]

While a studio's moment-to-moment vigilance concerning logistical and creative decisions was weakened on international productions, a closer look into the realities of foreign shoots reveals a more nuanced relationship between the Hollywood studio and the satellite film unit. What emerges is not a picture of filmmakers running away from the control of studio executives, but one of constant negotiation. Los Angeles–based studios attempted to promote Hollywood-style production standards from afar, as location film units tried to execute these directives against the pressure of new shooting conditions. Studios used several methods to supervise their film units abroad, which increased the likelihood that Hollywood production protocols would be followed. These methods included set visits by studio executives and managers; on-set proxies who represented the studios and reported back to them; cables and letters between the location unit and the Hollywood studio; and the decision to screen dailies in Hollywood before the filmmakers on location saw them.

With the growing ease of commercial airline travel in the 1950s, studio executives and production heads could fly to foreign locations to check on their companies' projects. Before Darryl Zanuck left Fox to become an independent producer in Europe, he was heavily involved in the studio's overseas productions, visiting active units throughout the world. In 1949 he used his studio's private C-47 plane to travel to London, Paris, Berlin, and Morocco, where Fox was engaged in five productions.[111] Likewise, the heads of Warner Bros., Republic, and Allied Artists all kept an eye on the planning and execution of their studios' productions abroad by dropping in on foreign locations.[112] However, visits from studio executives did not always guarantee a tight rein on filmmaking. Even though Fox executives went to Rome to keep track of spending, *Cleopatra* became the most expensive film up to that time due to aborted production plans in London, excessive building expenditures, and shooting delays associated with star Elizabeth Taylor's health.[113]

Compared to studio films, independent productions could appear to have more freedom from the supervision of their Hollywood financiers and distributors, but they were still somewhat beholden to Hollywood studios. Arthur Krim, head of United Artists, traveled to Europe to survey the various productions that his company was financing, including Sam Spiegel's *Melba* (1953) and Raymond Stross's *Shoot First* (1953), both filming in London. He also looked in on the Paris shoots of *Act of Love* and *Moulin Rouge*.[114] During Selznick's production of *A Farewell to Arms*, the film's coproducer and financer, Twentieth Century-Fox, was involved in making decisions about acquiring equipment and hiring labor in Italy.[115]

Studios also used on-location representatives to stay up to date on the latest shooting developments. For the complicated production of *Quo Vadis*, MGM had general manager Eddie Mannix supervise the troubled preproduction and early filming period, until the picture was on track.[116] Mannix replicated this supervision during the preproduction of *Ben-Hur*. Once production commenced, a string of other MGM executives followed with set visits.[117] Art director Edward Carfagno recollected that when *Ben-Hur* director William Wyler fell behind schedule, studio representatives traveled "to push him on."[118] For the productions of *Captain Horatio Hornblower* and *The Crimson Pirate* (1952), Teddington Studios manager Gerry Blattner kept Warner Bros. in Burbank informed on a range of matters, including shooting progress and hiring crew members.[119] Supervision by proxy helped to keep overseas productions running along the lines of a Hollywood studio.

Beyond personal contact, studios relayed their supervisory role through two important means. First, communication via letter and cable was key to ensuring that studio managers in Hollywood were informed of hiring, delays, and, most importantly, spending. In a letter to *Little Boy Lost* unit manager Bill Mull, Paramount's production manager Frank Caffey implored from Hollywood, "Please arrange to drop me a note religiously once a week as of course I am asked questions continuously."[120] Caffey's request suggests that he needed the foreign unit to be in constant contact with him because of his own accountability to his superiors. The other way to monitor production from a distance was to develop footage shot overseas in Hollywood, where executives and editors could then watch dailies to track filming progress and quality. On the Italian shoot of *Prince of Foxes*, Twentieth Century-Fox could have developed the dailies in the labs of Shepperton Studios, where the rushes for Fox's *I Was a Male War Bride* (1949) and *The Forbidden Street* (1949) were being processed. Instead, they were developed in Los Angeles to allow Darryl Zanuck to see the shooting results first.[121]

When wide-screen technologies were introduced, dailies became an effective way for studios to see how foreign units were handling the new format. With the advent of VistaVision, Paramount was particularly concerned with controlling how foreign location units employed its wide-screen process. The studio even attempted to shape the visual style of directors as authoritative as Alfred Hitchcock. When Hitchcock and his crew went to the south of France to shoot *To Catch a Thief*, the VistaVision process was still relatively new, having first been used a year earlier on Paramount's *White Christmas* (1954). The exposed footage of *To Catch a Thief* was processed at Technicolor in London, and then the dailies were shipped back to Hollywood, where Paramount personnel watched what was shot.[122] Because the projection of VistaVision films had not yet been fully standardized in commercial cinemas, the studio cabled the French location unit that they needed to compose shots somewhat loosely for the 1.85 aspect ratio so that human figures would also fit within a 1.66 ratio.[123] At the same time, Paramount wanted to ensure that the crew was filming with enough light to render shots in sharp focus, as VistaVision's benefit was its ability to produce great definition in the negative.[124] Cinematographer Robert Burks expressed concern that maintaining the backgrounds in sharp focus would be difficult because of Hitchcock's desire to capture "dramatic" close-ups.[125] In later years, Hitchcock articulated his thinking on how to shoot close-ups and asserted, "My argument has always been: Who wants to see around the close-up? Why should it be sharp behind the close-up? But there was always this aim, and this seemed to me to create an unreal effect—this yearning for the modeled figure, and this separation of the image from background."[126]

After the dailies of *To Catch a Thief* were reviewed at Paramount, studio production manager Frank Caffey cabled the French unit to express that the soft focus in the background of the close-up shots was "disturbing." He also advocated for waist-high framing captured with medium-focal-length lenses instead of shooting close-ups.[127] Throughout the production, Paramount pointed out the softness of some of the shots' backgrounds, noting that the scenes wouldn't cut together well.[128] Production manager "Doc" Erickson conveyed back to Paramount Hitchcock's concern over the studio's fixation on the shallow focus in the close-ups: "[Hitchcock] finds it very hard to believe that you can put across certain story points without actual close-ups."[129] Even though Hitchcock was resolute in his use of close-ups, additional wider shots and background plates were captured for protection.[130] While Erickson has suggested that Hitchcock did not heed the studio's advice, long shots are the most frequent framing in the movie.[131] Barry Salt's statistical analysis of Hitchcock's shot scales reveals that the director did in fact move away from close-ups in favor of more distant shots in his first three VistaVision motion pictures, starting with *To Catch a Thief*.[132] The resulting look of the film is evidence that for a director like Hitchcock, the studio could influence precise matters of style even as the distance between studios and location units was growing on international productions. The back-and-forth correspondence also indicates how a studio's supervision of overseas filmmaking could promote Hollywood stylistic conventions.

Ultimately, though, studios were more concerned with costs than the details of creative decisions on foreign shoots. In spite of the lack of day-to-day supervision, Hollywood filmmakers working abroad still adhered to the aesthetic norms of their domestic industry, even if certain stylistic features, namely location shooting, became more predominant on these productions. Whether they were journeymen such as *Little Boy Lost* director George Seaton or established masters such as Vincente Minnelli, these moviemakers depended on the creative solutions for big-budget filmmaking they had employed for decades in the studio system, especially in the face of the challenges of international production work.

While Hollywood had long thought globally in terms of its distribution reach, its postwar foreign film activity illustrates the intensification of a more international approach to production. Because of economic incentives, production infrastructure, and skilled film workers, the UK, Italy, and France became key staging grounds for Hollywood's move into overseas filmmaking. Meanwhile, changes were also taking place in the United States. Studios were cutting overhead as production was moving off the lot to locations across the country, a move that prompted adjustments in craft practices, as producers drew from a growing freelance labor pool. Overseas, these changes were amplified. Through Hollywood companies' ability to manage these changes and continue certain established filmmaking practices, the industry grew its international presence.

In the long run, the production centers of London, Rome, and to a lesser extent Paris profited from Hollywood's postwar investment in their labor and infrastructure. However, Hollywood's involvement in these production centers met some resistance. As noted above, labor groups in the UK, Italy, and France took issue with certain Hollywood film shoots in order to protect their jobs and pay. Italian director Roberto Rossellini delivered a more widespread complaint that Hollywood companies were driving up production expenses in the already-troubled Italian industry by inflating costs for studios, equipment, and labor.[133] Even some non-Italian producers criticized the increase in costs. Independent producer Gregor Rabinovitch accused Fox of overpaying Italian workers for its production of *Prince of Foxes*, making it more difficult for both Italian producers and Hollywood independents to finance filmmaking in Italy.[134]

In response, Darryl Zanuck defended these pay increases as a means to hire the best technicians possible and to pay a scale worthy of Fox, despite admitting to a huge savings in costs: "If any other producer or company wants to compete with us for the best Italian labor, he cannot expect to do it on a cut-rate wage scale, because 20th-Fox will not stoop to sweat-shop practices. We are not in Italy for the purpose of exploiting Italian labor or to make a 'Quickie' to cash in on another country's depressed condition."[135] Along these lines, correspondence for MGM's production of *Quo Vadis* suggests that the studio tried its best to not "derogate from the standard scales" and to work through Cinecittà's employment office when securing Italian labor.[136] The Italian government also tried to keep US companies from distorting local costs in order to avoid adversely affecting Italian companies trying to produce films.[137]

Production costs, in time, did rise in Italy due to the expensive epic films that Hollywood was producing.[138] From 1950 to 1952, *Daily Variety* reported, the price of film equipment and labor in Italy rose by one-third.[139] Producer Ilya Lopert complained that from 1948 to 1954, production costs had quadrupled.[140] By 1956, director Robert Rossen claimed that there was very little difference in production spending between Italy and the United States.[141] The Motion Picture Export Association also recognized the increasing cost of making films in Italy, but attributed the problem to a series of local conditions, including disorganized shoots, the high cost of Italian stars, an inflated Italian economy, and a time lag between production and the doling out of subsidies.[142] The Italian criticism lobbed against Hollywood continued into the 1960s, when two Italian newspapers were reported to have attacked the US industry for raising production costs to levels that local producers could not meet, along with enacting various unfair competitive strategies.[143]

In France, the industry took an ambivalent stance toward Hollywood productions. From one perspective, French studios and technicians felt that Hollywood films kept local technicians employed and well paid, and rarely took valuable studio space and equipment away from local films. From another perspective, some French producers and film unions felt that money made in the French market should be applied toward true French films rather than Hollywood films or Franco-US coproductions. French producers also feared that Hollywood's penchant for paying above wage scales could drive up production costs in their country. A general anti-Hollywood stance undergirded these attitudes, reinforced by vocal Communist groups that blamed the French industry's financial woes on the inundation of US films in France.[144]

Hollywood's involvement with the industries of the UK, Italy, and France can be understood through a dynamic of collaboration, compliance, and resistance from all sides. Hollywood productions ushered in pivotal changes to European film industries by bringing them into contact with US companies and financing, introducing new technologies, fostering coproduction deals, and contributing to the rebuilding of an infrastructure that had suffered during the war. Even if foreign industries profited from these activities, they were primarily undertaken out of Hollywood's self-interest so that it could build an overseas production network. Through a process of continuing Hollywood practices and adapting to foreign industries, Hollywood expanded its international production reach in order to navigate the changing industrial and cultural climates of the postwar era.

When in Rome

ROMAN HOLIDAY (1953)

"Italy is a place where it is 99% perspiration and 1% inspiration."

HENRY HENIGSON[1]

DURING THE EARLY STAGES OF *ROMAN HOLIDAY*'S preproduction, the film's general manager, Henry Henigson, wrote to producer-director William Wyler in Los Angeles to explain the trials of making a motion picture in Italy. Drawing on his experience of organizing productions abroad, Henigson pointed out some of the differences between working within the infrastructure of Hollywood and operating in European filmmaking centers:

> In the States we have large organizations thoroughly competent with vast resources at their immediate command, all of which is again backed by a general industrial situation within the city and often within the country. We have in the United States major industries at our beck and call. The Italian or European motion picture producing industry is not so constituted. All local production here is a relatively "hit-and-miss" affair. You know no "local" producers carry permanent staffs and hardly anyone connected with our business has any reasonable degree of industrial security as we know it. The result of this situation is one which makes for the inherent difficulties.[2]

Henigson's less than favorable assessment of the European film industries may have been intended to prepare Wyler for the worst. More broadly, Henigson's portrait lays bare some of the realities that Hollywood filmmakers faced when they went overseas in the postwar era.

Considering this situation, how did Wyler and company manage these "inherent difficulties" to produce the critical and commercial success of *Roman Holiday*? For Paramount, the film posed a challenge of supervision, since location shooting, studio work, and postproduction were completed in Rome. For Wyler, a major Hollywood filmmaker who had mastered studio-bound filmmaking, the production presented a different set of problems. As with John Huston, working overseas held political risks for a high-profile Hollywood liberal like Wyler. As a Jewish immigrant from the Alsace-Lorraine region and later a US Army Signal Corps officer who shot documentaries in Italy, Wyler brought considerable foreign experience with him.[3] But with *Roman Holiday*, the production was the first time he worked with foreign methods and an international crew. Although he was a central force in making organizational and artistic decisions due to his role as producer and director, the project depended on other major players. The film's general manager and various Hollywood technicians were indispensable figures in overcoming the hurdles of filmmaking abroad.

Over the years, *Roman Holiday* has become an exemplar of Hollywood's postwar international productions. It has received attention for its continental charm, the Roman backdrops, and its stars, Audrey Hepburn and Gregory Peck. It also holds an important place in film history because its extensive archival records chronicle the operation of an overseas production, offering a portrait of the countless decisions that shaped its making. In his 2009 book *Runaway Romances: Hollywood's Postwar Tour of Europe*, Robert R. Shandley uses some of these historical materials to argue that *Roman Holiday* was a "radical" undertaking that served as a "production model" for subsequent runaway productions because of its extensive use of locations and its completion of production and postproduction abroad. While the author puts forward convincing reasons why the movie was a significant runaway, it's unclear if future productions looked to it as a model for foreign filmmaking.[4]

Pace this explanation, I suggest that the film was, rather, a development on previous overseas productions. The correspondence for the film reveals that its general manager looked to his prior foreign experience while drawing from trade knowledge that Paramount supplied him with. Furthermore, production knowledge of foreign activities emerged piecemeal over multiple projects and adaptively addressed specific situations. At times, this knowledge crystallized in correspondence and the accumulated experience of each individual worker. Fundamentally, the production was an example of continuity and change. *Roman Holiday* reflected the Hollywood mode of international production, in which Paramount, Wyler, and his crew promoted studio practices while adapting to the conditions of filmmaking in Rome.

As with any production in a foreign setting, Paramount Studios faced the decision of whether to shoot the film in the United States, abroad, or some combination of the two. The commitment to execute the production entirely in Rome rested on a mixture of creative and economic factors. The film was originally going to be made in Hollywood, but as William Wyler explained to Paramount studio head Frank Freeman, "You can't build me the Colosseum, the Spanish Steps. I'll shoot the whole picture in Rome or else I won't make it."[5] He later elaborated, after a special screening of *Roman Holiday* for Los Angeles film students:

> I think you will realize that this subject matter, this story, if it had been made in Hollywood as was considered at one time, would not be the same picture by a long shot. If we had to build some of the sets, first of all, you couldn't afford to build some of the sets that you have seen, and if the background didn't look real, which they couldn't possibly, well, the characters would begin to look less real, the whole story would appear to be less real.[6]

To be sure, the creative urge to fill the screen with authentic Roman scenery was a key justification for why the producer-director wanted to make the film in Italy. For Wyler, reproducing Rome on a Hollywood back lot would have been inadequate, as well as too costly. Also, mixing second-unit location shots with studio process work that involved pre-filmed footage projected behind the actors would detract from the authenticity the story called for. "A process shot," noted Wyler, "even at its best, still looks phony in many cases."[7] Nevertheless, some of the movie's interiors were filmed at Cinecittà studios.

As is typical of public pronouncements about filmmaking, any discussion of money or its shaping of production decisions was absent. Even though authentic foreign locations were of great importance, the unblocking of frozen funds was also critical. The majority of financing came from frozen lire, but production-cost breakdowns reveal that additional funds were supplied by Paramount and Liberty Films, the latter an independent company that the studio owned.[8] Correspondence between Paramount and the production office at Cinecittà shows that the release of blocked lire rested upon the Italian authorities' script approval, which would slow up production.[9] Also, although cheaper Italian labor was probably an added inducement to making the film in Italy, production expenses were rising by 1952. Compared to when

Quo Vadis was shot in 1950, costs for equipment and labor at the time of *Roman Holiday* had increased by about a third.[10]

Another enticement for Wyler to work abroad was to take advantage of the eighteen-month tax loophole, despite the growing opposition to it from Hollywood unions. Like his friend John Huston and his star Gregory Peck, Wyler wanted to exploit the incentive. So he remained in Europe for the duration of *Roman Holiday*, including the postproduction phase. In a letter to MCA agent Jules Stein, he wrote: "The picture would not have been made in Rome if it had not been for the 18-month tax law and I am sure that everybody will agree that it would not be the same picture by far if it had been made in Hollywood."[11] Around this time, the promise of the tax benefit was in limbo as Congress moved to restrict allowable tax-free income, except for pay earned prior to December 31, 1952, but since Wyler's *Roman Holiday* salary was deposited just "under the wire" in late December 1952, the director reaped the rewards of the tax exemption.[12]

Beyond the bad publicity that Hollywood talent received for working overseas for tax reasons, Wyler's time abroad was a political gamble. Wyler, a cofounder (along with Huston) of the Committee for the First Amendment, found himself the victim of red-baiting tactics from the US press and anticommunist groups.[13] And the *Roman Holiday* production itself was not immune from bad press. A crisis of labor politics nearly erupted when an apocryphal news item about the shortcomings of the Italian crew was printed in gossip writer Louella Parsons's syndicated column: "From Rome comes word that Willie Wyler is having troubles getting 'Roman Holiday' on the screen. Italians no likee [*sic*] to work in the hot weather and take siestas every afternoon."[14] Disturbed by the matter, Henry Henigson wrote to Paramount to demand a retraction, emphasizing the Italians' cooperation: "These people are trying hard and striving to create a foreign production center."[15] Eventually Wyler cabled Parsons reiterating his full support of the hardworking Italians, portions of which the columnist reprinted, at which point the controversy seemed to fade.[16]

The episode testifies to the wider diplomatic nature of working overseas for Hollywood filmmakers, who needed to preserve positive relations with foreign industries and avoid a backlash from Hollywood unions and conservative commentators like Parsons. These factors were signs that shooting a film overseas was never an easy decision for filmmakers and studios. But the financial and creative motives to make the movie entirely in Rome were convincing enough to weather the risks. To surmount these obstacles and realize the project, Paramount needed to look to strategic contacts overseas.

FIGURE 11. General manager Henry Henigson (with his signature cigar) confers with actor Eddie Albert (center) and producer-director William Wyler (left) during the filming of *Roman Holiday* (1953). (Courtesy of UCLA Library Special Collections)

HENRY HENIGSON

The principal organizing force in bringing *Roman Holiday* to fruition was Henry Henigson (fig. 11), an exacting and budget-minded administrator whose responsibilities fulfilled many of the functions of a unit production manager while carrying certain executive privileges. He paved the way for the production to run smoothly away from the support of a Hollywood studio, and ensured that that same studio had a dependable proxy on the ground. A former Universal studio manager, Henigson had extensive foreign experience going back to the 1920s. Before working out of Universal's lot, he served as a company auditor in South America and then general manager of European distribution. In the 1930s he took on producing duties, first at Universal and then Paramount. In time he moved to MGM, which put him in charge of the studio's continental European productions.[17] In 1949 MGM sent him to Italy to study the setup for making *Quo Vadis*. His favorable assessment of

Cinecittà studios helped convince MGM to shoot the film in Rome.[18] Henigson served as business manager of the production, a position that granted him authority over organizational and financial matters.

Eddie Mannix, MGM's general manager, paid tribute to Henigson's work on *Quo Vadis*: "Without Henigson's great organizational ability and operational know-how, 'Quo Vadis' could not possibly have been made on such a grand scale or completed within the record-breaking time schedule that it was. The film itself will be a lasting monument to his industry."[19] While hailed by studio executives, Henigson's repute among crew members was less certain. Art director Edward Carfagno remembers him as a frugal manager during the production of *Quo Vadis*. Even though Carfagno worked well with him, he recalls that Henigson was unpopular because he was always concerned with the bottom line and the studio's interests.[20] This impression carried over to *Roman Holiday*, with some crew members, for instance assistant director Herbert Coleman, characterizing him as brusque and "ungracious."[21] French production manager Christian Ferry, who teamed up with Henigson in Morocco on MGM's *Saadia* (1954), remembered that the Italians called him *il sigaro* because of the omnipresent cigar in his mouth. But such accounts don't shed light on his influence on production in Italy, which was far-reaching. Ferry claimed that Henigson was partly responsible for "transplanting" a Hollywood-style division of labor to Italy. Bringing over key department heads from Hollywood helped him shape each department along the lines of a Hollywood studio.[22]

With his capacity to maintain Hollywood production standards abroad, Henigson was eventually assigned to manage the making of MGM's *The Devil Makes Three* (1952) in Austria and Germany. As this production wound down, Paramount hired him to organize *Roman Holiday* and set up a production base at Cinecittà. During the early stages of preproduction for *Roman Holiday*, Henigson took a break from his duties as production manager of *The Devil Makes Three* and spent three days in Rome along with Paramount staff who had traveled over from Los Angeles. They negotiated with the Italian government, US authorities, and the officials of Cinecittà, where they hired staff and crew and opened up offices in the studio's administration building.[23] Obtaining studio space and establishing a headquarters were crucial first steps to securing a foothold in the Italian production landscape.

In addition to his organizational skills, Henigson brought knowledge of film practices in Hollywood and abroad. Looking to his experience of

Quo Vadis, he implored various *Roman Holiday* departments to brace for any contingencies by studying the script to determine the requirements for construction and production materials.[24] He also recommended that the dailies process follow the one used on *The Devil Makes Three*, in which the rushes were developed in a local lab, with one copy remaining in Rome for the crew to view and another flown to Hollywood for Paramount executives to see.[25]

Henigson's correspondence with Wyler before the director's arrival in Rome reveals his thoroughness and attention to detail—and supports his reputation as a fussy production manager. Years of working abroad enabled him to anticipate potential filmmaking pitfalls and understand the idiosyncrasies of the local culture, from working with Italian chauffeurs to grasping the protocols of tipping.[26] As with many other Hollywood workers, Henigson's production knowledge advanced with each film shot overseas as he proceeded to work on MGM films such as *Saadia* in Morocco and *Bedevilled* (1955) in Paris. He then reprised his role as business manager on *Ben-Hur* (1959) at Cinecittà. During this last production, he suffered a stroke that forced him into retirement.[27] Throughout his postwar years abroad, MGM and Paramount had a trustworthy delegate in Henigson, who could bring some sense of standardization to the international production process. But even with the business manager's diligence, Paramount still had to exert some control over its production from a distance.

THE ROLE OF PARAMOUNT

Roman Holiday didn't begin as an in-house project at Paramount. The property belonged to Liberty Films, an independent production company started by directors Frank Capra, George Stevens, Wyler, and former Columbia executive Sam Briskin. But their venture was short-lived, owing to financial troubles, and they accepted a buyout from Paramount, the terms of which, Thomas Schatz claims, "severely limited their creative freedom and authority."[28] Capra, who originally planned to direct *Roman Holiday*, backed off from the project when Paramount reduced his budget. Wyler eventually took over, thereby fulfilling the contract that Paramount had inherited from Liberty, but (as noted above) with the stipulation that he would only make the film in Rome. Although working overseas gave the producer-director some latitude, the fact that this was a full-fledged studio production meant that Paramount held a supervisory role.

Paramount provided assistance in the form of its European offices, which facilitated the preliminary organization of the film. In the summer of 1951, Paramount's offices in Paris and London helped with the search for a lead actress. Eventually, the London branch arranged screen tests of Audrey Hepburn, which convinced Wyler to cast her.[29] Later, the London office secured equipment and film stock for the production.[30] Before a production office was established at Cinecittà, Wyler depended on Paramount's Rome office to carry out location scouting.[31] Even during production, Wyler and company used the Rome office for its projection room to watch dailies.[32] Also, in seeking permission to use the names of European newspapers in the film's press conference finale, the production worked with the Paramount offices in London, Paris, Madrid, Amsterdam, Stockholm, Frankfurt, and Zurich.[33]

One way that Paramount kept an eye on the *Roman Holiday* production was with visits from studio executives. During preproduction, staff executive Jacob Karp helped coordinate the film in Rome. Once shooting commenced, Paramount's president, Barney Balaban, paid a visit to the set. Then during postproduction, production supervisor Don Hartman dropped in on Wyler during a trip to check up on the studio's various film shoots in Europe.[34] Another means of supervision extended to viewing dailies so that the studio could evaluate filming progress. In a letter to Henigson, Frank Caffey explained the purpose of shipping dailies back to Hollywood: "The idea of seeing dailies here, as well as the cut film, as outlined, is simply to permit Don Hartman to be generally familiar with the picture as it is being shot and cut for whatever comments and suggestions he may care to make. . . . He will be looking for story points basically."[35] In response to the rushes, Hartman was mostly enthusiastic, complimenting Audrey Hepburn and commending the use of authentic settings. "I do not think we could ever have gotten such results by shooting in Hollywood," the supervisor admitted.[36]

As best it could, Paramount tried to rein in costs during production. Based on Henigson's updates, Karp was particularly concerned that Wyler's shooting methods resulted in too many takes and superfluous scenes. When the director wanted to shoot a night scene on a barge along the Tiber River, the studio expressed its concern about the time and expense.[37] Nevertheless, Wyler went ahead and shot the scene. Time and again, Karp looked to Henigson to control spending and keep Wyler "in line." In the general manager, Paramount found an employee for whom the administration of finances was a top priority. Still, Wyler had to answer to the studio directly. In a series of updates, Wyler defended his shooting progress and claimed that he was filming only what was necessary. His "excessive use of film" was due to improvisation, he insisted, which "helped the picture considerably."[38]

Ultimately, the endless and specific decisions that any filmmaker must make during shooting were left to the unit working in Rome. Interestingly, Wyler seemed to struggle with this newfound autonomy as he juggled his dual roles of producer and director. Expressing the difficulty of producing a film far from the Hollywood infrastructure, he wrote to his lawyer, "You cannot just press a button and get things done—you have to look after every detail yourself, and producing a picture really means what the word implies. You realize that a big studio organization certainly has its advantages in getting things done."[39] Within the shifting production conditions of foreign filmmaking, even a veteran Hollywood filmmaker like Wyler labored without the direct support of a familiar studio system. One way to maneuver this transition in production was to maintain some semblance of continuity with how films were made back in Hollywood.

CONTINUING HOLLYWOOD PRODUCTION PRACTICES

Confronted with a new production situation in Rome, Hollywood personnel promoted their filmmaking practices by sharing trade knowledge. Regular letter exchanges were essential to retaining some sense of studio control, and the techniques imparted in these exchanges were central to perpetuating Hollywood methods. In one letter sent to Henigson during preproduction, Frank Caffey outlined the basic filmmaking operations carried out at Paramount in response to Henigson's desire to follow studio protocol. Caffey relayed Paramount's procedures for filling out call sheets, daily production reports, script clerk notes, and camera reports, while providing samples of these materials. This information served as a model for the organizational structure of the different studio departments and how the departments processed this paperwork. Caffey appreciated the attempts to follow studio routines, and expressed his gratitude for Henigson's "desire to tie together the operation as it must be done in Rome with our records here at the Studio."[40]

More specialized technical knowledge was passed on by various Paramount department heads, again through correspondence. Paramount's director of sound recording and editorial head offered their recommendations on the kind of postproduction equipment available in Rome and what would have to be sent from the United States and England.[41] Paramount's assistant camera department head provided a detailed explanation for marking takes with the camera slate.[42] It is unclear to what extent this specific know-how was relayed to the technicians in Rome or whether the technicians were already familiar with these procedures, but what is certain is that Henigson was collecting this information in an attempt to shape the production according to Hollywood practices.

The most direct means of promoting Hollywood methods was by importing personnel familiar with them. A number of key Hollywood technicians served as department heads, ensuring that various segments of the Italian crew followed Hollywood practices. Paramount sent over editor Robert Swink, who had to organize the editorial department and train foreign personnel.[43] For director of photography, the studio employed Franz Planer, who had served as a cinematographer throughout Europe before immigrating to the United States to work in Hollywood. However, as was the case for most European productions, the director of photography had to take on certain gaffing duties, and the added tasks may have contributed to Planer eventually leaving the production; he complained that he had to spend the night prelighting the sets and locations and then shooting all day.[44] Eventually, French cinematographer Henri Alekan replaced him. While hiring Hollywood personnel helped ensure the preservation of Hollywood filmmaking methods, in certain cases, a technician might have to take on different responsibilities that mirrored the practices of the local industry.

The successful operation of the Hollywood crew was also contingent on its ability to collaborate with foreign personnel. Important to this process of cohesion was the crew's language skills. During the early stages of preproduction, Henigson wrote to Wyler and stressed the necessity of hiring bilingual workers rather than using interpreters. Drawing on his prior experience, he explained, "I do try to organize so we may have bi-lingual personnel with as much competence as we can obtain in each department, so that your requirements, and those of others, may be properly interpreted in a professional way. . . . It is economic and solid, and by experience successful."[45] As with any international production, efficiencies rested on a smooth flow of communication across the crew.

In the end, Hollywood practices were sustained through the combined efforts of general manager Henigson, who prepared the production in the mold of studio filmmaking, and Hollywood department heads, who brought some of the foreign workers into step with their accustomed ways of working. In recognition of these undertakings, Wyler remarked to the studio:

> The crew is willing and hard-working, with some key personnel bi-lingual. Henigson did a first-rate job of getting things organized, making arrangements with the unions, selecting people, etc. Without his experienced hand, we'd never have organized the production facilities and crews as rapidly and efficiently as we did. Our own Hollywood people have been doing a fine job and have adjusted themselves very well to operating in a foreign country. They are fighting for top quality all the way down the line and are a great help to me.[46]

Efficiency, organization, and communication were all essential to making the film in Rome. And to fully harmonize with the foreign crew, the Hollywood unit needed to conform to local methods in some respects.

DO AS THE ROMANS DO: ADAPTING TO LOCAL CIRCUMSTANCES

For Hollywood personnel, adapting to working in Rome sometimes meant managing the technical shortcomings of Italian services and equipment. When Paramount production supervisor Don Hartman complained about Wyler's shooting pace, Wyler enumerated various difficulties: "The current, the arcs, the generators, the cameras, the lab—all of these things at one time or another present some difficulty and cause for delay—never altogether but only one at a time."[47] Adjusting to these mishaps became a chance to increase productivity by further subdividing the labor. To save time and money, Wyler initiated a second-unit crew to shoot action scenes with doubles. But the results seem to have been mixed, since, according to the director, "Italian movie makers just don't know very much about the technique of shooting action film."[48] Nevertheless, Wyler's decision shows how economic concerns—namely, the need for increased efficiency—shaped production practices through the creation of a new department. Furthermore, the unforeseen conditions of foreign shooting did not bring about a unique solution, but the application of a proven Hollywood method, even though the results were unsatisfactory for Wyler.

The most striking local factor that the Hollywood unit had to acclimate to was location shooting, as the Roman locales presented both opportunities and

FIGURE 12. William Wyler, seated next to the camera, and crew capture actors Audrey Hepburn and Gregory Peck on Rome's Spanish Steps in front of a crowd of onlookers. (Courtesy of the Margaret Herrick Library, Academy of Motion Picture Arts and Sciences)

difficulties (fig. 12). Speaking to his cast and crew at the end-of-production "wrap" dinner, Wyler praised filming in Rome. Probably pandering to his audience, he declared, "I think Rome is without a doubt the greatest location in the world. . . . I can think of no time in my many years of picture-making where there was such a confusion of riches to choose from."[49] But working on location was also a challenge, so Wyler looked to Italian filmmakers Cesare Zavattini and Vittorio De Sica on how to best shoot street sequences.[50] Like other Neorealist filmmakers, Zavattini and De Sica had explored new expressions of realism by taking their cameras and stories out of the studio and into the Italian city streets.

In fact, Zavattini gave advice on early treatments of the film by Ben Hecht and the film's credited screenwriter, Ian McLellan Hunter, who acted as a front for blacklisted writer Dalton Trumbo. Zavattini's comments mostly concerned issues of action and characterization, but he also had suggestions on which Roman locations certain scenes could be set in. His take on the story sheds light on Hollywood versus Neorealist approaches to storytelling, which resulted in an odd juxtaposition for the Italian writer. He wrote, "This story, at least in the pages that I have read, has been written along the most professionally tried rules, but what embarrassed me a great deal was the violent clash found in the contrast between the operetta-like treatment of the story, let us say, and the environment in which the work develops, an environment which has its real streets, its real inhabitants, and its own real and immediate problems."[51] For Zavattini, Hollywood's heightened emotions, which were more pronounced in earlier drafts, seemed incompatible with the realism inherent in using authentic locations. For Wyler, conversely, the prospect of inserting pictorial realism into a traditional Hollywood romance likely sparked his interest in filming in Rome.

Working on location forced Wyler to give up the kind of technical capability—for instance controlling sound recording while shooting on the streets—that he had enjoyed for decades in the studio system. So for certain sequences, he brought his approach more in line with the Italian method of rolling the cameras without sound and then dubbing the voices later. He explained, "Here it has been necessary to shoot scenes and parts of scenes entirely silent, sometimes even without a guide track due to the fact that we had to work with concealed cameras. This will be time-consuming but should not be too costly as people here are experts at this kind of work and do it constantly."[52] Another complication was related to filming in authentic interiors, which imposed many technical restrictions on a director accustomed to commanding all the elements in a studio. Wyler expressed frustration over working inside the Palazzo Brancaccio: "Four walls, none of them wild [movable], no way to rig platforms for lights, makeshift installations of every sort, and to complicate matters, mirrors everywhere. For sound, we had to close all doors and windows, and with the lights on, the temperature rose a degree a minute—on some days we hit as high as 120 degrees!" Despite these limitations, Wyler concluded, "I feel that it was well worth the effort because we got stuff on the screen that would be virtually impossible to duplicate at home except for a fantastic price. We paid for what we got in sweat."[53]

In sum, Wyler and his crew were able to mix Hollywood production practices with filmmaking procedures more common in the local industry. By sharing trade knowledge, using Hollywood production heads, and training the foreign crew, Wyler and the Hollywood unit were able to maintain a way of working that had been developed and refined in the studio system, with minor variations due to slight differences in the division of labor and the demands of location filming. While operating away from the production center of Los Angeles was a hurdle for the production staff, the story and look of *Roman Holiday*, on the whole, still retain characteristic Hollywood aesthetics. The transcultural process of international filmmaking resulted in a look that emphasized locations that could not have been adequately re-created in Hollywood, but rendered in a way that did not stray from the conventions of Hollywood style, a dynamic explored in part III.

Style

CHAPTER 4

A Cook's Tour of the World

THE ART OF INTERNATIONAL LOCATION SHOOTING

IN 1932 MGM MADE *RED DUST*, a story of a rubber plantation owner who is torn between two women. Although set in Indochina, the film was shot on sets recycled from *Tarzan the Ape Man* (1932) at MGM's Culver City studios and back lot.[1] In 1953, MGM remade *Red Dust* as *Mogambo*, moving the story setting from Indochina to East Africa. In the remake, the film's exteriors were shot in British East African colonies and French Equatorial Africa, trading in the mutability of the studio for the fixedness of place.

Early in *Red Dust*, director Victor Fleming staged a key scene of arrival. On a mock river, a steamboat docks to deposit a surveyor and his wife, who plan to work for a rubber plantation owner named Carson. In this jungle setting erected around the half-acre lake on MGM's Lot One, a vaguely exotic locale is suggested by the murky river, the ramshackle steamer, and the tropical vegetation (fig. 13).[2] Carson (played by Clark Gable) wants to put on board a brash fugitive named Vantine and send her away. But she is smitten with Carson, and balks at having to depart. He misreads her hesitation and offers her money, thinking she wants payment for keeping him company (fig. 14), then to her chagrin abruptly says goodbye and heads to the boat to welcome his guests. Like many films of this era, foreign scenery was re-created in the studio and on back-lot sets, with production design and story working together to convey the film's overseas setting.

The remake, *Mogambo*, focuses on Victor (again played by Gable), a big-game hunter who makes his living capturing animals and selling them to zoos. Director John Ford shot the film in color and partly on location, emphasizing new story points and capitalizing on the authenticity of the East African backdrops. In the restaging of the arrival scene, the camera is situated farther back from the action to highlight a right-to-left recessional

FIGURES 13 AND 14

composition of the river and the wilderness in the background, all rendered in deep focus (fig. 15). A line of women in the foreground and men in the middle ground on the dock add to the slanted directionality. Replacing the character of Vantine is Kelly, who waits, sitting on her luggage as Victor explains his decision to send her packing. The film cuts to a series of alternating over-the-shoulder shots, in which the authentic backgrounds underscore the conflict between the two characters. Behind Kelly lies the river, down which Victor wants her dispatched (fig. 16). Behind Victor are a tangle of trees and a corner of his home, where Kelly would like to stay (fig. 17). As in *Red Dust*, Victor leaves Kelly so he can welcome his guests, an anthropologist and his wife, who have hired the hunter to take them on safari.

FIGURES 15 TO 17

Unlike the earlier film, Ford's version stays longer with Kelly, registering her disappointment and humiliation as she takes their place on the boat and departs.

In *Mogambo*, the script and Ford's direction shift the focus of the scene away from Gable's character onto Kelly, making her the fulcrum. This nuance is typical of the director's handling of character, but just as notable is the expressive use of locations. The Kagera River, the authentic backdrop, and the natural lighting give depth to the image through recessional compositions and deep focus. During the key exchange between Victor and Kelly, the backgrounds become reflections of their desires: Victor wants Kelly to leave downriver and she wants to stay with him in his home. Ford demonstrates how a real foreign location can be brought in line with Hollywood storytelling and style while holding expressive potential. The scene is not without its dubious aspects, though. The film consigns the welcoming locals to the status of decor—visual markers of supposed authenticity of place. As with many of Hollywood's postwar international productions, the film's move out of the studio into a foreign locale presented the location unit with technical and aesthetic challenges, along with the problem of representing the local culture. In taking on these challenges, the filmmakers looked to a common technique of overseas production that utilized real spaces to bring about visual interest and meaning. It's a vision of the world according to Hollywood.

Films like *Mogambo* are not radically different in terms of form and style from motion pictures made in Hollywood studios at the time. Hollywood filmmakers who went to Europe and other regions around the world did not turn out Neorealist films or movies under the sway of emerging new waves. While certain Hollywood filmmakers such as Jules Dassin acknowledged their debt to Italian Neorealism in their early overseas productions such as *Night and the City* (1950), the influence of Neorealism on Hollywood aesthetics and social concerns was modest.[3] Oftentimes, more proximate contexts like specific documentary experience or the semi-documentary cycle shaped Hollywood filmmakers' approach to realism.[4] Furthermore, unlike most of the new waves and realist movements, Hollywood films shot abroad were by and large big-budget affairs that took advantage of lower overseas costs to realize higher production values. As this book has argued, Hollywood overseas was able to make Hollywood-style films by developing an adaptable, transcultural filmmaking process. By continuing studio production practices while adjusting to foreign film industries, Hollywood filmmakers used that operational foundation to execute films that followed their own industry's aesthetic regimes.

Within this tendency of stylistic continuity, certain genres and film cycles became more pronounced. The emphasis on foreign settings and stories resulted in historical epics, semi-documentary war pictures, and romantic films about US nationals abroad. These stories operated within the norms of classical Hollywood storytelling: goal-driven characters and plots unfolding across a cause-and-effect chain of events. Similarly, the style of these films remained consistent with earlier decades, with editing shaped by continuity principles and audiovisual devices in the service of narrative.[5] However, one key stylistic element became more prominent in these films: location shooting. Many of these films offered postcard views of the world, provoking some film reviewers to call them "Cook's Tours," inspired by the nineteenth-century British travel agent Thomas Cook.[6] The task for Hollywood filmmakers working abroad was to capitalize on a location and bring it in line with the conventions of Hollywood aesthetics. Innovative directors and technicians could go further by turning the location into a bold pictorial and expressive element and eventually incorporating it into the aesthetics of wide-screen. By examining the interplay of convention and novelty across a diversity of locales, this chapter demonstrates that Hollywood filmmakers adhered to their prevailing standards of story and style even while rendering foreign locations in ways that were by turns odd, striking, or inventive. Unlike the previous section, which focused on production in the UK, Italy, and France, this chapter draws from a wider assortment of shooting sites to capture the truly global scope of postwar location shooting.

How can a visual element like a location, which exists in the real world, be analyzed systematically? Location shooting operates somewhere in the fuzzy realm between production design and cinematography. It shares with set design the ability to convey setting, but locations are real-world environments. Filmmakers must adapt to the particulars of these spaces, for instance unpredictable light and weather. Much like cinematography, the creative use of a location is based on selection, composition, the control of natural and artificial lighting, and the relation between character and background. Whether the location was a built environment (a city street, a building, a ruin) or a natural environment (a landscape, a mountain, a body of water), filmmakers had to work flexibly to incorporate these fixed spaces into the film frame and then shape them to satisfy stylistic and storytelling demands. By studying how filmmakers portrayed a location and set an action within it, my aim is to arrive at a better understanding of the composition tactics that Hollywood filmmakers drew from. I also want to show that locations, like other elements of film style, can fulfill multiple functions, including decoration, expressivity, symbolism, and narrative. The ability of locations to develop a story while realizing decorative, expressive, and symbolic tasks reveals that they, like other elements of film style, can have several functions at once.[7]

Important to reconstructing the continuities and changes of foreign location shooting are the reigning conventions of Hollywood style.[8] By looking at the conventions that were available to filmmakers as they shifted production abroad, we can identify some of the stable traditions of composition that directors and cinematographers turned to. Some of these compositional conventions inclined filmmakers to create vivid images with depth. Other conventions encouraged them to highlight foreground action and dialogue. Oftentimes, these two competing tendencies were reconciled by bringing locations into established patterns of shot development that moved from wider shots to closer ones. A broader menu of options and technologies also guided Hollywood filmmakers for how to approach representing a location. In any year from the late 1940s to the early 1960s, a filmmaker may have shot entirely on location, another may have mixed authentic exteriors with studio-bound interiors, and yet another may have shown foreign locations through rear projection. With all of these choices available, the following account of location filming is not a tidy chronicle of change or a teleological progression toward increased realism. This account is one of incremental shifts that points to how location shooting constituted a versatile stylistic practice that shaped postwar Hollywood aesthetics.

LOCATION SURVEYS

As Hollywood filmmakers moved into foreign territories, location surveys helped identify shooting locales with picturesque qualities that would fulfill story-setting requirements. This activity was essential to shaping the aesthetics of locations early in the production process. The survey was typically conducted before the core production unit traveled from Hollywood. The makeup of the survey team varied from film to film but generally included some combination of director, cinematographer, art director, and unit production manager. They would explore a location for specific shooting sites, using the script and visual references as guidelines along with tips from other filmmakers and production managers acquainted with the region.[9] The scouting team would then create a report detailing its production requirements and the characteristics of the location. These surveys could take place in stages: a preliminary trip might study the practical and visual offerings of a location, followed by a closer examination of the compositional possibilities once the locale was secured. Cinematographer Burnett Guffey summed up this procedure on Columbia's *Me and the Colonel* (1958), which was partly shot in France: "Previously, the area had been 'pre-scouted' by the producer, director and art director. They had selected tentative sites and general locations. Our group finalized everything. We pin-pointed each location, decided the direction we would shoot and at what time of day, and decided what additional set construction was necessary on the various locations."[10]

Another major consideration in deciding where to shoot was the weather—often the single greatest force affecting location shooting, especially outside the temperate climate of Southern California. In an *American Cinematographer* profile, Charles G. Clarke, who specialized in location work, ruminated on the technical challenges of "unfamiliar and unpredictable weather" while working on *The Barbarian and the Geisha* (1958) in Japan. "In Hollywood," he explained, "we know that if the day starts with a foggy overcast, it generally blows over by noon so that we have bright sun to work with in the afternoon. Here in Japan, as I have so often encountered elsewhere, the weather performs differently. One never knows quite what to expect."[11] Attempting to cope with the weather's unpredictability, some movie companies consulted the Motion Picture Division of the National Weather Institute in Los Angeles to obtain meteorological forecasts for a particular location. In anticipation of shooting *Little Boy Lost* (1953) and *To Catch a Thief* (1955) in France, Paramount depended on the National Weather Institute for "outlooks" that included data on cloud types, temperature, and precipitation.[12] Of course, weather is unpredictable, so despite these preparations, rain along the French Riviera interrupted the production of *To Catch a Thief*, forcing a number of planned exterior scenes to move to Paramount's Hollywood studio.

For the final selection of locations, filmmakers relied on survey reports and visual references such as photos and sketches that came from the scouting trips. Historically, Hollywood studios had long used location departments and the cataloguing of location photos to support off-the-lot filming.[13] International productions, however, operated in new territories where survey teams had to generate original material to bring to Hollywood studios and filmmakers, and the visual references started the process of how to think about composing shots on location. For *The Crimson Pirate* (1952), the production needed a location in the Mediterranean that could stand in for a Caribbean setting. Associate producer Norman Deming hunted along the Italian coastline and the islands of Capri, Sardinia, and Sicily, and the company eventually settled on Ischia, near Naples, which approximated a Caribbean island with its tropical-looking vegetation and buildings resembling Spanish colonial architecture. From this survey, Deming sent producer Harold Hecht a lengthy report on Ischia with accompanying drawings, photos, and a map detailing the angles from which the photos were taken.[14]

While location shooting usually recorded preexisting spaces, the art director was still important in the selection and alteration of the locale.[15] The task of the art director was to dress up a location in order to realize the prerequisites of story and cinematography, as well as match location exterior and studio interior shots. In the words of one Warner Bros. art director, "An outdoor set presents more of a challenge, or a problem. Once you've found the location for the set, your imagination has to begin working from the ground up. The terrain gets the first consideration in relation to the amount of sunlight it receives, what sort of background the distant horizon offers, and how well the topography of the ground fits into the requirements of the script."[16] The art director could then enhance the locale with supplemental constructions and set dressing. Guided by a sketch from Alfred Hitchcock, a survey team for *To Catch a Thief* selected a site in Monte Carlo for a waterfront restaurant. Art director "Mac" Johnson subsequently dressed a terrace adjacent to the film's fictional Bellini's restaurant for the exterior shots, while interiors were constructed on a Paramount soundstage.[17] By blending the real with the built, Hollywood's international location shooting favored a manufactured depiction of authentic locales. Filmmakers applied to location work some of the principles of design and construction that had been used in studios. This approach harkened back to the pioneering studio days, when filmmakers implemented a studio aesthetic in the real world. As Brian Jacobson has argued, the development of studio-based production practices prompted early moviemakers to apply a sensibility of "studio plasticity" to exteriors in Southern California, treating locations as malleable backdrops in much the same way that technicians were manipulating studio space to represent a diversity of settings.[18]

The location survey was thus the critical early step in a procedure that blended practical and aesthetic concerns to pave the way for Hollywood filmmakers to turn authentic locales into impactful visuals. From photographs and sketches to site visits, the fruits of these location inquiries began to shape how to shoot a location. Once the selection was complete, Hollywood film-makers in collaboration with their cinematographers and art directors began to make the creative decisions that would render locations pictorially interesting. A key consideration in planning the look of the film was how to balance location and studio work.

THE TECHNIQUES OF STUDIO WORK VERSUS LOCATION SHOOTING

During much of the studio-system era, filmmakers replicated foreign locales through set design and process shots. And even with the postwar proliferation of location filming in the United States and abroad, studio work remained important for interior scenes and capturing performances and audible dialogue that would be difficult to control on location. Within this studio tradition, rear projection continued to be an essential solution for producers who wanted to re-create exterior settings inside soundstages and avoid the technical and organizational challenges of principal photography on location: instead of traveling to a foreign city to shoot a scene of a couple talking while walking down a street or driving a car, the process photography department could re-create the scene in a studio with a background plate of stock footage or shots made especially for that project. This background footage was projected onto a translucent screen from behind, with the actors positioned in front of the screen and the camera facing the actors. In Andre DeToth's *Tanganyika* (1954), Universal saved on an expensive location trek by re-creating East African locales around Southern California and in a studio, where actors performed in front of rear-projection screens that displayed stock shots of wildlife (fig. 18).

Over the years, companies and technicians made various refinements to the practice, including upgrading techniques for lighting a set that used back projection and improving the luminosity of the rear-projected image.[19] All of these developments aimed to make shots using rear projection indistinguishable from non-process shots, but the system still tended to look artificial, partly due to the absence of realistic depth cues. Nevertheless, Hollywood's international productions continued to rely on rear projection because of its economic and logistical merits. Rear-projection scenes made in Hollywood or foreign studios became a common method for recording dialogue and traveling scenes. Because of the difficulty of recording sound and controlling lighting in exteriors, very often dialogue scenes began on location to establish

FIGURE 18. For the studio work on *Tanganyika* (1954), a camera films actor Van Heflin taking aim at a leopard in a rear-projected stock shot. (Courtesy of the Margaret Herrick Library, Academy of Motion Picture Arts and Sciences)

setting and highlight pictorialism, and then moved to the studio for closer views, where performance took precedence. The move from emphasizing pictorial beauty in establishing wide shots to breaking down the action in closer shots reflected a durable convention of classical style.[20]

This pattern plays out in John Huston's *We Were Strangers* (1949), which was shot at Columbia Studios and on location in Havana, where Cuban doubles stood in for the film's Hollywood leads. In one scene, a secret police agent stops a banker-turned-revolutionary on the street. In the wide shot, a double for Jennifer Jones walks through the city center as the agent's car pulls up alongside her (fig. 19). The shot indicates the setting and the spatial relationship of the characters. Pictorially, the image creates a diagonal thrust through the street, along a diminishing row of columns to the dome of Havana's Capitolio in the distance. When dialogue ensues, we cut to closer views of the film's principal actors in the studio, where rear projection shows the columned building from the previous shot and various Cuban passersby in the background (fig. 20). The switch from location to studio was not just

FIGURES 19 AND 20

a technical solution but also an economic one. A production could reduce costs by filming the wide shots and rear-projection background plates on location with extras, leaving the closer shots for the studios, where the paid extras were not needed.[21] In the case of *We Were Strangers*, the producers avoided the expense of flying the film's stars to Cuba by hiring doubles for the location wide shots.

One common use of rear projection was for driving scenes. The difficulty of sound recording, lighting, clearing roads, and the insurance risks of performing in moving vehicles frequently forced Hollywood productions to shoot these sequences on a soundstage. Studio technicians then had to coordinate the foreground action with the footage in the background plate so that changes in light and movement would be synchronized.[22] These driving scenes often began with establishing shots in an exterior, followed by a cut to a closer view of the car's occupants filmed in a studio in front of a background plate. Alfred Hitchcock opens *Stage Fright* (1950) with a succession of wide shots of London's Saint Paul's Cathedral and the surrounding bombed-out neighborhood as a convertible approaches from a distance. Each shot moves closer to the oncoming car, until the vehicle fills the screen as it drives over the camera (fig. 21). Then the scene jumps to the Associated British Picture Corporation's Elstree studio for a shot within the car of an uneasy-looking drama student and her friend, who explains how he has been pulled into a murder plot. On the rear-projection screen behind the actors, the streets of London trail behind (fig. 22).[23] This *in medias res* opening quickly sets up the London backdrop in the location wide shots and then uses the transition to the studio to focus our attention on the paranoia of the characters and the details of the murder intrigue. Through much of his career, Hitchcock, who opted for a precise breakdown of action, relied on rear projection to achieve a greater manipulation of screen action.[24]

While rear projection could translate to cost savings and increased control in the studio, continuity problems arose when filmmakers tried to match what were called "key" shots (background plates) and "straight" shots (non-process shots). The goal was to achieve visual continuity, so that the transition from a location shot to a studio shot would appear seamless. One efficient way to help harmonize location and studio footage was to schedule off-the-lot filming before the move to the soundstage. This was the case for the production of *To the Victor* (1948), which filmed its French locales prior to moving to the Burbank studio of Warner Bros. This plan enabled a crew to not only base the interiors on the exteriors but also re-create in the studio any scenes that were not shot on location because of delays, scheduling conflicts, or weather problems. To aid this process, reference footage was necessary. On the production of *Me and the Colonel*, a Moviola editing viewer was used on the set of Columbia Studios to screen footage filmed on location in France so that it could match what was already shot.[25] Not all productions followed this order, though, and the outcome could be complicated and costly. For *A Certain Smile* (1958), interiors at Fox Studios were shot before exteriors in France. The production had a Moviola on set so that director Jean

FIGURES 21 AND 22

Negulesco could watch interior footage and match it with the exteriors. However, certain sequences shot at Fox did not match with location work. Ultimately, because of weather problems in France, retakes and added scenes were completed back in Hollywood.[26]

From the late 1940s to the early 1960s, mixing location and studio work remained viable for international productions. The development of location shooting during this period does not reveal a linear evolution of realistic film styles, with filmmakers moving away from studio work toward

greater location shooting. The practice of location filming developed along-side competing technical tendencies. Some filmmakers favored heavy loca-tion shooting, while others replicated most foreign settings in the studio, with actual location shots appearing in background plates or as scene-transition shots. More films mixed the two, even into the 1960s with the turn to greater cinematic realism. Although a *Daily Variety* review compared Martin Ritt's *Paris Blues* (1961) to the French New Wave's authenticity of place, the film balances location shooting with extensive studio work.[27] It uses intricate studio sets as stand-ins for Parisian streets and rear-projection shots that take us from the deck of a *bateau mouche* excursion boat on the Seine to a film studio, where a background plate replicates the passing view from the river (fig. 23). Once again, studio filming makes up for the chal-lenges of location shooting, including sound problems and logistical setbacks.

The uneven advancement of location shooting is also clear when we observe that a number of early postwar international productions offered some of the most evocative location work. New technological developments had an important influence on these films by promoting a set of techniques that helped catalyze location shooting abroad.[28] Location shooting grew with new lighting methods and more portable lighting units, such as photofloods, which were easy to transport and could use the current from local utility lines instead of generators.[29] Other small but powerful lightweight lighting

FIGURE 24

units, such as Garnelites, Masterlites, and Colortran lamps, supported crews in illuminating location interiors and nighttime exteriors.[30] Another technical advance was a process called latensification, which increased the speed of film by exposing the negative to small amounts of light after the film was used in the camera but before development. The increased film speed was especially helpful in achieving photographic detail and density when shooting location interiors and night scenes with low light levels.[31] This process assisted a Fox crew in shooting scenes from the semi-documentary-inspired *The Big Lift* (1950) in Berlin's U-Bahn, where only a few added photofloods supplemented a subway train's practical lights to help with exposure.[32] The crew's ability to capture a critical moment of suspense in the tight, enclosed space of the subway car heightened the sense of anxiety and claustrophobia around a Soviet military search for smuggled goods among the passengers (fig. 24).

Many of these breakthroughs in technology and technique helped improve conditions for shooting on location. Once there, filmmakers had to figure out how to best portray a foreign setting and stage a scene within that space. Since many had worked in the studio system for decades, they did not discard the techniques that had sustained them. Even when faced with operating in often-uncharted territory and unpredictable exteriors, they did not start from scratch, but relied on shooting strategies and stylistic conventions that had worked in the past.

For Hollywood filmmakers, shooting in a studio or on a back lot with a constructed set commonly resulted in a finite number of angles from which a scene could be shot. But a location exterior, with its open space and intensified lighting, could offer more compositional options.[33] An *American Cinematographer* article enumerated:

> The problems encountered when shooting exterior scenes out of doors (some "exteriors" are shot indoors on the sound stage) arise, paradoxically, from the rather over-abundant generosity of Nature. That is to say, the chief concern in shooting exteriors is not so much to record on film the basically necessary photographic elements—lights, subject, etc.—but to *control* those elements, which have been so lavishly placed at our disposal, in order to obtain the best possible pictorial result.[34]

But filmmakers were not helpless in the face of so many creative and technical options. Rather, they looked to proven conventions for controlling how space was recorded.[35] In surveying a wide range of films shot on foreign locations in the postwar era, two dominant conventions of composition emerge: first, that an image should convey a sense of depth, and second, that backgrounds should not distract from the action. Balancing these tendencies, filmmakers depicted locations in visually attractive ways while taming that impulse in order to foreground dialogue and action. As the following examples demonstrate, locations fulfilled a decorative function while contributing to story and expression.

One of the rewards of shooting on location is that the available natural light of exteriors can accentuate depth that is rendered in sharp focus. Many filmmakers working overseas exploited this phenomenon to situate character and action in outdoor foreign localities. These filmmakers selected locations that brought out a sense of depth and simultaneously amplified it by deploying specific principles of composition, as illustrated in figure 19. A common approach was to enhance depth by creating diagonals running from one side of the foreground to the other side of the background. This recessional technique drew on earlier artistic traditions, from seventeenth-century painting to early nonfiction film actualities.[36] In his treatise on composition in the visual arts, Rudolf Arnheim described, "Diagonals, although dynamically active through their deviation from the Cartesian grid, perform like the trusses in a building. By cutting across the dichotomy of vertical vs. horizontal and mediating between the two dimensions, they add stability."[37] Picking up on this enduring feature of visual design, Hollywood cinematographers promoted the compositional device of recessional lines. One *American Cinematographer* article insisted, "Diagonal lines are more forceful and more pleasing to the eye than straight vertical or horizontal lines."[38] Another article recommended shooting a setting from an oblique angle, which "reveals the frame's depth, imparts a feeling of solidity and prevents it appearing simply as a cardboard cutout."[39]

Working on location, Hollywood filmmakers applied the recessive approach to give shots greater depth, often capturing elements of a locality from a slanted angle. In *Night and the City*, Jules Dassin stages the film's climax around London's Hammersmith Bridge, drawing on some compositional ideas he first explored in the location-heavy *The Naked City* (1948) a couple of years earlier. For the final shot of the movie, he uses the bridge's suspension cables to create a powerful sweep away from a crooked racketeer as his henchmen and car wait in the distance (fig. 25). Dassin shows how architecture in coordination with the placement of actors can create a diagonal trajectory within the shot, encouraging the viewer to zero in on particular points in the frame while stressing the depth of the image. Other filmmakers explored similar recessional compositions using nature or on-location set design to deepen the space.

Another means of bringing about increased depth was to layer foreground, middle ground, and background planes. Filmmakers used various facets of a setting such as nature, architecture, or even people to create multiple planes within a shot that produced overlapping depth cues. In his 1949 book *Painting with Light*, cinematographer John Alton suggested that a filmmaker can expand depth and indicate the relative size of objects by adding to the composition a foreground item that is darker than the background. For Alton, the objectives were to represent proper perspective and control where the viewer looks.[40] Patrick Keating connects this device to *repoussoir*, a painting technique of darkened foregrounds and brighter backgrounds that became standard in cinematography.[41] Using these approaches, a filmmaker could attain a sense of depth across the different planes while coaxing the viewer's eye to particular zones of the frame.

On location, some filmmakers practiced the layering option by positioning bodies in the foreground set off from location elements in the background

FIGURE 25

through a contrast of lighting. Early in Jacques Tourneur's *Berlin Express* (1948), a shot of a Parisian street café exhibits a staggered arrangement of patrons that proceeds to one of the film's lead characters, a government official, who rises from his seat (fig. 26). In the distance is the iconic Moulin Rouge windmill, which adds a visual anchor. In one brief shot, the layered bodies, the rising mid-ground motion, and the background buildings all work in tandem to efficiently produce a sense of depth. In *Man on a Tightrope* (1953), Elia Kazan calls upon a complex layering approach in extreme depth by staging a circus troupe's escape across the border from Czechoslovakia to Bavaria. The troupe's leader sneaks into a checkpoint sentry booth in the foreground as his circus caravan prepares for the border crossing in the background. In a dynamic shot that balances foreground and background, light and shadow, interior and exterior, the details of the getaway are presented in sharp focus (fig. 27). Kazan's layering technique becomes a way to achieve depth and keep various points of interest in play within the frame. Such shots help to realize various effects of location shooting: they enhance depth, allow for inventive compositions, and quickly establish setting and an authenticity of place.

Some filmmakers turned to other spatial strategies. Moving the camera on location could create a synthesis of mobile framing and background details to achieve a vigorous sense of depth. In John Huston's *Beat the Devil* (1954), a business schemer and an offbeat Englishwoman have a liaison on Ravello's

FIGURES 26 AND 27

Terrace of the Infinity, which overlooks the Amalfi coastline. At the beginning of the scene, the camera swoops down from an extreme long shot that takes in the characters and their brilliant surroundings (fig. 28), then moves in to frame a recessional perspective of the terrace they are standing on (fig. 29). This motion is reversed in a later scene as the two characters prolong their outing and the woman shares a plan to acquire uranium-rich land—an important plot point. The camera climbs upward from a medium shot of the couple sitting in a garden overlooking the sea to an extreme long shot that exposes a fellow swindler eavesdropping on their conversation. Production

FIGURES 28 AND 29

stills reveal that these mirrored camera movements were difficult to execute on the vertiginous locale, but they fulfill essential functions.[42] On a narrative level, they uncover consequential story information and shifting character knowledge. Visually, they emphasize the height of the perched locations and the spectacular scenery. Although these shots follow some of the conventions of depth composition, the sweeping camera moves attain an almost outlandish virtuosity.

FIGURE 30

In the above examples, exteriors provided the necessary lighting and space that could furnish images with a sense of depth. Working abroad, Hollywood companies tended to favor shooting exteriors, since outdoor filmmaking was easier to execute than location interiors, which could be replicated in a studio. However, some filmmakers made the most of the interiors of unique buildings, applying technical solutions and the same depth tactics employed for exteriors. For *Decision before Dawn* (1952), Anatole Litvak and cinematographer Franz Planer turned the interiors of European buildings into major locales using lighting and composition to maximize depth. Germany's Eberbach Abbey becomes a US Army headquarters, in which the play of light and the immersive perspective of a basilica's nave intensifies depth (fig. 30). In a parallel space, the Schleissheim Palace near Munich serves as a German outpost. Its decaying opulence echoes the decline of the German army. The film not only uses architecture to create depth, but also shows how one waxing army and another waning one were forced to take refuge in the unlikeliest of locales.

A problem of shooting within practical interiors was how to illuminate the space while keeping the set lights out of the camera's view. In a studio, movable walls and open-top sets allowed cinematographers to place lights almost anywhere. In a location interior, the director of photography and the lighting crew had to either maneuver within the confines of a room or work

FIGURE 31

out how to light a large interior space. The production of *Gigi* (1958) encountered these challenges when Vincente Minnelli wanted to shoot the Belle
Époque decor of the Parisian restaurant Maxim's, where mirrored walls reinforced a sense of depth but risked exposing production lighting, equipment,
and crew members. Moreover, all of this had to be accomplished in the
expansive framing of CinemaScope. At first, cinematographer Joseph
Ruttenberg considered covering the mirrors with black velvet, but Minnelli
countered, "The great thing about Maxim's—the signature of Maxim's—are
the mirrors and their art nouveau frames. You can see all the sections of the
room behind people. They give the whole room its character."[43] As a solution,
Ruttenberg shot with low-key lighting to cut down on the amount of equipment and placed suction cups on photofloods to allow for a more versatile
placement of lights. The cinematographer and director then synchronized
camera movement and the blocking of actors through the mirrored space to
generate shots that avoided unwanted reflections.[44] When man-about-town
Gaston shows off his young companion, Gigi, at Maxim's, the space becomes
a staging ground for the titular character's transformation from an ingénue
to a belle of Parisian high society. Minnelli and Ruttenberg worked with the
features of the restaurant to create multiple planes of visual interest (fig. 31).
The focus of the scene is the couple, planted in the foreground. The gossiping
onlookers sit in the middle ground. In the background are the intricate art
nouveau walls, whose mirrors expand the depth of the space by revealing a
dance floor. Here, Minnelli takes the colorful and intricate compositions
that he perfected on Hollywood soundstages into the real world by turning
these authentic locales into sumptuous sets that deliver a rich layering of

planes. As James Naremore suggests, Minnelli administers a "store-window sensibility" to the real space, a stylistic approach rooted in the director's experience as a Marshall Field's department-store window decorator.[45]

All of these strategies for conveying depth on location—recessive arrangements, multiplanar layering, and camera movement—risked working against a principle of Hollywood visuals and storytelling: that backgrounds should not distract from dialogue or divert the audience's attention away from the central action. As a 1947 *American Cinematographer* article pointed out, "We may borrow a thought from Ernst Lubitsch and Norman Bel Geddes, who say that if a background is so beautiful and commanding that it detracts from the action it is a crime."[46] In addition to lighting and focus, composition became a key technique to guide where the viewer looked within the frame. Another piece in *American Cinematographer* suggested, "The function of effective composition is to lead the eye directly to the most important point in the scene. For this reason, action should be so staged that the lines of the setting in which it is played will lead to the areas of greatest dramatic importance."[47] These zones of drama tend to be key actions and actors' faces, which convey essential bits of dialogue and the emotional register of a scene. Especially vital for a filmmaker on location was how to shoot a dialogue scene without letting the backdrop distract from important story information, yet at the same time achieve pictorial interest through the authentic locale—a key reason for mounting the production abroad.

Some filmmakers elected to capture dialogue entirely in foreign locales by balancing conversing characters in the foreground and a prominent location in the background within the same shot. In *Roman Holiday* (1953), William Wyler presents a key interaction on the Spanish Steps in Rome (figure 12 depicts the shooting of this scene). The director films a seemingly chance meeting between Princess Ann and newspaper reporter Joe Bradley in a medium-long shot with the baroque stairway leading up to the towering church of Santissima Trinità dei Monti (fig. 32). The shot records the encounter and introduces the pitched space. As the two sit down, the film cuts to a closer low-angle shot in which the characters and the church tower form a slight left-to-right recessional line (fig. 33). This composition inverts in the reverse angle, exhibiting a right-to-left slant from the reporter to the princess to a spherical ornament at the bottom of the steps (fig. 34). Applying continuity principles to location work, Wyler constructs this scene through editing while portraying the visual allure of the Roman site. The shot compositions prioritize dialogue and gestures and incorporate architecture at the edges of the frame for decoration and added depth. But at least one inadvertent background detail materializes: the drama of the passing clouds above the couple. For a director like Wyler, who favored staging scenes in deep focus, exterior location shooting provided the spatial depth and the abundance of lighting needed to achieve his preferred style while still upholding the conventions of continuity editing.

In *Three Coins in the Fountain* (1954), Jean Negulesco employs a similar approach for a dialogue scene, but this time he mixes location and studio work, all rendered in color and CinemaScope wide-screen. Like Wyler, the director exploits the scenic allure of Rome's famed landmarks in another commoner-royal interaction. Negulesco films a couple, an expatriate from the United States named Maria and a modern-day Italian prince, as they pull up near the Colosseum in a car. In a medium shot favoring Maria, the Colosseum on the left and the Arch of Constantine on the right frame the background (fig. 35). In the reverse angle that faces the prince, the ruins of the Temple of Venus and Roma in the background create recessional depth through a diagonal arrangement of columns and buildings (fig. 36). Once the conversation progresses and the scene moves to medium close-ups, the film shifts to the studio (fig. 37). Here, the performances could be better recorded and the surroundings do not compete with the significant information Maria imparts when she discloses her stratagem to seduce the prince. As with so many productions filmed overseas, this scene adheres to a pattern of wider shots achieved on location to establish place and highlight the decorative dimension of the space, followed by closer shots done in a studio, where the priority is on dialogue and the actors' faces. While cinematographers aimed to make this transition seamless by matching the lighting from locations to the studio shots, minor discontinuities are discernible. In this switch, the bright side-light and the shadows on Maria's face and blouse become softened with the help of studio lighting to magnify beauty. The time-honored conventions of glamour lighting—still prevalent if milder—override photographic fidelity.[48] Compared to the similar moment in *Roman Holiday*, this later scene demonstrates that even with the advent of new wide-screen technologies like CinemaScope, filmmakers still fell back on the control of studio work—a stylistic divergence in the meandering development of Hollywood realism.

The above two compositional conventions—the importance of creating depth in a shot and making sure that the backgrounds do not distract from

FIGURES 32 TO 34

FIGURES 35 TO 37

the central action—are competing aesthetic tendencies. As I will explore
further below, filmmakers frequently inserted the most flagrant uses of recessive and layering designs during moments of heightened action and pure
pictorialism. Over the course of conversations, recessive perspectives tended
to be more subdued as the camera cut to closer views of character interactions
either on location (see figs. 33, 34) or in a studio (see fig. 37). By following

tried-and-tested patterns of Hollywood aesthetics, these films fused differing location techniques to perform a variety of storytelling and stylistic tasks. With the application of wide-screen technologies to location work, filmmakers had to solve how to incorporate the new formats into prevailing aesthetic ideas.

WIDE-SCREEN LOCATIONS

As filmmakers continued to explore location shooting through the 1950s, new technological developments—for instance wide-screen—posed setbacks and advantages. Wide-screen's more expansive frame enabled intensified spectacle and realism in location shooting; early boosters of CinemaScope in fact wedded the format to epics shot on location. "CinemaScope is ideally suited to spectacle films in which most of the action can be played against huge outdoor panoramic vistas," one *American Cinematographer* commentary insisted.[49] John Belton similarly contends that CinemaScope "introduced a level of visual spectacle that often threatened to overwhelm the narrative. This threat could be contained only by a shift in terms of the kinds of films that were made—a shift to historical spectacle—which functioned to naturalize pictorial spectacle."[50] But early wide-screen films were not limited to historical epics; they featured all manner of stories.

The connection between wide-screen and foreign locations was forged in film after film, from nonfiction travelogues to fictional foreign-set motion pictures. The Cinerama process made use of foreign locales with *This Is Cinerama* (1952), depicting Italy, Scotland, and Spain, followed by more international views in *Cinerama Holiday* (1955) and *The Seven Wonders of the World* (1956). All of these films showcased foreign locations in a documentary-like episodic fashion, which had the effect of playing up the unique span of the medium. Other travelogues, such as the Oscar-winning short *Vesuvius Express* (1953), which recorded a Milan-to-Naples train ride, also created spectacle by marrying foreign locations with CinemaScope.[51] Some of the spectacle of these early wide-screen travelogues carried over into the fictional realm, too. Producer Michael Todd explored the creative possibilities of shooting foreign scenery in the Todd-AO format for *Around the World in 80 Days* (1956). Across Paris, Chinchón, London, Mexico City, and Bombay, the authentic locations accentuated the dimensions of Todd-AO even as this new format simultaneously punctuated the grandeur of foreign vistas.

Despite the aesthetic and technical potential of these new formats, filmmakers encountered a new set of limitations with the switch to wide-screen shooting. David Bordwell describes how CinemaScope ushered in an array of technical shortcomings, including image distortion, lenses that reduced sensitivity to light, and restrictions on composition and staging. Filmmakers developed various fixes, such as shooting farther back from actors to increase the depth of field and positioning actors side by side across the frame for clear dialogue exchanges.[52] Many of these problems and countermoves wound up in Twentieth Century-Fox's second CinemaScope film, *How to Marry a Millionaire* (1953), directed by Jean Negulesco. By the time *Three Coins in the Fountain* was filmed, Negulesco had worked out some of the glitches that befell his first CinemaScope feature. "A wide variety of shots became possible on the second film which were mechanically ruled out of the first," he claimed. "Lens, film stocks, process shots and editing requirements all have improved with general know-how in handling the medium."[53] In time, additional technologies and shooting practices helped address the imperfections of wide-screen. The emphasis on exterior shooting for international productions resulted in many strategies that helped filmmakers overcome these new formats' initial drawbacks.

One of the great benefits of shooting in outdoor locations was the high level of natural lighting that allowed cinematographers to heighten the depth of field. Wide-screen required more lighting, since the anamorphic lenses had longer focal lengths and reduced the transmission of light. Additional lighting was necessary to illuminate the vaster space composed by the broader frame.[54] Wide-screen productions shot on color film stock needed even more lighting than those on black-and-white stock to attain a greater depth of field. In this sense, exterior location shooting, with its bright natural lighting, served as an important remedy to the initial limitations of wide-screen and color. In Fox's *House of Bamboo* (1955), which was partly filmed in Japan, director Samuel Fuller exploited exterior lighting to produce startling CinemaScope compositions, such as a shot featuring the jutting feet of a corpse in the foreground and Mount Fuji behind. He also played out actions in long range, thanks to sunlight. At the film's climax, Japanese police and a US military agent chase a gangster up to an amusement park perched atop the Matsuya department store in Tokyo. Without an escape route, the gangster becomes increasingly desperate. He lashes out violently and fires multiple shots into a crowd gathered on the street many stories below. He shoots an innocent bystander, seen as a distant white figure falling to the ground (fig. 38). The film counterbalances this handling of depth with compositions

FIGURES 38 AND 39

that maximize the expanse of the CinemaScope format. As the gangster continues to shoot from atop a revolving fun-park Earth, the film captures the structure from a different angle to fill the wide-screen frame (fig. 39). Blending wide-screen, deep space, and the design of a singular location, Fuller delivers a bravura piece of action cinema.

As *House of Bamboo* proves, exterior location shooting helped filmmakers achieve a depth of field that had been difficult to produce in the studio while working in wide-screen. In the studio, CinemaScope initially made recessive compositions and linear perspectives more difficult. On location, a handful of filmmakers quickly revived these ideas. *Knights of the Round Table* (1954) was MGM's first foray into the format, and it was the first CinemaScope production to be shot in England. While much of the film relies on studio work and process shots, at times the movie combines location and wide-screen to attain compositions that play with the depth and length of the screen. After the death of King Arthur, a zigzag recessional shot links various points of interest (fig. 40). Percival stands in the foreground on the right. He watches Lancelot, who casts Arthur's Excalibur sword into the sea, in the

FIGURE 40

middle ground on the left. In the background, the Cornish cliffs of Tintagel occupy the right half of the frame. Unlike the relatively stilted compositions constructed within the studio, this location shot achieves greater depth and pictorial strength through natural lighting and expansive, authentic locales.

With the extra breadth of the wide-screen frame, filmmakers could capture architecture to stretch out recessive compositions into splashy diagonals that extended depth and width. An interplay of wide-screen and architecture is foregrounded in *Three Coins in the Fountain*. As it was one of Fox's first CinemaScope motion pictures to be shot abroad, the filmmakers sought to call attention to the new wide-screen technology. After the film's prologue tour of Roman fountains and then the credits, the movie proceeds to exploit architecture to emphasize the length of the screen and to elicit design principles that train the viewer's eyes to sweep across the CinemaScope frame. The story opens at Rome's modernist Termini train station, whose horizontal lines invite us to glance across the length of the frame (fig. 41). This perceptual push continues as the film cuts inside, to the arrival of Maria. She is first seen in the building's central gallery. Then in the ticketing hall, the camera composes for a slight left-to-right diagonal and a plunging perspective running down the undulating cantilevered roof as Maria looks for her ride (fig. 42). The movement of extras across the frame helps to accent the length of the wide-screen even as Maria remains the focal point. Like many wide-screen productions, the film captures locations in a way that reflected the rhetoric surrounding postwar wide-screen, which treated the new format as a participatory medium that created greater three-dimensionality.[55]

Filmmakers continued to play with the geometry of architecture in ways that could underscore the virtues of the wider frame. Mitchell Leisen, who

FIGURES 41 AND 42

had re-created Paris on Hollywood soundstages in films such as *Artists and Models Abroad* (1938) and *Arise, My Love* (1940), had the opportunity to actually work in the city on MGM's *Bedevilled* (1955). For the production, Leisen insisted, "an authentic Paris setting free of backlot 'French streets' and Stage 12 Latin Quarters, was mandatory."[56] Promoted as the first motion picture to be shot in Paris in CinemaScope, *Bedevilled* follows a novice priest who moves to Paris to join a seminary only to become involved with a nightclub singer. When the priest tracks down the mysterious singer at the Hôtel des Invalides, Leisen brings into play elements of the building's interior architecture that activate the visual features of CinemaScope. The priest approaches Napoleon's tomb, and the hemispherical opening fills the expanse of the frame. When he descends a staircase, the shot becomes a flourish of symmetry and linear perspective (fig. 43). Leisen demonstrates that not long after the spread of wide-screen, previous conventions of composition could be applied to authentic interiors, with distinctive results.

The above wide-screen examples come from CinemaScope films, but movie companies applied other processes to foreign location shoots. Alfred

FIGURES 43 and 44

Hitchcock validated the virtues of taking VistaVision cameras to foreign locales in *To Catch a Thief* and *The Man Who Knew Too Much* (1956). In the hands of certain film stylists, even more modest formats resulted in striking combinations of locations and wide-screen. Inaugurating the SuperScope process, Robert Aldrich shot *Vera Cruz* (1954) entirely in Mexico. Outdoors, the director uses Mexico's vegetation and colonial architecture to give images depth, often applying a mannered variant of the aforementioned compositional practices. In establishing shots, architectural details serve as visual embellishments. Arches in the foreground frame town plazas. In an inverted approach, slices of buildings appear in the background, adding a volumetric dynamism. Depth shots also turn into visual sport. Giant wooden doors opening onto a monastery dominate the sides of the frame, inviting viewers to appreciate a play of heights, from monk to officer on horseback to bell tower in the distance (fig. 44). Throughout the film, Aldrich pulls compositional elements from nature and architecture to create depth and an ornamental visual system. Some critics, however, did not appreciate the director's brazen style. In his landmark essay on wide-screen, Charles Barr criticized the film as "an absolute orgy of formalism," and panned Aldrich for pushing too much against Hollywood standards by flaunting the features of locations, which should have been at the service of narrative coherence. "If you notice it, it's bad," he wrote.[57] In spite of the critique, *Vera Cruz* indicates a common approach to foreign location shooting: Hollywood filmmakers followed compositional conventions, but there was room for variation, even bold deviations.

As many of these examples confirm, Hollywood filmmakers fairly quickly integrated wide-screen aesthetics into the practice of location shooting, often finding technical solutions that studio-bound filmmaking had previously inhibited. In films that aimed to highlight foreign locales, filmmakers were able to combine wide-screen and locations to produce compelling images that could not be found in rival entertainment forms, namely television. This unique attraction was foregrounded in the promotional discourse of these films, in which studios marketed spectacle and the representation of a geographic reality that was attained through new technologies. Promoting Richard Fleischer's *The Vikings* (1958), movie posters proclaimed, "Actually Filmed Amid the Ice-Capped Fjords of Norway and the Sea-Lashed Cliffs of Brittany! In Horizon Spanning Technirama and Magnificent Technicolor!" This rhetorical ballyhoo, which paired location shooting with wide-screen and color, hyped the ability of international productions to employ new technologies to render spectacular views from abroad.[58] For many filmmakers working globally, though, locations were not just about pure visual spectacle or a way to bring out the attributes of new wide-screen processes; filmmakers also sought to explore the conceptual and storytelling possibilities of foreign locations.

LOCATION AS AN EXPRESSIVE, SYMBOLIC, AND NARRATIVE ELEMENT

Beyond working out how to frame a foreign location or present an action in it, filmmakers needed to determine how it could be integrated into a scene in meaningful ways. For the majority of Hollywood international productions, the presentation of locations followed standard visual patterns. Filmmakers relegated them to the background during important conversations and actions, as the previous examples illustrate. However, some films deployed locations as visual motifs throughout the film, or used locales in expressive ways that not only amplified decorative appeal but added thematic weight to a scene or contributed to the narrative as well. As Fred Zinnemann declared, "The location is an actor, a dramatically active ingredient in itself."[59] A filmmaker's goal became focused on how to mobilize this element of style to reflect emotions, characters, and themes while remaining within the bounds of Hollywood stylistic norms. Location shooting thus moved beyond the decorative function of film style into the domain of expressivity, symbolism, and narrative.

For international productions made in the late 1940s, especially those shot in Germany, filmmakers exploited the sight of ruined cities to bring audiences an image of spectacle imbued with the horror of war. While viewers in the United States would have been familiar with cityscapes full of rubble from newsreels, magazines, and newspapers, portraying these scenes in 35mm as the backdrops to war-themed movies of intrigue and romance heightened the drama of the films. For the photographic-conscious technician, the mere documenting of rubble was insufficient. After all, newsreels had effectively recorded the ravages of war. To shoot a fictional story in front of ruins, filmmakers needed to make them more expressively cinematic.

For writer-director George Seaton, Germany's war-torn landscape offered grim sights that could be assimilated into a film in ways that were vivid and charged. In *The Big Lift*, he made use of the ruins of postwar Berlin as a constant background for an allegory of US-Germany postwar relations and a love story set against the Berlin Airlift.[60] A US sergeant falls for a *Trümmerfrau*, a rubble woman who earns her rations by cleaning up debris. Several of their encounters occur in front of bombed-out buildings, and Seaton allows for expressive flourishes with these backdrops. When the sergeant confronts the woman for lying about her past, her crestfallen look is mirrored in the section of a building that collapses behind her, appearing like an emotional punctuation mark (fig. 45). The moment is an extraordinary feat of production coordination and a daring use of a real locale to visualize what appears to be the character's inner state. But the scene is ultimately an instance of misdirection, as we eventually learn that the rubble woman is trying to manipulate the sergeant into marrying her so that she can go to the United States to reunite with her SS husband. Throughout the movie, Seaton mines the Berlin setting for visual analogues of love and betrayal.

FIGURE 45

Using locations as a reflection of a character's emotions was one possibility, but filmmakers also explored a tactic of contrast, in which the opposition of character and locality could bring to the fore certain intrinsic qualities in each. In *Boy on a Dolphin* (1957), Jean Negulesco went for both approaches. The character of Sophia Loren's sponge diver is developed through a series of associations with locations—nature, the sea, the island of Hydra—to dubiously suggest that she's an artless, earthy peasant. The visual scheme changes course when she travels to Athens to sell the eponymous undersea treasure and arranges to meet an archaeologist at an outdoor café. Now the camera captures a contrast: the fish-out-of-water sponge diver and the modern architecture of the Asteria restaurant and nightclub—a symbol of Athens's postwar modernization and a ready-made subject for the CinemaScope dimensions (fig. 46). Through a combination of location selection, staging, and composition, the shot achieves a meaningful juxtaposition. Like architecture, nature could move beyond expressivity to attain more symbolic qualities. In *The Brave One* (1956), the landscape of Mexico turns symbolic in the story of a young boy and his love for a bull that is being trained to fight in the ring. At times, the locations seem to manifest the boy's fears. When he runs through a field looking for his bull, a cactus forcefully dominates the frame, as if the Mexican terrain were a looming threat to the boy's innocence (fig. 47). Through a symbolic treatment of the locale, the trials and triumphs of this coming-of-age tale find resonance in the rural landscape that the boy must navigate.

FIGURES 46 and 47

Filmmakers could similarly explore the meaning of place by playing with the color and tone of locations for symbolic purposes. For *The Nun's Story* (1959), Fred Zinnemann created a visual juxtaposition between a European and an African setting, against which he told the story of a nun who moves from Belgium to its colony, the Belgian Congo, where she struggles to reconcile her nursing talents with her devotion to the humbling rules of her congregation. The director originally wanted to shoot the scenes of Belgium in black and white and the Congo sequences in color, "so that the austerity of Europe would contrast with the bursting tropical fertility of the African scenes."[61] But Warner Bros. executives opposed this artistic choice, and as a compromise, Zinnemann and cinematographer Franz Planer shot the Belgian scenes in muted colors, embodied in the black-and-white nun habits, and the Congo scenes in richer colors. Of course, the idea that the Congo symbolizes "tropical fertility" and a place that provokes the nun's inner life points to a troubling colonialist imaginary that was common in Hollywood films shot in Africa and their contemporaneous reception, as evidenced by *American Cinematographer*'s production report: "In dazzling contrast to the convent sequences are the scenes shot in the Belgian Congo. The verdant lushness of the foliage itself, the foaming turbulence of jungle rivers, the colorful trappings of the natives—all combine to produce an almost kaleidoscopic effect. In psychological contrast to the earlier sequences one is made strikingly aware that here is life—primitive, violent, surging with color."[62] The filmmakers succeed in transforming the locations into arresting visuals, but the film and the aesthetic discourse surrounding it exemplify how real people and places can be relegated to racist symbols and elements of decor.[63]

Faced with working in new environments, Hollywood filmmakers opted to exploit locations for decorative functions, but also leveraged them for expressive and symbolic purposes in a manner once reserved for other elements of mise-en-scène, such as costume and decor. Through these approaches, locations became a vital element of a film's visual design. A number of the abovementioned examples also reveal how authentic locales could contribute to developing the narrative in ways both subtle and overt. Filmmakers could incorporate locations into a film's narrative structure in an integrated manner while still conforming to the conventions of Hollywood aesthetics.

Like many elements of style in Hollywood cinema, formal principles suggested that locations should be at the service of storytelling. Despite the prominence of locations in films shot abroad, they rarely are pure spectacle or mere episodic travelogues, as is the case in the nonfiction Cinerama films. Motivated by story and character action, the presentation of location is narrativized. Even during the unfolding of a scene, the location takes on a secondary status during key pieces of dialogue and action, falling in line with the narrational characteristics of Hollywood classicism. Typically, the beginnings and endings of classical Hollywood films tend to be the most stylized passages, in which a technique such as a camera move or a music cue draws attention to itself. In overseas productions, a film might commence with a montage of location shots. At a more local narrative level, the openings and endings of scenes become occasions of overt narration.[64] During these moments, wide shots of locations that accent pictorialism might appear before moving to tighter shots of conversations captured in a studio, where dialogue and performance are stressed. In this fashion, these films give prominence to locations during episodes when classical conventions had always permitted a greater degree of showiness.

Film beginnings provided Hollywood filmmakers with the maximum opportunity to flaunt locations. These segments are typically frontloaded with foreign environments to clearly establish the setting for the audience. A setting's connection to authentic locales can be reinforced with a credit title that announces where the film was shot. Mirroring the movie's advertising campaign, the credits for *The Man on the Eiffel Tower* (1950) give "the City of Paris" fifth billing, after the film's four lead actors, over a shot of the Eiffel Tower in the far background. In some cases, an opening credit gives thanks to local authorities who supported location shooting. *Kim* (1951) carries the acknowledgment, "To the Government of India and His Highness the Maharajah of Jaipur, and His Highness, the Maharajah of Bundi, we express our deep appreciation for the facilities afforded us in filming this picture in India." Credit sequences can also salute the participation of foreign talent. Over an East African landscape, a title card at the beginning of *Mogambo* credits the Samburu, Wagenia, Bahaya and M'Beti peoples. These movies recognize the authorities and communities that the filmmakers worked with while simultaneously underscoring the film's authenticity for the audience.

When films set in foreign lands start with montage sequences of locations, these views provide visual evidence of the link between story and authentic setting. Designer David Bass describes these passages as the proof of "really being there" traditionally provided by postcards and tourist snapshots.[65] This sense of "being there" permeates Fox's *Three Coins in the Fountain*, which commences with a four-minute prologue featuring the film's titular theme song played over shots of Rome's many fountains. The travelogue effect not only spotlights the CinemaScope format, but roots the film in authenticity as well. After that success, Fox attempted the same visual and production strategies on *Boy on a Dolphin*, gathering some of the same crew, including director Jean Negulesco and cinematographer Milton Krasner. Once again, the film kicks off with a travelogue montage, this time featuring a lineup of Greek islands. In both movies, foregrounding these location shots enforces various narrative and perceptual goals. The locations inaugurate the setting, emphasize the fact that the film was shot in a real locale, and prime the audience to take notice of authentic foreign sights throughout the film.

Once a movie's plot begins, filmmakers faced the narrative challenge of how to motivate showing locations. Some of the examples of dialogue scenes above illustrate how locales could be accentuated and then tamed through

FIGURE 48

conventions of shot patterns, moving from long shots to closer shots. Discrete arcs of action might provoke a more conspicuous presentation of locations, which could be driven by genre. In musicals, filmmakers could embed these spaces into sequences such as song-and-dance numbers, which had traditionally allowed for moments of flashy style in Hollywood cinema. In *Funny Face* (1957), director Stanley Donen shows off iconic Parisian localities during the musical performance of "Bonjour Paris" and then an on-location fashion shoot. The urban chase could also be an opportunity to narrativize an eye-catching exhibition of place. A feature of silent film comedies and postwar domestic location work, chases allowed filmmakers to apply familiar compositional practices.[66] In *The Man on the Eiffel Tower*, the geography of Paris is cut up into angular perspectives as two cops pursue a petty thief. As he runs through various landmarks, each shot becomes an occasion to showcase the symmetry and linear perspectives formed by the city's grand avenues and urban landscape. Some shots convey a stunning show of depth. When the thief ducks into the columned forecourt of the Palais-Royal, the architecture forms an impressive central vanishing point (fig. 48). By activating locations through the chase, the spectacle of place is naturalized and brought in line with the conventions of Hollywood narrative. Like other studio filmmakers working overseas, actor-director Burgess Meredith exploits the play of perspectives built into architecture and city planning to produce forceful compositions that enhance the action.

Chases and musical numbers show how locations can be incorporated into a narrative in contained ways within sequences, but filmmakers could explore locations at a broader level, too. Many international productions motivated locations by following prototypical story structures in which real locales materialize as characters pursue their goals. These stories could be a globe-trotting trip (*Around the World in 80 Days*), a land journey (*Berlin Express, Escapade in Japan* [1957], *The Sundowners* [1960], *The Big Gamble* [1961]), a sea voyage (*The Crimson Pirate, Mutiny on the Bounty* [1962]), an African expedition (*King Solomon's Mines* [1950], *The African Queen* [1952], *Mogambo, Killers of Kilimanjaro* [1960]), a treasure hunt (*Plunder of the Sun* [1953], *Valley of the Kings* [1954]), or a military mission (*Decision before Dawn, Bitter Victory* [1958], *The Longest Day* [1962]). These story lines of movement drive the visualization of authentic foreign locations and make the advance through environments an integral part of a film's unfolding drama. In stories set in cities, the urban tour becomes the justification for views of built spaces.

A final consideration of *Roman Holiday* expresses how location shooting can highlight a distinct sense of place while being central to the film's tour plot. Despite some consultation with Italian filmmakers and extensive location work, William Wyler's emphasis on the landscape of Rome does not result in Neorealist narrative forms, in which causality is loosened and narrative development becomes episodic.[67] Instead, the depiction of the Eternal City conforms to the conventions of Hollywood storytelling: the pursuit of sharply defined goals (Princess Anne's desire to explore the city) inspires the progression through the urban environment. The movement through Rome is further encouraged by reporter Joe Bradley's attempt to steal candid photos of her in the most un-royal of circumstances in real places. Rome's landmarks (the Trevi Fountain, the Spanish Steps, a café by the Pantheon, the Colosseum, the grand avenues, the Mouth of Truth, the barges along the Tiber River) become sites where the princess can delight in her newfound freedom and the electrifying vibrancy of a big city. Through a synthesis of story and style, Wyler maps the narrative of *Roman Holiday* onto its locations. In the end, the director captures Roman scenery to realize various functions, turning the city into a lively playing space while still maintaining the coherence of Hollywood storytelling.

As the preceding examples indicate, early in the postwar era filmmakers were already finding ways to incorporate locales into stories so that they conformed to the conventions of Hollywood aesthetics. At the same time, these filmmakers made the location expressive or decoratively interesting. On a broader level, locations—whether serving as symbolic spaces or as signposts for narrative development—became components of the drama rather than serving as mere backdrops. By motivating an overt display of location through certain standard story structures, filmmakers were able to assimilate the spectacle of place into the narrative.

POSTWAR HOLLYWOOD FILM STYLE

Just as postwar Hollywood underwent a transitional phase in its business practices and organization, film style during this period was also in flux, characterized by its eclecticism.[68] Motion pictures in Technicolor and then Eastman Color were made alongside black-and-white films. Across the 1950s, aspect ratios expanded and contracted, moving from the classic, squarer Academy ratio to Cinerama, CinemaScope, VistaVision, and an array of other wide-screen systems. Films featured studio work and location footage, shot in the United States and abroad. Hollywood's international productions contributed in crucial ways to the diversity of postwar film style.

While foreign location shooting was shaped by Hollywood stylistic conventions, the mixing of Hollywood and foreign creative personnel points to transcultural dimensions at the production level. However, as I have explained, these films on the whole were Hollywood products because of a more international mode of production that allowed motion-picture companies to preserve established studio practices while adapting to the conditions of overseas locations. Moreover, in order to naturalize the presentation of foreign location shooting, these companies generated stories about expeditions, city tours, and other travel themes, which prompted the display of place. Within these story parameters, Hollywood filmmakers looked to enduring compositional principles to guide them as they increasingly moved off the studio lot in the postwar era.

The development of location filming during this period, though, is neither a story of rigid stylistic continuity nor one of radical departure. Ultimately, it demonstrates measured change. Foreign location shooting contributed to gradual shifts in Hollywood aesthetics by promoting a set of practices that drew on existing stylistic conventions while gesturing to the naturalistic film trends that would strengthen in the 1960s and 1970s. Like the move toward a more adaptable and transcultural means of making films explored in the earlier chapters, moviemakers' ability to navigate stylistic continuity and change contributed to building a more global production operation. To get a closer look at how filmmakers negotiated the style, technology, and logistics of location shooting, a case study of *Lust for Life* (1956) follows.

Mental Spaces and Cinematic Places

LUST FOR LIFE (1956)

"Our work in the studio, though it included many of our biggest dramatic scenes, was less exciting than on the locations, where we had the constantly thrilling sense of feeling the same burning sun, treading the same dry earth and reacting to the same violent colors that had helped drive Vincent into madness three-quarters of a century earlier."

JOHN HOUSEMAN[1]

BY THE MID-1950S, AS INTERNATIONAL PRODUCTIONS were more and more frequent, filmmakers were thinking through how to incorporate locations in ever more novel ways. When the opportunity arose in 1955 to make an adaptation of Irving Stone's 1934 Vincent van Gogh biography *Lust for Life*, producer John Houseman and director Vincente Minnelli contemplated making foreign locales integral to the film's visual design and narrative trajectory. The story, after all, was about an artist who dedicated his life to painting the world he perceived in new, expressionistic styles. So, they drafted a letter to MGM production executive J. J. Cohn in anticipation of the second-unit crew's trip to Arles, France, to shoot footage for the film's springtime sequences. The letter laid out a summary of the movie's visual concept, which was meant to guide the work in Arles, and articulated how the film's locations extended beyond serving as mere setting or conveying pictorial beauty to in fact "bear an important and even vital psychological relationship to the story."[2] Far more than just decorative, the locations would be a reflection of the painter's inner life and an essential component of the film's narrative. As a sign of how foundational locations were to the project, the letter was written before writer Norman Corwin started work on the script. No doubt, Houseman and Minnelli's visual ideas would shape much of the project's development.

MGM had been thinking of making this movie for a decade. In 1945 the studio bought the rights to Stone's biography of the Dutch painter with the provision that the film would be made within ten years. Considerable time passed, but eventually the project drew the interest of Minnelli and Houseman, who convinced MGM executive Dore Schary to approve the production in late February 1955, with only nine months left before the rights would revert back to Stone.[3] Despite this impending deadline, the filmmakers committed to shooting the exteriors in authentic locations in Europe, a goal that was complicated by the fact that Minnelli was obligated to work on *Kismet* (1955) until the middle of July. In the meantime, Houseman, associate producer Jud Kinberg, and various MGM personnel began organizing the international production, with location work set for Europe followed by interiors at MGM's Culver City studio. In addition, original van Gogh paintings had to be found around the world to be filmed for incorporation into the movie.[4]

Initially released in art houses, the film epitomized postwar middlebrow tastes with its portrayal of the life of a popular artist. It was not unlike John Huston's Toulouse-Lautrec biopic, *Moulin Rouge* (1953), whose success MGM hoped to reproduce. While *Lust for Life* generated its share of detractors (film critic Manny Farber called it, and its kind, "heroic garbage"), the movie's approach to authentic locations made it more than just a run-of-the-mill biopic.[5] Shot in the mid-1950s, after Hollywood had established a foothold in the Western European production landscape, the motion picture provides insight into how Minnelli and Houseman conceived of foreign locales as decorative and expressive elements. *Lust for Life* also shows how these filmmakers meaningfully integrated locations into the movie's narrative in a manner that conformed to the conventions of Hollywood storytelling.

SURVEYING AND SHOOTING LOCATIONS

After Houseman and Minnelli devised the visual concept for the locations and while the script was still being developed, a small survey team traveled through Europe to begin preproduction arrangements. The goal was to scout locations and shoot second-unit footage for the springtime scenes. The group included unit production manager William Kaplan, cinematographer Joseph Ruttenberg, and MGM art director Edward Carfagno. For portions of the location trek, script supervisor Sylvette Baudrot, along with a small assistant camera crew, accompanied the team to keep track of camera reports for the second-unit filming and to help match locations with van Gogh's paintings.[6] To guide the cinematographic work and the choice of locales, the unit used the visual ideas in the memo compiled by Houseman and Minnelli, as well as diagrams created by the director. Then the producer followed up with a letter that offered additional guidelines for filming in Brussels, the Borinage, Nuenen, Paris, Arles, and Auvers-sur-Oise.[7] In particular, Houseman highlighted the importance of capturing the original wheat fields of Auvers, where van Gogh painted his last pieces and shot himself. However, many of the original sites where the artist lived and worked either had been transformed or no longer existed, pointing to the difficulty of trying to re-create the past in authentic present-day locations.[8]

The survey team gathered footage to be incorporated into the final picture, such as the blooming cherry blossoms in Arles. Technicians on the trip also experimented with various methods for photographing locations. Baudrot remembered that Ruttenberg tested varying film stocks to see which could best replicate van Gogh's paintings.[9] The footage was then flown to MGM Studios in Culver City, where Houseman, Minnelli, and executives viewed the dailies. The location reconnaissance trip yielded reports, photos, and sketches that would aid the first unit once they arrived in Europe. The scouting group researched the flowering and harvesting of various crops in France in order to understand how the landscape would look after principal photography began.

In early July, as Minnelli finished *Kismet*, Houseman flew to London and then to Paris to help prepare the production in anticipation of filming during the ripening of the wheat fields in Auvers-sur-Oise. A crew of mostly British and French personnel was assembled, headed by production manager Julien Derode and transportation captain Christian Ferry. British cinematographer Freddie Young was responsible for the exterior shooting in Europe, while Hollywood cinematographer Russell Harlan was in charge of matching the interior work in Culver City. Throughout the preproduction stage, MGM looked to its offices in Paris, Amsterdam, and Brussels to assist in organizing the film. Even though this was a continental project, Paris became a center to coordinate the location work, and the city's Studio Francoeur supplied production offices for Minnelli and the managerial staff.[10] Once production commenced later in the summer, the shooting start date was inaugurated with an advertisement in the pages of *Daily Variety* that highlighted the film's authenticity of place. The ad simply reported, "The production of 'Lust for Life' started Monday in the actual scenes of Van Gogh's Life . . . France, Belgium and Holland."[11] The announcement reveals how by the 1950s, production conditions were increasingly becoming selling points and a way to add value to films. The commencement of shooting itself became one of many events in the production process that could be promoted for a movie's advertising campaigns.

From the start, the cast and crew worked in reverse chronological story order, traveling through Europe in a caravan of production vehicles. They began in Auvers, where van Gogh committed suicide, then moved to Arles, where the painter had his most fertile period. Next came Paris, where he was exposed to the work of the Impressionists, then to the village of Nuenen in the Netherlands, where he returned to his childhood home to focus on his painting. The location unit finished in the coal-mining region of the Borinage in Belgium, where van Gogh worked as a preacher.[12] As the unit moved from one spot to another, the director and his collaborators improvised with shooting locations, incorporating evocative sights as they discovered them or taking inspiration from the extant correspondence between Vincent and his brother, Theo van Gogh. In his memoir, Houseman recollected, "Occasionally Minnelli would be so entranced by some place he saw during the day that [associate producer] Jud [Kinberg] and I would sit up all night digging something out of the letters or writing a new scene that could be shot in the location we had just discovered."[13] According to Minnelli, as the crew searched for locations, the unit compared van Gogh's original paintings with the film sites. They positioned Kirk Douglas, who portrayed the artist, within the landscape from the appropriate vantage point that would then be shot.[14] This time-consuming approach was done in the face of resistance from the MGM production department, which attempted to limit any extra time and expense that accrued during the location work, resulting, according to Houseman, in "screams of anguish that emanated daily from Culver City."[15] In spite of MGM's attempts to manage the shooting progress, the location unit took the time to attentively capture the various landscapes in meaningful ways and to cinematically re-create many of the artist's iconic paintings.[16]

PAINTING WITH CAMERAS

By the mid-1950s, filmmakers had a varied toolbox to use on locations, but creative decisions and market pressures competed to elevate certain technologies over others. For *Lust for Life*, the crew opted to use Ansco Color to render the authentic locations and mimic van Gogh's vibrant color palette for the reproduction of the artist's paintings. Ansco was a high-speed, fine-grained stock that became the basis for MGM's Metrocolor process.[17] Houseman and

Minnelli learned that Eastman Kodak, which by the mid-1950s dominated the supply of color film in Hollywood, had "so attenuated and prettified its colors" that the colors that characterized so many of van Gogh's paintings could not be achieved.[18] Ansco, on the other hand, could emulate the colors that the filmmakers desired. However, because of Kodak's monopoly on film stock, Ansco had stopped producing 35mm film. The filmmakers, though, were able to track down enough remaining Ansco film to shoot the picture and convince the company to establish a lab in Houston, Texas, to process the movie. To view dailies, the location team had to wait for the exposed footage to go from the south of France to Paris and then to Houston, where it was developed. The rushes were subsequently sent to Los Angeles, where MGM executives viewed the footage to monitor the look and progress of the production. Finally, the dailies were flown back to the south of France.[19] While this process was more roundabout than most foreign location shoots, the studio's tracking of the footage followed a pattern established by many other international productions.

Less in line with the filmmakers' vision was the picture's wide-screen format. Initially, Houseman and Minnelli resisted the idea of shooting in CinemaScope, preferring to work in the traditional Academy aspect ratio. "If ever a picture shouldn't have been filmed in Cinemascope [sic]," argued Minnelli, "it was *Lust for Life*, since the dimensions of the wider screen bear little relation to the conventional shape of paintings."[20] Houseman felt similarly, recalling, "By 1955 this ridiculous process, adopted and publicized by Fox in its desperation, had swept the industry. Over the protest of every respectable filmmaker, the vermiform screen had triumphed: every large movie-house in the Western world was installing the hateful lenses; every major studio had given the order that all high-budget pictures must henceforth be shot in the new ratio."[21] Houseman and Minnelli resisted the prevailing notion that wide-screen and locations worked well together, but MGM president Arthur Loew overruled them, and the picture was shot in CinemaScope. While Minnelli used the wider canvas to create compositions that force the viewer's eyes to scan the frame, the shots tend to be static, with van Gogh seated or standing in the central zone of the frame against a beautiful landscape as he paints. Intensifying the depth of the images seemed to be more important than filling the shots' length. As with other filmmakers working in the format, Minnelli utilized recessional lines, the layering of planes, and natural light to amplify depth.

Another goal of filming in authentic foreign locations for Minnelli and his collaborators was staging scenes in locales that could bring to life the

FIGURE 49

iconic sites of van Gogh's work. By placing Kirk Douglas within some of the
original settings of the paintings, Minnelli could attain a sense of authenticity and create visual parallels between the paintings and the film's mise-en-
scène. "My plan," explained the director, "was to re-create the subject matter
of Van Gogh's paintings, not as frozen tableaux, but within an everyday context."[22] The paintings, therefore, became a reference point for re-creating the
landscape, the figures, and the colors of the original work, from the mill in
Water Mill at Kollen near Nuenen (1884) to the woman in *Fisherman's Wife
on the Beach* (1882). In recording Douglas painting the drawbridge of *Langlois
Bridge at Arles* (1888), Minnelli managed to achieve recessional depth with
the slanted bridge and the pair of trees in the distance (fig. 49). Even though
the bridge from the painting no longer existed, the setting conjures a sense of
fidelity.[23] The connections between the locations and the sceneries of van
Gogh's paintings were also played up in the marketing of the film. MGM
assembled a behind-the-scenes featurette on the location work, which was
exhibited in schools and universities.[24] The short, entitled *Van Gogh:
Darkness into Light* (1956), shows Minnelli and his crew either filming in the
genuine settings of the paintings or using ingenuity to alter them to look like
the real thing. Whether by means of selection and composition or via reconstruction, these location shots are in the end fabrications, a studio-set aesthetic applied to the real world. As visual theorist Griselda Pollock suggests
of the film, van Gogh's "paintings are carefully and faithfully reconstructed
as *sets*, so that Van Gogh becomes virtually a figure in his own paintings."[25]

In sum, Houseman and Minnelli attempted to find a cinematic analogue
of van Gogh's artwork through a synthesis of character, painting, and location. In conceiving of these location shots, the filmmakers were searching for

FIGURE 50

imagery that they envisioned would equal the vitality that van Gogh brought to his work. For the springtime sequence in Arles, Houseman explained, "The mood we seek to capture is not lyrical but exultant, climatic, with the strength, the boldness and the urgency with which Van Gogh impaled them on his canvas." The producer concluded by advocating an approach that conflated van Gogh's painting with how the film would stylistically portray the artist: "We are dealing with the story of one of the greatest creative artists—a human volcano of boldness and imagination—and the camera need not be shy about the scope of its pallette [*sic*] or the vigor of its brush strokes."[26] Using a film's story as a metaphor for its making was a long-standing convention of how filmmakers talked about their work and how movies were promoted. A fusion of form and content was also reflected in the ways that the locations could be folded into the movie's narrative.

THE PSYCHOLOGY AND MOTIVATION OF LOCATIONS

As Houseman and Minnelli expressed in their original conception of the film, the aesthetic objective of the overseas work was to move beyond thinking of locations as mere ornamental elements, and treat them as central to the development of story and character—as methods to fulfill expressive and narrative functions. The journey structure helps motivate foregrounding the locations. When van Gogh moves to a new town—the Borinage, Nuenen, Arles, Auvers-sur-Oise—it becomes an inspiration for his paintings. The wanderings around Europe follow a development in the film's atmosphere and color, reflecting the changes in the painter's life. Houseman articulated this evolution: "*Lust for*

FIGURE 51

FIGURE 51

Life will be essentially the story of a painter who progressed from darkness to light—from the literal darkness of black, grim coal mines to the dazzling sunlight of Provence; from the murky, labyrinthine gloom of his own uncertainty and lack of confidence, to the ultimate triumph of his powers and talent."[27] Minnelli and his crew took the idea of visual progression and inscribed it into the movie's succession of landscapes and colors.

Throughout this journey, locations become expressions of van Gogh's mental states. An aspiring preacher, he is placed by an evangelical committee in the mining town of the Borinage, a ruthless environment characterized by the stark landscapes and drab colors of industrial spaces and slag heaps (fig. 50). The soot-covered atmosphere becomes a manifestation of the painter's inner turmoil as he pursues the life of a preacher instead of his artwork. While the job is meaningful, it is creatively empty. Convinced by his brother, Theo, to move back home to Nuenen, van Gogh throws himself into painting by reproducing the pastoral scenery of his hometown, full of deep greens and browns. These artistic pursuits develop as he continues to hone his craft, eventually focusing on new subject matter, such as workers toiling on the land. After a brief stay in Paris with Theo, van Gogh moves to Arles in the south of France, whose beauty and vibrant colors seem to erupt when the painter opens his windows to the blossoming of trees. "It will be in Arles, for the first time," explained Houseman, "that we burst into the luxuriant light and brilliant color that characterized the greatest period of his work."[28]

The Arles section of the film represents van Gogh's most prolific period, when the environment's heady mixture of colors, landscapes, and people inspires his work. The artist thrives in the open spaces, where he tries out new forms and colors, such as mounds of golden yellow haystacks (fig. 51). Here, the progression of the film's visuals and the painter's mental states reaches its apotheosis, having transitioned from slag heaps to wheat fields, from darkness to light. For the filmmakers, the Arles segments serve as more than a travelogue of southern French vistas—or, as Houseman put it, "It is not a Cinerama tour of pretty fields." Instead, these scenes become a reflection of the painter's subjectivity and a "dramatic event" for van Gogh. The producer elaborated, "The spring material will be integrated into the final film not from the viewpoint of some neutral observer, but as the *experience* of our central figure—to whom landscapes and seasons and all manifestations of Nature meant vastly more than a series of pretty picture post-cards: they were his blood and guts. He lived and died for what he saw in the moods of nature and in its many colors and textures and forms."[29] The filmmakers meld geography and mental space, making the landscape a reflection of the artist's inner drama. This relationship continues into the last section of the film. After a mental breakdown and a fight with his friend, the painter Paul Gauguin, van Gogh enters a sanatorium in Auvers-sur-Oise, where the golden hues of the wheat fields spark his late work and fuel a return to madness.

The link between geographic place and mental space exists largely at the level of expressionism and symbolism, but the development of this link is also structural, giving the film its rough form. Locations play another narrative role, in which the filmmakers motivate the display of localities through van Gogh's artistic preoccupations and his character's psychology. The painter is drawn to landscapes and laborers who work the land, subject matter that connects him to outdoor surroundings. This concern also has a psychological component. One of his worst fears is being confined indoors, where, without direct contact with the environment of his paintings' settings, he cannot work. In effect, his need for the artistic inspiration that comes from the outdoors encourages his presence in real-world locations, thereby driving the prominent presentation of scenery. As the film portrays, van Gogh's great tragedy is the vicious cycle in which his work is driven by his madness and in turn intensifies his madness. This dilemma crystallizes at the climax of the film, as he paints what some critics believe to be one of his last works, *Wheatfield with Crows* (1890), which illustrates the birds that fly around the landscape of Auvers-sur-Oise (fig. 52). The atmosphere, as if come to life, seems to accost van Gogh—a materialization of how his feverish painting sessions feed his mania. The landscape plays a part in that vicious cycle, at once inspiring and overwhelming him. Unable to cope with his mental anguish, he walks to a nearby tree, scrawls a suicide note, pulls out a pistol,

FIGURE 52

and fires. Throughout the movie, the filmmakers blend location and character to create a portrait of an artist stimulated by the world around him but too psychically fragile to exist in it.

The location shooting for *Lust for Life* proved that working in authentic locales could galvanize the creative process. As the epigraph to this case study reveals, Houseman felt that the crew thrived on making a movie in the same environs where van Gogh once lived and painted. For Minnelli, the production was "the most thrilling and stimulating creative period" of his life.[30] As an example of location filming, this case study sheds light on the logistics that went into shooting a story in some of its authentic settings, but it also indicates how locations can fulfill various functions. In *Lust for Life*, the filmmakers re-created van Gogh's paintings through the decorative appeal of real spaces. They also found a way to narrativize the locations and make them expressive by treating landscapes as reflections of the artist's creative evolution and his fluctuating psychological state. Minnelli and Houseman managed to do all this by falling back on production strategies and aesthetic conventions that had long sustained them.

Epilogue

SUNKEN MOVIE RELICS

AT THE BOTTOM OF THE OCEAN, ABOUT NINETY MILES southeast of Cape Hatteras, North Carolina, sits the ship built for the 1962 MGM film *Mutiny on the Bounty*. The vessel was a replica of the original eighteenth-century, three-masted tall ship HMS *Bounty*, which had sailed under the command of William Bligh from England to Tahiti before being burned by mutineers. After serving as a floating movie studio and set for *Mutiny on the Bounty*, the fully operational ship went on to have an active life. It functioned as a tourist attraction and an education center, and it appeared in TV shows like *Flipper* (1964–67), movies such as *Pirates of the Caribbean: Dead Man's Chest* (2006), and even an adult film called *Pirates* (2005). Sadly, its undersea situation was the result of a modern-day tragedy. In late October 2012, as Hurricane Sandy was barreling toward the Eastern Seaboard, the *Bounty* was sailing from Connecticut to Florida to make an appearance at a fundraiser. Against others' better judgment, the captain believed that the vessel would fare better out on the ocean than docked. The crew charted an easterly course to evade the superstorm, but soon found themselves drawn southwest into the storm system in a tempestuous zone known as the Graveyard of the Atlantic. Sixty-mile-per-hour winds and thirty-foot waves battered the *Bounty*. Once the ship's water removal system malfunctioned and the engine shut down, the crew sent out a Mayday call. Fourteen crew members were rescued by the Coast Guard, but the ship's captain and one crew member tragically died.[1] The toll of Hurricane Sandy on the *Bounty*, not to mention countless communities from the Caribbean up through the Eastern Seaboard, was devastating.

Far less grave, the sinking of the ship brought an end to the fabled history of a movie prop that, in many ways, embodied the extravagance of postwar

Hollywood's international ventures. Whereas this book opened with a call to excavate the histories of Hollywood's runaway productions, I bring it to a close with a historical dredging and a nod to today. A brief consideration of *Mutiny on the Bounty* dredges up a piece of Hollywood history. It also uncovers the pitfalls of international productions: faraway locations could present unexpected bad weather, and exacerbate the outcomes of poor management and unchecked egos, despite the dazzling beauty that they might bring to a film. Based on the 1932 novel, which was in turn based on real-life events, the film *Mutiny on the Bounty* recounts the journey of the HMS *Bounty*, under the stewardship of Captain William Bligh in the 1780s, from England to the South Pacific in search of coveted breadfruit to export to the Caribbean to feed slaves. After stopping off at the island of Tahiti for several months, the crew, led by Fletcher Christian, stages a mutiny in response to Bligh's authoritarian rule.

The motion picture reflected a studio strategy of remaking old properties. For instance the success of *Ben-Hur*, the 1959 remake of the 1925 original, inspired MGM to greenlight films such as *Cimarron* (1931 and 1960) and *The Four Horsemen of the Apocalypse* (1921 and 1962). *Mutiny on the Bounty* was a remake of the studio's 1935 version, which had been filmed in French Polynesia, Catalina Island in Southern California, and the Culver City lot. The 1962 version was made in the mold of *Ben-Hur*: a big-budget overseas production, shot in the MGM Camera 65 wide-screen format by cinematographer Robert Surtees, who had won acclaim and an Oscar for his work. The movie would again be filmed by Surtees in the same format with a few technical improvements, now credited as Ultra Panavision 70, on the islands of Tahiti, Bora Bora, and Mo'orea. As with many overseas productions before it, location shooting involved an international cast and crew with local labor hired from Tahiti and personnel brought over from Hollywood, London, and Paris.

MGM initially tried to follow the established pattern of accomplishing location work first and then moving into the studio to tackle interiors, closer shots, and scenes that couldn't be executed abroad. However, the realities of working on a remote location complicated this plan. Shooting commenced in late November of 1960 under the direction of British filmmaker Carol Reed. He had made some Hollywood-backed European movies, but *Mutiny on the Bounty* would be his first large-scale studio production. Despite weather outlooks and reports from the location survey team about the impending rainy season, which even Captain Bligh had described in his logbooks, MGM approved the location unit to commence work. The situation was made worse by a delay in the construction of the *Bounty* replica, which pushed the South Pacific shoot even further into the winter months. Tahiti had no soundstages for "cover" sets to offset the rainy periods, which meant that days would go by with little to no filming. After a couple of months of unsuccessful shooting, the endless rain eventually forced the studio to postpone the production. Cast and crew retreated to Hollywood to wait out the wet weather, and Carol Reed left the picture. While some reports claimed that MGM fired him, other news items suggested that he quit.[2] Whatever the case, the accumulation of delays, lack of filming progress, and tensions with star Marlon Brando made the situation unworkable. In late winter of 1961, production resumed at Culver City, now under the guidance of Lewis Milestone, a veteran Hollywood director, who was tasked with getting the shoot back on track. In March, the location unit returned to Tahiti. The production pressed on through the summer in the face of more bad weather, the deaths of a couple of cast and crew members, and time-wasting tactics from Brando. By the end of the summer, the location unit and some of the cast returned to MGM for studio work. Finally, after almost eleven months since filming commenced, the production wrapped in the fall of 1961.

With a negative cost of around $20 million, *Mutiny on the Bounty* was one of the most expensive films made up to that time. In the end, it earned only $9.8 million in North America, significantly under its total budget.[3] The deficit contributed to MGM's overall financial losses in the early 1960s.[4] The impact on the islands that hosted the location work was also unfavorable. According to the film's promotional materials, the production added more than $2 million to the economy of Tahiti and hired around seven thousand residents on an island of some thirty thousand inhabitants.[5] However, some reports faulted MGM for hiring locals at day rates rather than weekly or monthly rates, which left many with a lack of stable work.[6] Despite attempts by the local government to regulate prices and salaries, community leaders and the local press complained that MGM was inflating the prices of transportation and gas. On top of that, the cast and crew monopolized precious accommodations and drove up the prices of hotels and rentals. To many locals, the MGM production felt like an invasion.[7] Eventually, signs reading "MGM go home" popped up around the island.[8]

Blame for the film's problems was cast on all sides. MGM president Joseph Vogel attributed the misfortunes to the holdup in building the *Bounty*, bad weather, and difficulties with the film's directors.[9] Lewis Milestone, for his part, held studio management responsible for continuing with production despite an unfinished script.[10] The director, like many others, also pointed the finger at Marlon Brando.[11] As the shooting dragged on, the popular and trade press began to report on the film's spiraling costs, many attributing the budget overruns to Brando's antics and unprofessionalism.[12] Defending himself, the actor assigned fault to the studio's underestimation of the location costs and the fact that the production commenced with an incomplete screenplay.[13] Ironically, the substantial financing of the film was contingent on the casting of Brando, who was at the time one of the most bankable stars in Hollywood, but it was his participation that drove costs up.[14] Because the production went on for so long, Brando's $5,000-a-day overtime fee kicked in, swelling his extra pay to $750,000 above his $500,000 baseline salary.[15] The press and the history books would deem the movie a fabulous flop.

While much of film history focuses on successful motion pictures and business practices, examining the flops can also tell us a lot about how the industry functioned. The financial failure of *Mutiny on the Bounty* and the endless challenges of its making expose the perils of international production. For the film industry, the production represented a cautionary tale of foreign location shooting's out-of-control expenses. It also signaled the extravagance that would persist in the 1960s, as Hollywood was making fewer but bigger-budget productions such as *Cleopatra* (1963), *The Greatest Story Ever Told* (1965), and *The Sound of Music* (1965).[16] A mix of box-office bombs and impressive hits, these films garnered high profiles, but they carried heavy financial risks. Ultimately, *Mutiny on the Bounty* helped usher in a phase of contradictory impulses in the history of runaway production. For financial reasons, Hollywood in the 1960s began to support more domestic productions while investing in more foreign films from the United Kingdom, Italy, and France. At the same time, it continued with the production bloat— embodied by *Mutiny on the Bounty*—that would contribute to the woes that led to a slump in the US film industry by the end of the decade.

As this book has made evident, *Mutiny on the Bounty* exemplified several consequential postwar shifts in filmmaking. The means of financing diversified, the personnel became more international, and the locations spanned the world. Remarkably, though, these productions were very much in line with US film industrial practices in terms of organization and execution. By both adapting to the conditions of foreign locations and employing Hollywood craft practices and stylistic regimes, producers delivered products that were, for the most part, consistent with what was being made domestically.

From a global perspective, these productions brought significant modifications to the foreign regions where they were made. While much more research remains to be done about the experience of overseas workers and industries involved in Hollywood production and the long-term effects of Hollywood's presence in foreign countries, let me gesture toward some prominent changes. One of the outcomes of Hollywood's production work in Western Europe was the rebuilding of filmmaking infrastructures that had been damaged during the war. By investing in studios and employing European crews, Hollywood companies arguably contributed to laying the foundation for French, Italian, and British film industries to grow in the 1950s and 1960s. But this investment was primarily done to expand Hollywood's global production network, a move that met with both resistance and endorsements from foreign labor groups.

Ironically, by helping to build up these industries abroad, Hollywood strengthened its own competition. For many in Hollywood, however, putting money into foreign industries after the war was necessary to reach short-term goals. Twentieth Century-Fox president Spyros Skouras made the case that US investment in international productions would help restore film industries abroad, which would have the upshot of easing remittance restrictions overseas for Hollywood companies.[17] Moreover, the renovation of filmmaking infrastructures in Western Europe, funded in part by studios' frozen earnings, helped support foreign studios and technicians, which US film companies could then use. At the same time, Hollywood capitalized on many financial inducements that were intended for other industries while also raising production costs. While the far-ranging power of Hollywood is not in dispute in this study, my examination has sought to show how the hegemony of Hollywood production worked abroad. It did not simply command foreign film industries; it was an adaptive process that conformed to local circumstances and needs so that Hollywood companies could satisfy their self-serving objectives.

Despite the conflicts that did arise, these collaborations persisted throughout the 1950s and into the 1960s, foretelling some of the practices of contemporary international production work. Today's global Hollywood is characterized by synergistic multinational conglomerates whose film financing, production, and distribution activities are vigorous and diversified. Within this context, runaway production has taken root in new areas of industrial agglomeration: cities and regions in Canada, Australia, New Zealand, Central and Eastern Europe, and China.[18] Additionally, the proliferation of film commissions and location trade shows throughout the world, along with new tax incentives and coproduction deals, have facilitated Hollywood's overseas media-making enterprises. This continued decentralization of film activities may be a sign of the deficiency of a term like "runaway production" when it becomes difficult to identify a center to run away from.[19]

These more recent location sites, however, have a far more mutable status than their postwar predecessors. In the past, foreign locations often played themselves, a fact that was key to the films' style and selling point. Today, a foreign location might play itself, but more often it serves as a substitute for another setting, either real or make-believe. Ben Goldsmith and Tom O'Regan make the case that in the contemporary global film industry, "the built and natural environments of a place are valued as much for what they can stand in for, what they can be bent/reshaped to represent, as they are valued for themselves."[20] Now the old debates about justifying runaway production by appealing to authentic location arguments are isolated. The economic factors for running away from Hollywood are a given. Locations in the United States and abroad aim to serve as one-stop shops of services and natural and built environments that can meet the needs of any major production.

Nonetheless, even within these more recent developments, some of the attributes of Hollywood's postwar international productions endure. Interaction and communication among Hollywood and foreign personnel remains central to how these films are executed. Hollywood craft practices and technologies continue to circulate abroad while also reconfiguring according to local conditions. Foreign locations, while far more changeable, still attract Hollywood productions for economic and aesthetic reasons. All of these matters, which were so crucial in the postwar era, remain critical components of the process of globalization and film production. Although the specific economic and geopolitical mechanisms of today's globalization may differ from yesterday's internationalism, unpacking Hollywood's postwar runaway productions can help us better understand the transcultural exchanges of our interconnected world.

Appendix

HOLLYWOOD'S INTERNATIONAL
PRODUCTIONS, 1948–1962

THE FOLLOWING IS A LIST OF HOLLYWOOD PRODUCTIONS that were shot abroad in the postwar era. The productions were identified by surveying more than 5,400 movie titles from the *American Film Institute Catalog*, which remains one of the best databases for Hollywood features. The list is organized by the year of the films' US theatrical release. The information for each title includes the primary Hollywood studio or established US-based independent film company. These firms sometimes functioned as the production company, but more often as the financier and distributor of the movie, as was becoming the norm in the postwar period. The name of the director follows. Subsequently, I include the foreign locales where the film's principal photography took place—either in whole or in part—whether it was shot on location, made in a foreign studio, or both.

At the risk of engaging in an exercise of splitting hairs, I have attempted to identify the region that hosted the location or studio work as accurately as possible. Most of these locales represent countries, but in some cases I include territories, such as Greenland, Hong Kong, Puerto Rico, and the US Virgin Islands, which offered their own economic and production incentives. I do not include the incorporated US territories of Alaska and Hawaii, which received statehood in 1959. Whenever possible, I use the historical names of countries, including the European colonies and territories in Africa, Asia, and Oceania, to foreground the geopolitics of the period and the colonial ties that US film companies exploited. I also make a distinction between locations in East and West Germany after the creation of the two states in 1949. However, "Germany" is the location listed when the *AFI Catalog* does not identify the exact German locale and the region's filming sites could not be verified.

Aside from the above points, what merits inclusion in the appendix? The list focuses on fiction feature films, in which a Hollywood studio or a proven US independent company had a significant financial and organizational stake, eventually releasing the motion picture in the United States. Reflecting the book's criteria for defining a Hollywood international production, these movies are directed by individuals with experience in Hollywood. However, in some instances, a motion picture directed by a foreign filmmaker who was based in a foreign industry is included if a major Hollywood studio or US movie company was the primary producing entity. This is the case with the United Artists / Hecht-Lancaster production of *Trapeze* (1956), directed by British filmmaker Carol Reed, as well as for a handful of Disney productions that were released by RKO and eventually Disney's distribution arm Buena Vista—keep in mind that the distributors are listed below. Thus, Disney's *Swiss Family Robinson* (1960), directed by British filmmaker Ken Annakin, qualifies. Where the lines of division become murkier are productions directed by British filmmakers and backed by Hollywood producers who ran British companies, such as Sam Spiegel's Horizon Pictures and Irving Allen and Albert "Cubby" Broccoli's Warwick Films. Most of these companies' movies had a more distinctly British production setup, so they've been left off the list. Whenever possible, the following titles have been cross-checked with viewings, reviews, and research materials to show the array of productions that Hollywood was undertaking abroad.

1948

Berlin Express (RKO | Jacques Tourneur | France, Germany)
Captain from Castile (Fox | Henry King | Mexico)
The Emperor Waltz (Paramount | Billy Wilder | Canada)
Escape (Fox | Joseph L. Mankiewicz | UK)
A Foreign Affair (Paramount | Billy Wilder | Germany)
The Iron Curtain (Fox | William Wellman | Canada)
Mystery in Mexico (RKO | Robert Wise | Mexico)
Northwest Stampede (Eagle-Lion | Albert S. Rogell | Canada)
Sealed Verdict (Paramount | Lewis Allen | various European locations)
The Search (MGM | Fred Zinnemann | Germany, Switzerland)
So Evil My Love (Paramount | Lewis Allen | UK)
Sofia (Film Classics | John Reinhardt | Mexico)

Tarzan and the Mermaids (RKO | Robert Florey | Mexico)

To the Ends of the Earth (Columbia | Robert Stevenson | China, Cuba, Egypt)

To the Victor (Warner Bros. | Delmer Daves | France)

The Treasure of the Sierra Madre (Warner Bros. | John Huston | Mexico)

Women in the Night (Film Classics | William Rowland | Mexico)

1949

The Big Steal (RKO | Don Siegel | Mexico)

Black Magic (United Artists | Gregory Ratoff | Italy)

Border Incident (MGM | Anthony Mann | Mexico)

Canadian Pacific (Fox | Edwin L. Marin | Canada)

Edward, My Son (MGM | George Cukor | UK)

The Forbidden Street (Fox | Jean Negulesco | UK)

I Was a Male War Bride (Fox | Howard Hawks | Germany, UK)

Johnny Stool Pigeon (Universal | William Castle | Mexico)

Outpost in Morocco (United Artists | Robert Florey | Morocco)

Pirates of Capri (Film Classics | Edgar G. Ulmer | Italy)

Prince of Foxes (Fox | Henry King | Italy)

The Red Danube (MGM | George Sidney | Austria, Italy)

Tokyo Joe (Columbia | Stuart Heisler | Japan)

Under Capricorn (Warner Bros. | Alfred Hitchcock | UK)

We Were Strangers (Columbia | John Huston | Cuba)

1950

American Guerrilla in the Philippines (Fox | Fritz Lang | Philippines)

The Avengers (Republic | John H. Auer | Argentina)

The Big Lift (Fox | George Seaton | East and West Germany, Portugal)

The Black Rose (Fox | Henry Hathaway | Morocco, UK)

Conspirator (MGM | Victor Saville | UK)

Deported (Universal | Robert Siodmak | Italy)

Give Us This Day (Eagle-Lion | Edward Dmytryk | UK)

The Hasty Heart (Warner Bros. | Vincent Sherman | UK)

Killer Shark (Monogram | Budd Boetticher | Mexico)

Kill or Be Killed (Eagle-Lion | Max Nosseck | Portugal)

King Solomon's Mines (MGM | Compton Bennett, Andrew Marton | Belgian Congo, Kenya, Tanganyika, Uganda)

A Lady without Passport (MGM | Joseph H. Lewis | Cuba)

The Man on the Eiffel Tower (RKO | Burgess Meredith | France)

The Miniver Story (MGM | H. C. Potter, Victor Saville | UK)

The Mudlark (Fox | Jean Negulesco | UK)

Night and the City (Fox | Jules Dassin | UK)

One Way Street (Universal | Hugo Fregonese | Mexico)

Samson and Delilah (Paramount | Cecil B. DeMille | Algiers, Morocco)

Sarumba (Eagle-Lion | Marion Gering | Cuba)

Stage Fright (Warner Bros. | Alfred Hitchcock | UK)

Three Came Home (Fox | Jean Negulesco | North Borneo)

Time Running Out (United Artists | Frank Tuttle | France)

Treasure Island (RKO | Byron Haskin | UK)

Under My Skin (Fox | Jean Negulesco | France, Italy)

The White Tower (RKO | Ted Tetzlaff | France)

1951

The 13th Letter (Fox | Otto Preminger | Canada)

Adventures of Captain Fabian (Republic | William Marshall, Robert Florey | France)

The Brave Bulls (Columbia | Robert Rossen | Mexico)

Bullfighter and the Lady (Republic | Budd Boetticher | Mexico)

Calling Bulldog Drummond (MGM | Victor Saville | UK)

Captain Horatio Hornblower (Warner Bros. | Raoul Walsh | France, UK)

The Desert Fox (Fox | Henry Hathaway | France, Germany, UK)

Fugitive Lady (Republic | Sidney Salkow | Italy)

Happy Go Lovely (RKO | H. Bruce Humberstone | UK)

I'll Never Forget You (Fox | Roy Baker | UK)

The Kangaroo Kid (Eagle-Lion | Lesley Selander | Australia)

Kim (MGM | Victor Saville | India, Pakistan)

The Light Touch (MGM | Richard Brooks | Italy, Tunisia)

Lucky Nick Cain (Fox | Joseph Newman | Italy, UK)

The Magic Face (Columbia | Frank Tuttle | Austria)

The Man with My Face (United Artists | Edward J. Montagne | Puerto Rico)

My Outlaw Brother (Eagle-Lion | Elliot Nugent | Mexico)

No Highway in the Sky (Fox | Henry Koster | UK)

On the Riviera (Fox | Walter Lang | France)

Pardon My French (United Artists | Bernard Vorhaus | France)

Quebec (Paramount | George Templeton | Canada)

Quo Vadis (MGM | Mervyn LeRoy | Italy)

September Affair (Paramount | William Dieterle | Italy)

Tarzan's Peril (RKO | Byron Haskin | Kenya, Mexico, Tanganyika, Uganda)

Teresa (MGM | Fred Zinnemann | Italy)

Three Steps North (United Artists | W. Lee Wilder | Italy)

Tokyo File 212 (RKO | Dorrell and Stuart McGowan | Japan)

1952

5 Fingers (Fox | Joseph L. Mankiewicz | Turkey)

The African Queen (United Artists | John Huston | Belgian Congo, Uganda, UK)

Another Man's Poison (United Artists | Irving Rapper | UK)

Assignment—Paris (Columbia | Robert Parrish | France, Hungary)

Babes in Bagdad (United Artists | Edgar G. Ulmer | Spain)

Bal Tabarin (Republic | Phil Ford | France)

The Crimson Pirate (Warner Bros. | Robert Siodmak | France, Italy, UK)

Decision before Dawn (Fox | Anatole Litvak | West Germany)

The Devil Makes Three (MGM | Andrew Marton | Austria, West Germany)

Diplomatic Courier (Fox | Henry Hathaway | Austria, France, Italy, Romania)

The Fighter (United Artists | Herbert Kline | Mexico)

The Gambler and The Lady (Lippert | Patrick Jenkins, Sam Newfield | UK)

Geisha Girl (Realart | George Breakston, C. Ray Stahl | Japan)

The Green Glove (United Artists | Rudolph Maté | France)

Hong Kong (Paramount | Lewis R. Foster | Hong Kong)

The Hour of 13 (MGM | Harold French | UK)

Island of Desire (United Artists | Stuart Heisler | Cuba, Jamaica, UK)

The Jungle (Lippert | William Berke | India)

Kangaroo (Fox | Lewis Milestone | Australia)

The Miracle of Our Lady of Fatima (Warner Bros. | John Brahm | Portugal)

Monsoon (United Artists | Rod Amateau | India)

One Big Affair (United Artists | Peter Godfrey | Mexico)

Oriental Evil (Classic Pictures | George Breakston, C. Ray Stahl | Japan)

Pandora and the Flying Dutchman (MGM | Albert Lewin | Spain, UK)

The Quiet Man (Republic | John Ford | Ireland)

Scotland Yard Inspector (Lippert | Sam Newfield | UK)

The Snows of Kilimanjaro (Fox | Henry King | France, Kenya, Spain, Tanganyika)

Storm Over Tibet (Columbia | Andrew Marton | Tibet)

The Story of Robin Hood and His Merrie Men (RKO | Ken Annakin | UK)

Stronghold (Lippert | Steve Sekely | Mexico)

Way of a Gaucho (Fox | Jacques Tourneur | Argentina)

When in Rome (MGM | Clarence Brown | Italy)

Where's Charley? (Warner Bros. | David Butler | UK)

Willie and Joe Back at the Front (Universal | George Sherman | Japan)

1953

Act of Love (United Artists | Anatole Litvak | France)

Affair in Monte Carlo (Monogram | Victor Saville | Monaco, UK)

All the Brothers Were Valiant (MGM | Richard Thorpe | Jamaica)

Bad Blonde (Lippert | Reginald LeBorg | UK)

Blowing Wild (Warner Bros. | Hugo Fregonese | Mexico)

Captain Scarlett (United Artists | Thomas H. Carr | Mexico)

Decameron Nights (RKO | Hugo Fregonese | Italy, Spain, UK)

Egypt by Three (Filmakers Releasing | Victor Stoloff | Egypt)

Fort Algiers (United Artists | Lesley Selander | Morocco)

The Hindu (United Artists | Frank Ferrin | India)

I Confess (Warner Bros. | Alfred Hitchcock | Canada)

I'll Get You (Lippert | Seymour Friedman | UK)

Ivanhoe (MGM | Richard Thorpe | UK)

The Juggler (Columbia | Edward Dmytryk | Israel)

Laughing Anne (Republic | Herbert Wilcox | UK)

Little Boy Lost (Paramount | George Seaton | France)

The Man from Cairo (Lippert | Ray H. Enright | Italy)

Man on a Tightrope (Fox | Elia Kazan | West Germany)

Martin Luther (Louis de Rochemont Associates | Irving Pichel | West Germany)

The Master of Ballantrae (Warner Bros. | William Keighley | Italy, UK)

Melba (United Artists | Lewis Milestone | UK)

Mission over Korea (Columbia | Fred F. Sears | Japan, Korea)

Mogambo (MGM | John Ford | Belgian Congo, French Equatorial Africa, French West Africa, Kenya, Tanganyika, Uganda, UK)

Moulin Rouge (United Artists | John Huston | France, UK)

My Cousin Rachel (Fox | Henry Koster | UK)

Never Let Me Go (MGM | Delmer Daves | UK)

Niagara (Fox | Henry Hathaway | Canada)

No Time for Flowers (RKO | Don Siegel | Austria)

Plunder of the Sun (Warner Bros. | John Farrow | Mexico)

Return to Paradise (United Artists | Mark Robson | Western Samoa)

Rogue's March (MGM | Allan Davis | India)

Roman Holiday (Paramount | William Wyler | Italy)

Sailor of the King (Fox | Roy Boulting | UK)

Sea Devils (RKO | Raoul Walsh | UK)

Second Chance (RKO | Rudolph Maté | Mexico)

Shoot First (United Artists | Robert Parrish | UK)

Sombrero (MGM | Norman Foster | Mexico)

The Sword and the Rose (RKO | Ken Annakin | UK)

Terror on a Train (MGM | Ted Tetzlaff | UK)

That Man from Tangier (United Artists | Robert Elwyn | Morocco, Spain)

Treasure of the Golden Condor (Fox | Delmer Daves | Guatemala)

Trent's Last Case (Republic | Herbert Wilcox | UK)

White Witch Doctor (Fox | Henry Hathaway | Belgian Congo)

1954

20,000 Leagues under the Sea (Buena Vista | Richard Fleischer | Bahamas, Jamaica)

The Barefoot Contessa (United Artists | Joseph L. Mankiewicz | Italy)

Beat the Devil (United Artists | John Huston | Italy, UK)

Beau Brummell (MGM | Curtis Bernhardt | UK)

Betrayed (MGM | Gottfried Reinhardt | Netherlands, UK)

The Black Knight (Columbia | Tay Garnett | Spain, UK)

The Black Pirates (Lippert | Allen H. Miner | El Salvador)

Carnival Story (RKO | Kurt Neumann | West Germany)

Cease Fire (Paramount | Owen Crompton | Korea)

Crest of the Wave (MGM | John and Roy Boulting | UK)

Crossed Swords (United Artists | Milton Krims | Italy)

Duel in the Jungle (Warner Bros. | George Marshall | Northern Rhodesia, South Africa, UK)

The Egyptian (Fox | Michael Curtiz | Egypt)

Elephant Walk (Paramount | William Dieterle | Ceylon)

Fire over Africa (Columbia | Richard B. Sale | Spain, UK)

Flame and the Flesh (MGM | Richard Brooks | Italy, UK)

Garden of Evil (Fox | Henry Hathaway | Mexico)

The Golden Mistress (United Artists | Abner Biberman | Haiti)

Hell below Zero (Columbia | Mark Robson | UK)

His Majesty O'Keefe (Warner Bros. | Byron Haskin | Fiji)

Hondo (Warner Bros. | John Farrow | Mexico)

Knights of the Round Table (MGM | Richard Thorpe | Ireland, UK)

Knock on Wood (Paramount | Melvin Frank, Norman Panama | Switzerland, UK)

The Last Time I Saw Paris (MGM | Richard Brooks | France)

Night People (Fox | Nunnally Johnson | West Germany)

Operation Manhunt (United Artists | Jack Alexander | Canada)

Prince Valiant (Fox | Henry Hathaway | UK)

Rhapsody (MGM | Charles Vidor | France, Switzerland)

Rob Roy the Highland Rogue (RKO | Harold French | UK)

Rose Marie (MGM | Mervyn LeRoy | Canada)

Saadia (MGM | Albert Lewin | Morocco)

The Saint's Girl Friday (RKO | Seymour Friedman | UK)

Saskatchewan (Universal | Raoul Walsh | Canada)

The Scarlet Spear (United Artists | George Breakston, C. Ray Stahl | Kenya)

Secret of the Incas (Paramount | Jerry Hopper | Peru)

Sitting Bull (United Artists | Sidney Salkow | Mexico)

Three Coins in the Fountain (Fox | Jean Negulesco | Italy)

Trouble in the Glen (Republic | Herbert Wilcox | UK)

Twist of Fate (United Artists | David Miller | France, UK)

Valley of the Kings (MGM | Robert Pirosh | Egypt)

Vera Cruz (United Artists | Robert Aldrich | Mexico)

The White Orchid (United Artists | Reginald LeBorg | Mexico)

1955

The Americano (RKO | William Castle | Brazil)

Angela (Fox | Dennis O'Keefe | Italy)

Battle Cry (Warner Bros. | Raoul Walsh | Puerto Rico)

Bedevilled (MGM | Mitchell Leisen | France)

The Bridges at Toko-Ri (Paramount | Mark Robson | Japan, Korea)

A Bullet for Joey (United Artists | Lewis Allen | Canada)

Captain Lightfoot (Universal | Douglas Sirk | Ireland)

Cross Channel (Republic | R. G. Springsteen | UK)

The Deep Blue Sea (Fox | Anatole Litvak | UK)

The End of the Affair (Columbia | Edward Dmytryk | UK)

The Far Country (Universal | Anthony Mann | Canada)

Footsteps in the Fog (Columbia | Arthur Lubin | UK)

Fury in Paradise (Gibraltar Motion Picture Distributors | George Bruce | Mexico)

Gentlemen Marry Brunettes (United Artists | Richard B. Sale | France, Monaco, UK)

The Green Buddha (Republic | John Lemont | UK)

Green Fire (MGM | Andrew Marton | Colombia)

House of Bamboo (Fox | Samuel Fuller | Japan)

Land of the Pharaohs (Warner Bros. | Howard Hawks | Egypt, Italy)

A Life in the Balance (Fox | Harry Horner | Mexico)

The Littlest Outlaw (Buena Vista | Roberto Gavaldón | Mexico)

Long John Silver (Distributors Corp. of America | Byron Haskin | Australia)

Love Is a Many-Splendored Thing (Fox | Henry King | Hong Kong)

The Magnificent Matador (Fox | Budd Boetticher | Mexico)

Mambo (Paramount | Robert Rossen | Italy)

Othello (United Artists | Orson Welles | Italy, Morocco)

A Prize of Gold (Columbia | Mark Robson | UK, West Germany)

The Purple Plain (United Artists | Robert Parrish | Ceylon, UK)

Quentin Durward (MGM | Richard Thorpe | France, UK)

The Racers (Fox | Henry Hathaway | Belgium, France, Italy, Monaco, Switzerland, West Germany)

The Rains of Ranchipur (Fox | Jean Negulesco | Pakistan)

Robbers' Roost (United Artists | Sidney Salkow | Mexico)

Secret Venture (Republic | R. G. Springsteen | UK)

Seven Cities of Gold (Fox | Robert Webb | Mexico)

Silent Fear (Gibraltar Motion Picture Distributors | Edward L. Cahn | Mexico)

Soldier of Fortune (Fox | Edward Dmytryk | Hong Kong, Macao)

Special Delivery (Columbia | John Brahm | West Germany)

The Tall Men (Fox | Raoul Walsh | Mexico)

They Were So Young (Lippert | Kurt Neumann | Italy, West Germany)

Three Stripes in the Sun (Columbia | Richard Murphy | Japan)

To Catch a Thief (Paramount | Alfred Hitchcock | France, Monaco)

The Treasure of Pancho Villa (RKO | George Sherman | Mexico)

Ulysses (Paramount | Mario Camerini | Italy)

Untamed (Fox | Henry King | Ireland, South Africa)

The Warriors (Allied Artists | Henry Levin | UK)

White Feather (Fox | Robert Webb | Mexico)

1956

23 Paces to Baker Street (Fox | Henry Hathaway | UK)

Alexander the Great (United Artists | Robert Rossen | Spain)

The Amazon Trader (Warner Bros. | Tom McGowan | Brazil)

The Ambassador's Daughter (United Artists | Norman Krasna | France)

Anastasia (Fox | Anatole Litvak | Denmark, France, UK)

Around the World in 80 Days (United Artists | Michael Anderson | France, India, Mexico, Pakistan, Spain, Thailand, UK)

Bandido (United Artists | Richard Fleischer | Mexico)

The Beast of Hollow Mountain (United Artists | Edward Nassour, Ismael Rodríguez | Mexico)

Bhowani Junction (MGM | George Cukor | Pakistan, UK)

The Brave One (RKO | Irving Rapper | Mexico)

The Cockleshell Heroes (Columbia | José Ferrer | Portugal, UK)

Comanche (United Artists | George Sherman | Mexico)

The Come On (Allied Artists | Russell Birdwell | Mexico)

Crowded Paradise (Tudor Pictures | Fred Pressburger, Ben Gradus | Puerto Rico)

Curucu, Beast of the Amazon (Universal | Curt Siodmak | Brazil)

Daniel Boone, Trail Blazer (Republic | Albert C. Gannaway, Ismael Rodríguez | Mexico)

Dark Venture (First National Film Distributors | John Calvert | Kenya, Mozambique)

Flame of the Islands (Republic | Edward Ludwig | Bahamas)

Flight to Hong Kong (United Artists | Joseph Newman | Hong Kong, Japan, Macao)

Foreign Intrigue (United Artists | Sheldon Reynolds | Austria, France, Monaco, Sweden)

Helen of Troy (Warner Bros. | Robert Wise | Italy)

Huk! (United Artists | John Barnwell | Philippines)

Invitation to the Dance (MGM | Gene Kelly | UK)

The Last Frontier (Columbia | Anthony Mann | Mexico)

Let's Make Up (United Artists | Herbert Wilcox | UK)

Lisbon (Republic | Ray Milland | Portugal)

Lum and Abner Abroad (Howco Productions | James V. Kern | France, Monaco, Yugoslavia)

Lust for Life (MGM | Vincente Minnelli | Belgium, France, Netherlands)

Magic Fire (Republic | William Dieterle | West Germany)

Manfish (United Artists | W. Lee Wilder | Jamaica)

The Man Who Knew Too Much (Paramount | Alfred Hitchcock | Morocco, UK)

Massacre (Fox | Louis King | Mexico)

Moby Dick (Warner Bros. | John Huston | Ireland, Portugal, Spain, UK)

The Mountain (Paramount | Edward Dmytryk | France)

No Place to Hide (Allied Artists | Josef Shaftel | Philippines)

Port Afrique (Columbia | Rudolph Maté | Morocco, UK)

The Proud and the Profane (Paramount | George Seaton | Puerto Rico, US Virgin Islands)

The River Changes (Warner Bros. | Owen Crompton | West Germany)

Run for the Sun (United Artists | Roy Boulting | Mexico)

Serenade (Warner Bros. | Anthony Mann | Mexico)

Shadow of Fear (United Artists | Albert S. Rogell | UK)

The Sharkfighters (United Artists | Jerry Hopper | Cuba)

Star of India (United Artists | Arthur Lubin | Italy, UK)

The Teahouse of August Moon (MGM | Daniel Mann | Japan)

The Ten Commandments (Paramount | Cecil B. DeMille | Egypt)

Track the Man Down (Republic | R. G. Springsteen | UK)

Trapeze (United Artists | Carol Reed | France)

War and Peace (Paramount | King Vidor | Italy)

Wetbacks (Gibraltar Motion Picture Distributors | Hank McCune | Mexico)

A Woman's Devotion (Republic | Paul Heinreid | Mexico)

1957

20 Million Miles to Earth (Columbia | Nathan Juran | Italy)

Abandon Ship (Columbia | Richard B. Sale | UK)

Affair in Havana (Allied Artists | Laslo Benedek | Cuba)

The Barretts of Wimpole Street (MGM | Sidney Franklin | UK)

Beyond Mombasa (Columbia | George Marshall | Kenya, UK)

The Big Boodle (United Artists | Richard Wilson | Cuba)

The Black Scorpion (Warner Bros. | Edward Ludwig | Mexico)

Boy on a Dolphin (Fox | Jean Negulesco | Greece, Italy)

Escapade in Japan (Universal | Arthur Lubin | Japan)

A Farewell to Arms (Fox | Charles Vidor | Italy)

Fire Down Below (Columbia | Robert Parrish | Trinidad and Tobago, UK)

Funny Face (Paramount | Stanley Donen | France)

The Happy Road (MGM | Gene Kelly | France)

Heaven Knows, Mr. Allison (Fox | John Huston | Trinidad and Tobago)

Hidden Fear (United Artists | Andre DeToth | Denmark)

Interlude (Universal | Douglas Sirk | Austria, West Germany)

Island in the Sun (Fox | Robert Rossen | Barbados, Grenada, Trinidad and Tobago, UK)

Istanbul (Universal | Joseph Pevney | Turkey)

Joe Butterfly (Universal | Jesse Hibbs | Japan)

Lady of Vengeance (United Artists | Burt Balaban | UK)

Legend of the Lost (United Artists | Henry Hathaway | Italy, Libya)

Let's Be Happy (Allied Artists | Henry Levin | UK)

The Little Hut (MGM | Mark Robson | Italy, Jamaica, UK)

The Living Idol (MGM | Albert Lewin | Mexico)

Love in the Afternoon (Allied Artists | Billy Wilder | France)

Love Slaves of the Amazons (Universal | Curt Siodmak | Brazil)

The Monte Carlo Story (United Artists | Samuel Taylor | Italy, Monaco)

The Pride and the Passion (United Artists | Stanley Kramer | Spain)

The Prince and the Showgirl (Warner Bros. | Laurence Olivier | UK)

The Rising of the Moon (Warner Bros. | John Ford | Ireland)

The River's Edge (Fox | Allan Dwan | Mexico)

Saint Joan (United Artists | Otto Preminger | UK)

Sayonara (Warner Bros. | Joshua Logan | Japan)

Sea Wife (Fox | Bob McNaught | Jamaica, UK)

The Seventh Sin (MGM | Ronald Neame | Hong Kong)

Something of Value (MGM | Richard Brooks | Kenya)

The Spirit of St. Louis (Warner Bros. | Billy Wilder | Canada, France, Greenland, Ireland, Spain)

Stopover Tokyo (Fox | Richard L. Breen | Japan)

The Story of Esther Costello (Columbia | David Miller | UK)

The Sun Also Rises (Fox | Henry King | France, Mexico, Spain)

Tarzan and the Lost Safari (MGM | H. Bruce Humberstone | Kenya, UK)

Ten Thousand Bedrooms (MGM | Richard Thorpe | Italy)

The Tijuana Story (Columbia | Leslie Kardos | Mexico)

Tip on a Dead Jockey (MGM | Richard Thorpe | Spain)

Until They Sail (MGM | Robert Wise | New Zealand)

The Vintage (MGM | Jeffrey Hayden | France)

1958

The 7th Voyage of Sinbad (Columbia | Nathan Juran | Spain, UK)

Another Time, Another Place (Paramount | Lewis Allen | UK)

The Barbarian and the Geisha (Fox | John Huston | Japan)

Bitter Victory (Columbia | Nicholas Ray | France, Libya)

Bonjour Tristesse (Columbia | Otto Preminger | France, UK)

The Bravados (Fox | Henry King | Mexico)

The Brothers Karamazov (MGM | Richard Brooks | France, UK)

A Certain Smile (Fox | Jean Negulesco | France)

Curse of the Demon (Columbia | Jacques Tourneur | UK)

Diamond Safari (Fox | Gerald Mayer | South Africa)

Enchanted Island (Warner Bros. | Allan Dwan | Mexico)

Flaming Frontier (Fox | Sam Newfield | Canada)

Fräulein (Fox | Henry Koster | West Germany)

From the Earth to the Moon (Warner Bros. | Byron Haskin | Mexico)

Gigi (MGM | Vincente Minnelli | France)

Harry Black and the Tiger (Fox | Hugo Fregonese | India)

High Hell (Paramount | Burt Balaban | Switzerland, UK)

Hong Kong Affair (Allied Artists | Paul F. Heard | Hong Kong)

The Hunters (Fox | Dick Powell | Japan)

I Accuse! (MGM | José Ferrer | Belgium, UK)

Indiscreet (Warner Bros. | Stanley Donen | UK)

The Inn of the Sixth Happiness (Fox | Mark Robson | UK)

Island Women (United Artists | William Berke | Bahamas)

Kings Go Forth (United Artists | Delmer Daves | France)

The Last of the Fast Guns (Universal | George Sherman | Mexico)

Lost Lagoon (United Artists | John Rawlins | various Caribbean islands)

The Lost Missile (United Artists | Lester Wm. Berke | Canada)

Machete (United Artists | Kurt Neumann | Puerto Rico)

Manhunt in the Jungle (Warner Bros. | Tom McGowan | Brazil, Peru)

Maracaibo (Paramount | Cornel Wilde | Venezuela)

The Mark of the Hawk (Universal | Michael Audley | Nigeria, UK)

Me and the Colonel (Columbia | Peter Glenville | France)

The Naked and the Dead (Warner Bros. | Raoul Walsh | Panama)

Naked Earth (Fox | Vincent Sherman | Uganda, UK)

The Old Man and the Sea (Warner Bros. | John Sturges | Bahamas, Cuba, Ecuador, Panama, Peru)

Paris Holiday (United Artists | Gerd Oswald | France)

Paths of Glory (United Artists | Stanley Kubrick | West Germany)

The Quiet American (United Artists | Joseph L. Mankiewicz | Italy, Vietnam)

Raw Wind in Eden (Universal | Richard Wilson | Italy)

The Reluctant Debutante (MGM | Vincente Minnelli | France)

The Roots of Heaven (Fox | John Huston | Belgian Congo, France, French Equatorial Africa)

The Safecracker (MGM | Ray Milland | UK)

Seven Hills of Rome (MGM | Roy Rowland | Italy)

Sierra Baron (Fox | James B. Clark | Mexico)

South Pacific (Fox | Joshua Logan | Fiji)

Spanish Affair (Paramount | Don Siegel | Spain)

Spy in the Sky! (Allied Artists | W. Lee Wilder | Netherlands)

Ten Days to Tulara (United Artists | George Sherman | Mexico)

A Time to Love and a Time to Die (Universal | Douglas Sirk | West Germany)

Tom Thumb (MGM | George Pal | Mexico, Netherlands, UK)

The Vikings (United Artists | Richard Fleischer | France, Norway, West Germany)

Villa! (Fox | James B. Clark | Mexico)

Wolf Dog (Fox | Sam Newfield | Canada)

The Young Lions (Fox | Edward Dmytryk | France, Germany)

The Angry Hills (MGM | Robert Aldrich | Greece, UK)

Ben-Hur (MGM | William Wyler | Italy)

The Blue Angel (Fox | Edward Dmytryk | West Germany)

Counterplot (United Artists | Kurt Neumann | Puerto Rico)

Count Your Blessings (MGM | Jean Negulesco | France, UK)

Desert Desperadoes (RKO/State Rights | Steve Sekely | Egypt, Italy)

The Devil's Disciple (United Artists | Guy Hamilton | UK)

The Diary of Anne Frank (Fox | George Stevens | Netherlands)

Face of Fire (Allied Artists | Albert Band | Sweden)

For the First Time (MGM | Rudolph Maté | Austria, Germany, Italy)

The Giant Behemoth (Allied Artists | Eugène Lourié | UK)

Gideon of Scotland Yard (Columbia | John Ford | UK)

Green Mansions (MGM | Mel Ferrer | British Guiana, Colombia, Venezuela)

Holiday for Lovers (Fox | Henry Levin | Brazil)

The House of the Seven Hawks (MGM | Richard Thorpe | Netherlands, UK)

It Started with a Kiss (MGM | George Marshall | Spain)

Jet over the Atlantic (Inter Continent Releasing | Byron Haskin | Mexico)

John Paul Jones (Warner Bros. | John Farrow | France, Spain, UK)

The Journey (MGM | Anatole Litvak | Austria)

Journey to the Center of the Earth (Fox | Henry Levin | UK)

The Last Blitzkrieg (Columbia | Arthur Dreifuss | Netherlands)

Libel (MGM | Anthony Asquith | UK)

The Little Savage (Fox | Byron Haskin | Mexico)

The Man Who Understood Women (Fox | Nunnally Johnson | France)

The Mouse that Roared (Columbia | Jack Arnold | UK)

The Naked Maja (United Artists | Henry Koster | Italy)

Never So Few (MGM | John Sturges | Burma, Ceylon, India)

The Nun's Story (Warner Bros. | Fred Zinnemann | Belgian Congo, Belgium, Italy)

On the Beach (United Artists | Stanley Kramer | Australia)

The Scavengers (Valiant Films | John Cromwell | Hong Kong, Macao, Philippines)

The Sheriff of Fractured Jaw (Fox | Raoul Walsh | Spain, UK)

Solomon and Sheba (United Artists | King Vidor | Spain)

The Son of Robin Hood (Fox | George Sherman | UK)

Surrender–Hell! (Allied Artists | John Barnwell | Philippines)

Tarzan's Greatest Adventure (Paramount | John Guillermin | Kenya, UK)

Ten Seconds to Hell (United Artists | Robert Aldrich | East and West Germany)

Third Man on the Mountain (Buena Vista | Ken Annakin | Switzerland, UK)

The Two-Headed Spy (Columbia | Andre DeToth | UK, West Germany)

The Wonderful Country (United Artists | Robert Parrish | Mexico)

The Young Land (Columbia | Ted Tetzlaff | Mexico)

1960

The 3 Worlds of Gulliver (Columbia | Jack Sher | Spain, UK)

The Angel Wore Red (MGM | Nunnally Johnson | Italy)

Battle of Blood Island (Filmgroup | Joel M. Rapp | Puerto Rico)

Bluebeard's Ten Honeymoons (Warner Bros. | W. Lee Wilder | France, UK)

Bobbikins (Fox | Robert Day | UK)

A Breath of Scandal (Paramount | Michael Curtiz | Austria, Italy)

Crack in the Mirror (Fox | Richard Fleischer | France)

Dinosaurus! (Universal | Irvin S. Yeaworth Jr. | US Virgin Islands)

A Dog of Flanders (Fox | James B. Clark | Belgium, Netherlands)

The Enemy General (Columbia | George Sherman | France, Italy, Netherlands)

Esther and the King (Fox | Raoul Walsh | Italy)

Exodus (United Artists | Otto Preminger | Cyprus, Israel)

Five Branded Women (Paramount | Martin Ritt | Austria, Italy)

For the Love of Mike (Fox | George Sherman | Mexico)

G.I. Blues (Paramount | Norman Taurog | West Germany)

Hell to Eternity (Allied Artists | Phil Karlson | Japan)

It Started in Naples (Paramount | Melville Shavelson | Italy)

Kidnapped (Buena Vista | Robert Stevenson | UK)

Killers of Kilimanjaro (Columbia | Richard Thorpe | Kenya, Tanganyika, UK)

The Last Voyage (MGM | Andrew L. Stone | Japan)

Last Woman on Earth (Allied Artists | Roger Corman | Puerto Rico)

Macumba Love (United Artists | Douglas Fowley | Brazil)

The Magnificent Seven (United Artists | John Sturges | Mexico)

Man on a String (Columbia | Andre DeToth | Soviet Union, West Germany)

The Night Fighters (United Artists | Tay Garnett | Ireland)

Once More, With Feeling! (Columbia | Stanley Donen | France)

Scent of Mystery (Michael Todd Jr. | Jack Cardiff | Spain)

The Secret of the Purple Reef (Fox | William Witney | Puerto Rico)

September Storm (Fox | Byron Haskin | Spain)

Seven Thieves (Fox | Henry Hathaway | France, Monaco)

Sink the Bismarck! (Fox | Lewis Gilbert | UK)

Song Without End (Columbia | George Cukor, Charles Vidor | Austria)

Sons and Lovers (Fox | Jack Cardiff | UK)

Spartacus (Universal | Stanley Kubrick | Spain)

Suddenly, Last Summer (Columbia | Joseph L. Mankiewicz | Spain, UK)

The Sundowners (Warner Bros. | Fred Zinnemann | Australia, UK)

Sunrise at Campobello (Warner Bros. | Vincent J. Donehue | Canada)

Surprise Package (Columbia | Stanley Donen | Greece, UK)

Swiss Family Robinson (Buena Vista | Ken Annakin | Trinidad and Tobago, UK)

Tarzan the Magnificent (Paramount | Robert Day | Kenya, UK)

The Unforgiven (United Artists | John Huston | Mexico)

Village of the Damned (MGM | Wolf Rilla | UK)

1961

Armored Command (Allied Artists | Byron Haskin | West Germany)

Atlas (Filmgroup | Roger Corman | Greece)

The Big Gamble (Fox | Richard Fleischer | France, Ireland, Ivory Coast, UK)

The Big Show (Fox | James B. Clark | Denmark, West Germany)

The Canadians (Fox | Burt Kennedy | Canada)

Come September (Universal | Robert Mulligan | Italy)

Creature from the Haunted Sea (Filmgroup | Roger Corman | Puerto Rico)

Cry for Happy (Columbia | George Marshall | Japan)

El Cid (Allied Artists | Anthony Mann | Italy, Spain)

Fanny (Warner Bros. | Joshua Logan | France)

Francis of Assisi (Fox | Michael Curtiz | Italy)

Go Naked in the World (MGM | Ranald MacDougall | Mexico)

Goodbye Again (United Artists | Anatole Litvak | France)

Gorgo (MGM | Eugène Lourié | Ireland, UK)

The Grass Is Greener (Universal | Stanley Donen | UK)

Greyfriars Bobby (Buena Vista | Don Chaffey | UK)

The Happy Thieves (United Artists | George Marshall | Spain)

Journey to the Seventh Planet (American International Pictures | Sidney Pink | Denmark)

Judgment at Nuremberg (United Artists | Stanley Kramer | West Germany)

Karate, the Hand of Death (Allied Artists | Joel Holt | Japan)

King of Kings (MGM | Nicholas Ray | Spain, UK)

The Last Sunset (Universal | Robert Aldrich | Mexico)

Marines, Let's Go! (Fox | Raoul Walsh | Japan)

A Matter of Morals (United Artists | John Cromwell | Sweden)

Most Dangerous Man Alive (Columbia | Allan Dwan | Mexico)

Mysterious Island (Columbia | Cy Endfield | Spain, UK)

Nikki, Wild Dog of the North (Buena Vista | Jack Couffer, Donald Haldane | Canada)

One, Two, Three (United Artists | Billy Wilder | East and West Germany)

On the Double (Paramount | Melville Shavelson | UK)

Paris Blues (United Artists | Martin Ritt | France)

Pepe (Columbia | George Sidney | Mexico)

Portrait of a Sinner (American International Pictures | Robert Siodmak | UK)

Question 7 (Louis de Rochemont Associates | Stuart Rosenberg | West Germany)

Romanoff and Juliet (Universal | Peter Ustinov | Italy)

The Roman Spring of Mrs. Stone (Warner Bros. | José Quintero | Italy, UK)

The Savage Innocents (Paramount | Nicholas Ray | Canada, Greenland, UK)

The Secret Ways (Universal | Phil Karlson | Austria, Switzerland)

The Steel Claw (Warner Bros. | George Montgomery | Philippines)

Then There Were Three (Parade Releasing | Alex Nicol | Italy)

Town Without Pity (United Artists | Gottfried Reinhardt | Austria, France, West Germany)

The World of Suzie Wong (Paramount | Richard Quine | Hong Kong, UK)

1962

The 300 Spartans (Fox | Rudolph Maté | Greece)

Almost Angels (Buena Vista | Steven Previn | Austria)

Barabbas (Columbia | Richard Fleischer | Italy)

The Bashful Elephant (Allied Artists | Dorrell and Stuart McGowan | Austria)

Big Red (Buena Vista | Norman Tokar | Canada)

Bon Voyage! (Buena Vista | James Neilson | France)

The Counterfeit Traitor (Paramount | George Seaton | Denmark, Sweden, West Germany)

Damon and Pythias (MGM | Curtis Bernhardt | Italy)

East of Kilimanjaro (Parade Releasing | Arnold Belgard, Edoardo Capolino | Uganda)

Escape from East Berlin (MGM | Robert Siodmak | West Germany)

The Four Horsemen of the Apocalypse (MGM | Vincente Minnelli | France)

Freud (Universal | John Huston | Austria, West Germany)

Geronimo (United Artists | Arnold Laven | Mexico)

Gigot (Fox | Gene Kelly | France)

A Girl Named Tamiko (Paramount | John Sturges | Japan)

Hatari! (Paramount | Howard Hawks | Tanganyika)

Hemingway's Adventures of a Young Man (Fox | Martin Ritt | Italy)

In Search of the Castaways (Buena Vista | Robert Stevenson | UK)

It Happened in Athens (Fox | Andrew Marton | Greece)

Jessica (United Artists | Jean Negulesco | Italy)

Light in the Piazza (MGM | Guy Green | Italy, UK)

Lisa (Fox | Philip Dunne | Netherlands, UK)

Lolita (MGM | Stanley Kubrick | UK)

The Longest Day (Fox | Ken Annakin, Andrew Marton, Gerd Oswald, Bernhard Wicki | France, UK)

The Manster (Lopert Pictures | George Breakston, Kenneth Crane | Japan)

Merrill's Marauders (Warner Bros. | Samuel Fuller | Philippines)

Mutiny on the Bounty (MGM | Lewis Milestone | French Polynesia)

My Geisha (Paramount | Jack Cardiff | Japan)

No Man Is an Island (Universal | John Monks, Jr., Richard Goldstone | Philippines)

The Pigeon That Took Rome (Paramount | Melville Shavelson | Italy)

Reptilicus (American International Pictures | Sidney Pink | Denmark)

The Road to Hong Kong (United Artists | Norman Panama | UK)

Rome Adventure (Warner Bros. | Delmer Daves | Italy)

Samar (Warner Bros. | George Montgomery | Philippines)

Satan Never Sleeps (Fox | Leo McCarey | UK)

The Spiral Road (Universal | Robert Mulligan | Suriname)

Taras Bulba (United Artists | J. Lee Thompson | Argentina)

Tarzan Goes to India (MGM | John Guillermin | India)

Tender Is the Night (Fox | Henry King | France, Italy, Switzerland)

Two Weeks in Another Town (MGM | Vincente Minnelli | Italy)

When the Girls Take Over (Parade Releasing | Russell Hayden | Puerto Rico)

The Wonderful World of the Brothers Grimm (MGM | Henry Levin, George Pal | West Germany)

NOTES

PROLOGUE: MOVIE RUINS

1. All film title years correspond to the movie's US release and derive from the *American Film Institute Catalog*, https://catalog.afi.com.

2. Vivian Sobchack explores the excavation of the buried sets of Cecil B. DeMille's *The Ten Commandments* (1923) in California's Guadalupe-Nipomo Dunes as an allegory of historiography in "What Is Film History?, or, the Riddle of the Sphinxes," in *Reinventing Film Studies*, ed. Christine Gledhill and Linda Williams (London: Arnold, 2000), 300–315.

3. Throughout this study, I refrain from using the terms "America" or "American" to refer to the United States, its products, or its peoples to avoid an ethnocentric position that privileges the United States above North and South America. Unless I'm quoting or using these terms as part of a proper name, I instead employ the "United States," or "US" as a modifier, as in the US motion picture industry. A similar concern is raised by Ruth Vasey in *The World According to Hollywood, 1918–1939* (Madison: University of Wisconsin Press, 1997), 232n9.

INTRODUCTION: "HAVE TALENT, WILL TRAVEL"

1. Steven Bingen, Stephen X. Sylvester, and Michael Troyan, *MGM: Hollywood's Greatest Backlot* (Solana Beach, CA: Santa Monica Press, 2011), 250.

2. Michael Curtin and Kevin Sanson, eds., *Precarious Creativity: Global Media, Local Labor* (Oakland: University of California Press, 2016).

3. One prominent feature story is Ted Johnson, "Fighting the Flight," *Variety*, August 27, 2013, 22–27.

4. Janet Staiger, "The Director-Unit System: Management of Multiple-Unit Companies after 1909," in David Bordwell, Janet Staiger, and Kristin Thompson, *The Classical Hollywood Cinema: Film Style and Mode of Production to 1960* (New

York: Columbia University Press, 1985), 121–23; Eileen Bowser, *The Transformation of Cinema, 1907–1915* (Berkeley: University of California Press, 1990), 150–65; Gary W. Harner, "The Kalem Company, Travel and On-Location Filming: The Forging of an Identity," *Film History* 10, no. 10 (1998): 188–207.

5. Janet Staiger, "The Director-Unit System," 125; Juan Antonio Ramírez, *Architecture for the Screen: A Critical Study of Set Design in Hollywood's Golden Age*, trans. John F. Moffitt (Jefferson, NC: McFarland, 2004), 16–21.

6. Barry Salt, *Film Style and Technology: History and Analysis* (London: Starwood, 1992), 210; Mark Shiel, *Hollywood Cinema and the Real Los Angeles* (London: Reaktion, 2012), 163.

7. Dorothy B. Jones, "Hollywood's International Relations," *Quarterly of Film Radio and Television* 11, no. 4 (Summer 1957): 370.

8. Harold Hecht, "Locationing Is Broadening," *Hollywood Reporter: Twenty-Fourth Anniversary Issue*, November 12, 1954, section IV. Other variations of this saying existed.

9. William Lafferty, "A Reappraisal of the Semi-Documentary in Hollywood, 1945–1948," *Velvet Light Trap* no. 20 (Summer 1983): 22–26; Sheri Chinen Biesen, *Blackout: World War II and the Origins of Film Noir* (Baltimore: Johns Hopkins University Press, 2005).

10. David Bordwell, "Deep-Focus Cinematography," in *The Classical Hollywood Cinema*, 349–50; Barry Salt, *Film Style and Technology*, 229–30, 241–45; Thomas Schatz, *Boom and Bust: American Cinema in the 1940s* (Berkeley: University of California Press, 1997), 333.

11. "$640,000 Saved on Location Shots for 8 Films," *Daily Variety*, November 29, 1948, 16.

12. "20th Filming 'Fox' Here, Not Africa; Economy Move," *Daily Variety*, December 20, 1950, 2.

13. Thomas Schatz, *Boom and Bust*, 379–81; Andrew Tracy, "Documentary and Democracy in *Boomerang!* and *Panic in the Streets*," and Patrick Keating, "Elia Kazan and the Semidocumentary: Composing Urban Space," in *Kazan Revisited*, ed. Lisa Dombrowski (Middletown, CT: Wesleyan University Press, 2011), 133–62.

14. Herb A. Lightman, "New Horizons for the Documentary Film," *American Cinematographer*, December 1945, 442.

15. James Agee, "The New Pictures," *Time*, September 15, 1947, 103.

16. For the value of using proximate causal contexts as a framework for studying production and film style, see David Bordwell, Janet Staiger, and Kristin Thompson, *The Classical Hollywood Cinema*, especially "Preface" and the "Technology, Style, and Mode of Production" chapter.

17. "Zanuck Sees Actual Locale Lensing as B.O. Stimulant and TV Antidote," *Daily Variety*, July 19, 1951, 1, 4.

18. "Irving Allen Opines H'wood's Future Lies in Int'l Production," *Daily Variety*, January 6, 1954, 3.

19. In a publication of the Society of Motion Picture Art Directors, an article on *The Desert Fox* discusses the need to seamlessly match studio work with foreign

locales, which "were known from the personal experiences of millions of American Servicemen, the British Commonwealth, and to both German and French audiences." Herman Blumenthal, "'Desert Fox': Maurice Ransford, Art Director," *Production Design*, October 1951, 14.

20. John Alton, *Painting with Light* (1949; repr., Berkeley: University of California Press, 1995), 69.

21. William Perlberg, "What Do You Mean? Run-Away Production!," *Journal of the Screen Producers Guild* 6, no. 7 (December 1960): 7.

22. Irving Bernstein, *Hollywood at the Crossroads* (Hollywood: American Federation of Labor Film Council, 1957), 48.

23. Irving Bernstein, *Hollywood at the Crossroads*, 49–50.

24. Peter Lev, *The Fifties: Transforming the Screen 1950–1959* (Berkeley: University of California Press, 2003), 150. Another study in turn relied on Lev's use of Bernstein's data; see Toby Miller, Nitin Govil, John McMurria, Richard Maxwell, and Ting Wang, *Global Hollywood 2* (London: BFI, 2005), 133.

25. Bernstein defines an "American-interest" film as "a picture financed in whole or in part by American money (perhaps money earned by a U.S. company in a foreign country) and produced by an American company; but the labor that produces it is foreign, with the frequent exception of the director and two or three leading actors, and the film is shot in a foreign country." Irving Bernstein, *Hollywood at the Crossroads*, 48.

26. Murray Schumach, "Paramount Gives Hollywood Hope," *New York Times*, September 25, 1962, 32.

27. But already by 1964, this committee was dissolved. Camille K. Yale, "Runaway Film Production: A Critical History of Hollywood's Outsourcing Discourse" (PhD diss., University of Illinois at Urbana-Champaign, 2010), 102–3.

28. For summaries of these reasons see Murray Schumach, "Hollywood Sees a Rise in Filming," *New York Times*, October 8, 1962, 18; "'Back to Hollywood' Upbeat," *Film Daily*, October 17, 1962, 1, 4; Stanley W. Penn, "Back to Hollywood: Movie Makers Produce More Films in the U.S. as Foreign Costs Rise," *Wall Street Journal*, November 6, 1962, 1.

29. Dale Olson, "Campaigning in Studio, Brown Hits 'Runaway' (Natch)," *Daily Variety*, October 18, 1962, 3.

30. Camille K. Yale, "Runaway Film Production," 104.

31. "SEG's 'Greatest' Victory in 'Runaway' Fight," *Daily Variety*, May 16, 1962, 1, 7; "AFL-CIO Helps Sell 'Spartacus' Tix as Part of Its 'Runaway' Campaign," *Daily Variety*, January 18, 1961, 3.

32. Quoted in Dale Olson, "Campaigning in Studio, Brown Hits 'Runaway' (Natch)," *Daily Variety*, October 18, 1962, 3. However, the French press decried the film's back-lot Paris. Antoine De Baecque, ed., *Paris by Hollywood* (Paris: Flammarion, 2012), 189.

33. Murray Schumach, "Hollywood Sees a Rise in Filming," *New York Times*, October 8, 1962, 18.

34. Murray Schumach, "Actors to Waive Salary Increase," *New York Times*, November 13, 1962, 43. Nonetheless, certain producers, such as Stanley Kramer,

argued that it was not union wages that helped keep production overseas but the high salaries of stars. See Art Ryon, "Kramer Says Producers Can Blame Themselves for Rising Film Costs," *Los Angeles Times*, November 14, 1962, A1.

35. Thomas Guback, *The International Film Industry: Western Europe and America since 1945* (Bloomington: Indiana University Press, 1969), 171.

36. Thomas Guback, *The International Film Industry*, 176–78.

37. Murray Schumach, "Producer Fears Hollywood Doom," *New York Times*, February 8, 1962, 22. After being blacklisted in Hollywood, Foreman fled to England, where he resided through the 1950s and 1960s. For more on Foreman and other Hollywood exiles see Rebecca Prime, *Hollywood Exiles in Europe: The Blacklist and Cold War Film Culture* (New Brunswick, NJ: Rutgers University Press, 2014); Rebecca Prime, "'The Old Bogey': The Hollywood Blacklist in Europe," *Film History* 20, no. 4 (2008): 474–86; Larry Ceplair and Steven Englund, *The Inquisition in Hollywood: Politics in the Film Community, 1930–1960* (Urbana: University of Illinois Press, 2003), 396–425.

38. Nathan Golden, the chief of the Department of Commerce's Motion Picture Division, had pointed out this risk early on. "New Rival in Europe Is Seen," *Daily Variety*, September 13, 1949, 8; "Golden Says Prod Abroad Suicidal," *Hollywood Reporter*, September 13, 1949, 1, 5.

39. Tino Balio, *The Foreign Film Renaissance on American Screens, 1946–1973* (Madison: University of Wisconsin Press, 2010).

40. Peter Lev, *The Euro-American Cinema* (Austin: University of Texas Press, 1993).

41. Irving Bernstein, *Hollywood at the Crossroads*; Thomas Guback, *The International Film Industry*; Peter Lev, *The Fifties*.

42. Kristin Thompson, *Exporting Entertainment: America in the World Film Market 1907–34* (London: BFI, 1985).

43. Ruth Vasey, *The World According to Hollywood, 1918–1939* (Madison: University of Wisconsin Press, 1997).

44. Douglas Gomery, *The Hollywood Studio System: A History* (London: BFI, 2005), 178–83; John Trumpbour, *Selling Hollywood to the World: U.S. and European Struggles for Mastery of the Global Film Industry, 1920–1950* (Cambridge, England: Cambridge University Press, 2002); Ian Jarvie, *Hollywood Overseas Campaign: The North Atlantic Movie Trade, 1920–1950* (Cambridge, England: Cambridge University Press, 1992).

45. One proponent of internationalism in understanding international history is Akira Iriye. See his *Global Community: The Role of International Organizations in the Making of the Contemporary World* (Berkeley: University of California Press, 2002).

46. In *The International Film Industry*, Thomas Guback studies how the United States used film to strengthen its cultural and economic domination overseas in the postwar era. Similar assessments are made in David W. Ellwood and Rob Kroes, eds., *Hollywood in Europe: Experience of Cultural Hegemony* (Amsterdam: VU University Press, 1994); Victoria de Grazia, "Mass Culture and Sovereignty: The

American Challenge to European Cinema, 1920–1960," *Journal of Modern History* 61, no. 1 (March 1989): 53–87.

47. Peter Lev, *The Euro-American Cinema*; Geoffrey Nowell-Smith and Steven Ricci, *Hollywood and Europe: Economics, Culture, National Identity, 1945–95* (London: BFI, 1998); Giuliana Muscio, "Invasion and Counterattack: Italian and American Film Relations in the Postwar Period," in *"Here, There and Everywhere": The Foreign Politics of Popular Culture*, ed. Reinhold Wagnleitner and Elaine Tyler May (Hanover, NH: University Press of New England, 2000), 116–31; Vanessa Schwartz, *It's So French! Hollywood, Paris, and the Making of Cosmopolitan Film Culture* (Chicago: University of Chicago Press, 2007); Ken Provencher, "Bizarre Beauty: 1950s Runaway Production in Japan," *Velvet Light Trap* no. 73 (Spring 2014): 39–50.

48. The ongoing globalization of Hollywood and contemporary runaway productions are examined in Toby Miller et al., *Global Hollywood 2*; Greg Elmer and Mike Gasher, eds., *Contracting Out Hollywood: Runaway Productions and Foreign Location Shooting* (Lanham, MD: Rowman and Littlefield, 2005); Ben Goldsmith and Tom O'Regan, *The Film Studio: Film Production in the Global Economy* (Lanham, MD: Rowman and Littlefield, 2005); Janet Wasko and Mary Erickson, eds., *Cross-Border Cultural Production: Economic Runaway or Globalization?* (Amherst, NY: Cambria, 2008); Courtney Brannon Donoghue, *Localising Hollywood* (London: BFI, 2017).

49. Elizabeth Ezra and Terry Rowden, eds., *Transnational Cinema, The Film Reader* (London: Routledge, 2006); Will Higbee and Song Hwee Lim, "Concepts of Transnational Cinema: Towards a Critical Transnationalism in Film Studies," *Transnational Cinemas* 1, no. 1 (2010): 7–21.

50. John Thornton Caldwell, *Production Culture: Industrial Reflexivity and Critical Practice in Film and Television* (Durham, NC: Duke University Press, 2008); Vicki Mayer, Miranda J. Banks, and John T. Caldwell, eds., *Production Studies: Cultural Studies of Media Industries* (New York: Routledge, 2009); Petr Szczepanik and Patrick Vonderau, eds., *Behind the Screen: Inside European Production Cultures* (New York: Palgrave, 2013); Miranda Banks, Bridget Conor, and Vicki Mayer, eds., *Production Studies, The Sequel!: Cultural Studies of Global Media Industries* (New York: Routledge, 2015).

51. Other studies that take what I consider a transcultural approach to film industries include Vanessa Schwartz, *It's So French!*; Ben Goldsmith, Susan Ward, and Tom O'Regan, *Local Hollywood: Global Film Production and the Gold Coast* (St. Lucia: University of Queensland Press, 2010); Nitin Govil, *Orienting Hollywood: A Century of Film Culture between Los Angeles and Bombay* (New York: New York University Press, 2015).

52. Vicki Mayer, *Below the Line: Producers and Production Studies in the New Television Economy* (Durham, NC: Duke University Press, 2011); Erin Hill, *Never Done: A History of Women's Work in Media Production* (New Brunswick, NJ: Rutgers University Press, 2016).

53. Peter Lev, *The Fifties*; John Belton, *Widescreen Cinema* (Cambridge, MA: Harvard University Press, 1992).

54. Vanessa Schwartz, *It's So French!*; Robert R. Shandley, *Runaway Romances: Hollywood's Postwar Tour of Europe* (Philadelphia: Temple University Press, 2009); Barton Palmer, *Shot on Location: Postwar American Cinema and the Exploration of Real Place* (New Brunswick, NJ: Rutgers University Press, 2016).

55. David Bordwell, Janet Staiger, and Kristin Thompson, *The Classical Hollywood Cinema*; Scott Higgins, *Harnessing the Technicolor Rainbow: Color Design in the 1930s* (Austin: University of Texas Press, 2007); Patrick Keating, *Hollywood Lighting from the Silent Era to Film Noir* (New York: Columbia University Press, 2010).

56. For the benefit of norms as a concept see David Bordwell, "An Excessively Obvious Cinema," in *The Classical Hollywood Cinema*, 3–11.

1. ALL THE WORLD'S A STUDIO: THE DESIGN AND DEBATES OF POSTWAR "RUNAWAY" PRODUCTIONS

1. "Hollywood Goes to Rome," *Collier's*, March 6, 1948, 18–19.

2. "Hollywood in Italy," *New York Times Magazine*, September 25, 1949, 24–25.

3. "Hollywood Now Reigns over Vast International Domain," *Los Angeles Times*, January 2, 1953, E130.

4. "Hollywood Studio—The World," *New York Times*, January 4, 1953, SM18.

5. "Metro Will Shoot Five Pix on Far Away Locations," *Daily Variety*, June 21, 1948, 9; "Zanuck Talks of Big Prod'n Abroad," *Daily Variety*, August 30, 1948, 12; "California Solons Fite Quota," *Daily Variety*, March 31, 1949, 5.

6. "SAG Beef Is Planned on Foreigners," *Daily Variety*, April 6, 1949, 1, 6.

7. "Zanuck Delays His Return to H'wood," *Daily Variety*, September 12, 1949, 1, 2.

8. "'Runaway' Boycott before AFL Council," *Hollywood Reporter*, September 26, 1949, 3; "AFL Report on Pix Abroad Is Delayed," *Daily Variety*, September 27, 1949, 2.

9. This was an argument made by the labor-management coalition the Motion Picture Industry Council. "Pressures Induce O'Seas Prod'n," *Daily Variety*, December 11, 1953, 1, 8.

10. A. H. Allen, "Mirrors of Motordom," *Steel*, February 8, 1943, 67–68.

11. Edwin Niederberger, "The Aggressor: Inflation," *America*, May 18, 1946, 133; "Ties Future to Economics," *Motion Picture Daily*, November 14, 1946, 24.

12. The article states that overseas filming "long has been dubbed 'runaway' production by laborites." But this seems to be one of the first mentions of the term in the film trades. "AFL Council to Ask Gov't Act on Films Made Abroad," *Hollywood Reporter*, February 15, 1949, 14.

13. "AFL Council Moves vs. Overseas Prod.," *Motion Picture Daily*, September 26, 1949, 1, 5; "AFL Report on Pix Abroad Is Delayed," *Daily Variety*, September 27, 1949, 2.

14. Ben Pearse, "How the Movies Get Their Money out of Europe," *Saturday Evening Post*, November 27, 1954, 43; Thomas Guback, *The International Film*

Industry: Western Europe and America since 1945 (Bloomington: Indiana University Press, 1969), 120–21.

15. "Activities Abroad of the Motion Picture Association of America," March 17, 1953, Italy Motion Pictures (1950–1955), State Department Records, National Archives and Records Administration, College Park, Maryland (hereafter NARA).

16. "Activities Abroad of the Motion Picture Association of America."

17. "Leo's Foreign Biz Perks," *Daily Variety*, February 10, 1949, 1, 5.

18. Thomas Guback, *The International Film Industry*, 121–22.

19. "Majors Use Iced Coin to Expand," *Daily Variety*, February 25, 1948, 1, 13.

20. "Lesser Learns 'Tarzans' Can Be Lensed More Profitably Here Than in Africa," *Daily Variety*, June 18, 1951, 4.

21. "20th Buys Story with Iced Coin," *Daily Variety*, April 27, 1949, 1; "Metro Buys Thriller with Iced Money," *Daily Variety*, May 25, 1949, 1.

22. W. N. Walmsley Jr. to the secretary of state, June 11, 1949, Italy Motion Pictures (1945–1949), State Department Records, NARA; David Forgacs and Stephen Gundle, *Mass Culture and Italian Society from Fascism to the Cold War* (Bloomington: Indiana University Press, 2007), 137.

23. Ben Pearse, "How the Movies Get Their Money out of Europe," *Saturday Evening Post*, November 27, 1954, 43.

24. "Tax Deal Big U.S. Victory," *Daily Variety*, March 12, 1948, 1, 6.

25. Various cables and correspondence, August 1947, Great Britain Motion Pictures (1945–1949), State Department Records, NARA.

26. "No Bundles for Britain," *Daily Variety*, August 11, 1947, 1; "'Wait and See' Stand Taken by Movie Industry," *Los Angeles Times*, August 13, 1947, 7; "Three More UA Prods Halting Pix Because of British Tax," *Daily Variety*, August 15, 1947, 1; Thomas F. Brady, "British Tax Frightens Hollywood," *New York Times*, August 17, 1947, 59.

27. "Memorandum of Agreement between His Majesty's Government in the United Kingdom of Great Britain and Northern Ireland and the Motion Picture Industry of the United States of America dated 11th March, 1948" (London: His Majesty's Stationery Office, 1948). Trade press coverage of the deal can be found in "Cash Deal with Britain," *Daily Variety*, March 11, 1948, 1, 10. The agreement would be renewed and modified in the coming years. See Sue Harper and Vincent Porter, *British Cinema of the 1950s: The Decline of Deference* (Oxford: Oxford University Press, 2003), 5–6.

28. "Memorandum of Agreement," 5–7.

29. "Majors Due for Heavy Production in England," *Daily Variety*, March 12, 1948, 6.

30. "Hollywood Indies in Rush to Get British Stage Space," *Daily Variety*, March 24, 1948, 1, 6.

31. The frozen reserves would replenish once Fox started earning more abroad. "20th Thaws $10 Million," *Daily Variety*, October 6, 1949, 1, 8.

32. Frank McCarthy, "Italy: General Situation," 1947; W. N. Walmsley Jr. to the secretary of state, September 23, 1947, both in Italy Motion Pictures (1945–1949), State Department Records, NARA.

33. Harold L. Smith, press release, January 4, 1947, France Motion Pictures (1945–1949), State Department Records, NARA.

34. US Embassy in Paris to the secretary of state, August 11, 1948, France Motion Pictures (1945–1949), State Department Records, NARA.

35. In Italy, SIMPP was part of early postwar Italian-US film accords, but then left out of a 1954 agreement between the MPEA and the Associazione Nazionale Industrie Cinematografiche e Affini. See correspondence from SIMPP president Ellis Arnall to Renato Gualino, October 6, 1954, Italy Motion Pictures (1950–1955), State Department Records, NARA.

36. "UA Seeking Gov't Loan in Britain," *Daily Variety*, November 2, 1948, 1, 7.

37. "Kramer Suggests Indie Pool on Pix in Britain," *Daily Variety*, March 26, 1948, 8.

38. "Kramer Advised to De-Ice Funds in England," *Daily Variety*, November 2, 1949, 15; "Kramer Buys 'De Bergerac' with Frozen British Coin," *Daily Variety*, November 9, 1949, 3.

39. "Group Talks to Truman on British Film Barrier," *Los Angeles Times*, April 2, 1949, 3; Camille K. Yale, "Runaway Film Production: A Critical History of Hollywood's Outsourcing Discourse" (PhD diss., University of Illinois at Urbana-Champaign, 2010), 48–59.

40. Camille K. Yale, "Runaway Film Production," 56–57.

41. "Hearings before the Subcommittee on the Impact of Imports and Exports on American Employment of the Committee on Education and Labor House of Representatives, 87th Congress, 1st and 2nd Sessions" (Washington, DC: United States Congress, 1962), 473.

42. Quoted in "Roy Brewer Explains IA's 'Runaway' Pix Complaint," *Hollywood Reporter*, February 2, 1953, 8.

43. "U.S. Film Biz in Europe Is Up 15 Percent; Coin Is Easier," *Daily Variety*, November 4, 1949, 1; "H'Wood out of Deep Freeze," *Daily Variety*, April 12, 1950, 1, 11. One article proposed that increased tourism helped unfreeze earnings by improving local economies: "Hot U.S. Tourist Biz Abroad May Thaw Pix Coin," *Daily Variety*, May 19, 1955, 3.

44. Thomas Guback, *The International Film Industry*, 166.

45. "La Loi d'aide temporaire au cinéma," *La Technique Cinématographique*, September 2, 1948, 364 ; Colin Crisp, *The Classic French Cinema, 1930–1960* (Bloomington: Indiana University Press, 1993), 77; "Eady Plan Will Yield H'Wood $5,000,000," *Daily Variety*, August 6, 1951, 2. See also Thomas Guback, *The International Film Industry*, 165–66.

46. Frank McCarthy, "Italy: General Situation," 1947, Italy Motion Pictures (1945–1949), State Department Records, NARA.

47. E. Jan Nadelman to the Department of State, March 3, 1950, Italy Motion Pictures (1950–1954), State Department Records, NARA.

48. Rebecca Prime, *Hollywood Exiles in Europe: The Blacklist and Cold War Film Culture* (New Brunswick, NJ: Rutgers University Press, 2014), 40.

49. Robert B. Parke to the Department of State, July 5, 1957, Great Britain Motion Pictures (1955–1959), State Department Records, NARA; W. P. Robinson, "The American Producer in England," in *Syllabus and Forms on American Motion Picture Production in Foreign Countries* (Los Angeles: Beverly Hills Bar Association and USC School of Law, May 9, 1959), 1–2; Sue Harper and Vincent Porter, *British Cinema of the 1950s*, 30.

50. "'Not Cheaper to Shoot Abroad, but Financing Easier': Cohen," *Daily Variety*, October 5, 1962, 1, 4.

51. Christopher Brunel, "Who Benefits from the Eady Plan?," *Cine-Technician*, November–December 1952, 144; "Briton Blast U.S. Producer Eady Plan Use," *Daily Variety*, July 9, 1958, 2.

52. F. W. Allport to Ralph D. Hetzel, March 27, 1956, Great Britain Motion Pictures (1955–1959), State Department Records, NARA. Several months later, Davis seemed to reverse his position by expressing his support of Hollywood's interests in the British industry. See Robert B. Parke to the Department of State, August 24, 1956, Great Britain Motion Pictures (1955–1959), State Department Records, NARA.

53. Charles Frank, "The Case for Co-Productions," *Film and TV Technician*, April 1957, 56.

54. "Entertainment Motion Pictures—35mm—United Kingdom," January 15, 1951, Great Britain Motion Pictures (1950–1954), State Department Records, NARA.

55. "SAG Charges Pressure by O'Sea Gov'ts," *Daily Variety*, November 25, 1953, 1, 9.

56. "AFL Council Asks U.S. Eady Plan," *Daily Variety*, April 7, 1958, 1, 4.

57. Dale Olson, "Campaigning in Studio, Brown Hits 'Runaway' (Natch)," *Daily Variety*, October 18, 1962, 3.

58. "House Unit Sees 'Runaways' Linked to Foreign Subsidies," *Motion Picture Herald*, June 13, 1962, 15.

59. For an overview of the hearings see Camille K. Yale, "Runaway Film Production," 89–100.

60. For information on the French and Italian subsidies see Tino Balio, *United Artists: The Company That Changed the Film Industry* (Madison: University of Wisconsin Press, 1987), 276–78, 282–84.

61. Thomas Guback, *The International Film Industry*, 167.

62. Thomas Guback, *The International Film Industry*, 167; F. W. Allport to Eric Johnston, September 24, 1946, Great Britain Motion Pictures (1945–1949), State Department Records, NARA; Jonathan Stubbs, "'Blocked' Currency, Runaway Production in Britain and *Captain Horatio Hornblower* (1951)," *Historical Journal of Film, Radio and Television* 28, no. 3 (August 2008): 342.

63. "King Bros. Form Prod'n Companies in England, Italy to Duck Quotas," *Daily Variety*, September 5, 1952, 1, 4. It is unclear if the King Brothers ever produced films through these subsidiaries.

64. Thomas Guback, *The International Film Industry*, 167–68.

65. "Eady Moves near Tie with France and Italy: Karp," *Daily Variety*, May 26, 1961, 1, 4; "MGM Forms French Firm with Bar," *Daily Variety*, December 21, 1960, 32.

66. Peter Lev, *The Euro-American Cinema* (Austin: University of Texas Press, 1993), 24; Tino Balio, *United Artists*, 279–82.

67. Gianni Manca, "Certain Relevant Aspects of the Production of Films in Italy by Foreign Producers," in *Syllabus and Forms on American Motion Picture Production in Foreign Countries*, 12.

68. John F. L. Ghiardi to J. M. Colton Hand, November 25, 1957, Italy Motion Pictures (1955–1959), State Department Records, NARA.

69. Tim Bergfelder, "The Nation Vanishes: European Co-Productions and Popular Genre Formula in the 1950s and 1960s," in *Cinema and Nation*, ed. Mette Hjort and Scott MacKenzie (New York: Routledge, 2002), 139–52.

70. Peter Lev, *The Fifties: Transforming the Screen 1950–1959* (Berkeley: University of California Press, 2003), 154. For an overview of France's coproduction requirements see "La réglementation des co-productions avec l'étranger," *La Technique Cinématographique*, October 21, 1948, 417.

71. Edwin Schallert, "International Picture Plans Enlarging; Movie Set Building Downtown," *Los Angeles Times*, November 21, 1949, B9.

72. Rebecca Prime, *Hollywood Exiles in Europe*, 40–41, 44–45.

73. "Joint Int'l Production Looks Set to Stay, Sez French Producer Sarrut," *Variety*, July 26, 1950, 19.

74. "Selznick and Korda Pair Up," *Daily Variety*, May 18, 1948, 4.

75. "20th Closes Deal for French Pictures by Graetz," *Daily Variety*, December 28, 1948, 1, 9.

76. "Par Will Co-Produce Pix in Italy," *Daily Variety*, December 5, 1952, 1, 9; "Ponti, de Laurentiis Here for Par Parley," *Daily Variety*, October 5, 1953, 2.

77. Tino Balio, *United Artists*, chapters 7–9; Tino Balio, *The Foreign Film Renaissance on American Screens, 1946–1973* (Madison: University of Wisconsin Press, 2010), chapter 12.

78. Gerry Blattner to R. J. Obringer, March 22, 1951; F. W. Witt. to Gerry Blattner, May 21, 1951; Gerry Blattner to Steve Trilling, August 31, 1951, *The Crimson Pirate* (Steve Trilling Files), Warner Bros. Archive, University of Southern California, Los Angeles (hereafter Warner Archive).

79. Gerry Blattner to Steve Trilling, January 12, 1952, *The Crimson Pirate* (Steve Trilling Files), Warner Archive.

80. The TMZ is an area with a thirty-mile radius centered at the intersection of Beverly and La Cienega Boulevards, the original headquarters of the Association of Motion Picture and Television Producers. Film unions have used this zone to calculate pay rates and driving distances. Allen J. Scott, *On Hollywood: The Place, The Industry* (Princeton, NJ: Princeton University Press, 2005), 124–25.

81. Vincent Porter, "All Change at Elstree: Warner Bros., ABPC and British Film Policy, 1945–1961," *Historical Journal of Film, Radio and Television* 21, no. 1 (2001): 5–35.

82. "Disney's 'Treasure' Qualifies under British Quota," *Daily Variety*, April 26, 1949, 5; "Bobby Driscoll Pays, but with Shaved Coin," *Daily Variety*, October 26, 1949, 8.

83. Gene Moskowitz, "In Paris," *Daily Variety*, October 16, 1956, 3.

84. "Tie 'Runaway' to Gold Standard," *Daily Variety*, January 10, 1961, 1, 14; "Resolution on Runaway Production," February 9, 1961, Hollywood AFL Film Council File, AMPTP Records, Margaret Herrick Library, Academy of Motion Picture Arts and Sciences, Beverly Hills (hereafter AMPAS Library).

85. Studio Hamburg advertisement, *Daily Variety*, July 13, 1962, 5.

86. Throughout this book I attempt to use the historical names of countries where Hollywood films were shot. At times, these names refer to European colonies. The goal is not only to evoke the historical context of the filming locations but to also highlight the complex and troubling realities that Hollywood productions were working in and sometimes exploiting.

87. "'Black Rose' Leaves Morocco for London," *Daily Variety*, June 17, 1949, 10; "'Black Rose' on British Bandwagon," *Daily Variety*, November 15, 1949, 3.

88. Harold Myers, "Col, Foreman Forego Eady 'Victors' Coin," *Daily Variety*, December 3, 1962, 1, 4.

89. Sylvette Baudrot and Isabel Salvani, *La Script-Girl* (Paris: La Femis, 1989), 80; Sylvette Baudrot, interview with author, December 18, 2010, Paris.

90. "'It's Better in U.S.'—Welles," *Daily Variety*, April 3, 1956, 1, 11.

91. "Resolution on Runaway Production," February 9, 1961, Hollywood AFL Film Council File, AMPTP Papers, AMPAS Library.

92. "AFL Gets 'Tough' on Runaway Pix," *Daily Variety*, April 6, 1955, 1, 4; "Lensers Demand H'wood Crews on U.S.-Originated Pix O'Seas," *Daily Variety*, March 21, 1958, 6.

93. "AFL May Ask Label on Foreign-Made Pix," *Daily Variety*, March 21, 1950, 3.

94. Hollywood AFL Film Council release, July 28 [possibly 1952], Hollywood AFL Film Council File, AMPTP Papers, AMPAS Library.

95. "State Labor OK's 'Runaway' Label," *Daily Variety*, August 14, 1959, 1, 4.

96. "AFL-Pushed Bill to Tag Foreign Pix Appears Doomed," *Daily Variety*, April 8, 1960, 1, 4; William Ornstein, "IA Plugs 'Made In' Tag for Pix," *Daily Variety*, April 18, 1962, 1, 15.

97. Roger Cantagrel, "Les communistes regentent-ils le cinéma français?," *Le Figaro*, February 15, 1952, 6.

98. Buck Harris, Hollywood AFL Film Council release, March 31, 1959, Hollywood AFL Film Council File, AMPTP Papers, AMPAS Library.

99. "Hollywood Unionists See 'Red' in All-Out Rage over Runaway Subsidy," *Variety*, October 24, 1962, 26.

100. "Awake, America!" pamphlet, n.d., Hollywood AFL Film Council File, AMPTP Records, AMPAS Library.

101. Camille K. Yale, "Runaway Film Production," 59–61.

102. Rebecca Prime, *Hollywood Exiles in Europe*, 59–82; Rebecca Prime, "'The Old Bogey': The Hollywood Blacklist in Europe," *Film History* 20, no. 4 (2008): 474–86.

103. The process for importing foreign actors to the United States was not simple. A US film company had to file a McCarran-Walter Act Petition with the Immigration and Naturalization Service, whose approval was then forwarded to the State Department and the foreign US Embassy or Consulate for the allocation of visas. The procedure is explained in Max L. Raskoff to Herbert Coleman, April 22, 1955, *The Man Who Knew Too Much* (Herbie Coleman), Alfred Hitchcock Papers, AMPAS Library.

104. "Roy Brewer Explains IA's 'Runaway' Pix Complaint," *Hollywood Reporter*, February 2, 1953, 8.

105. Al St. Hilaire, "To Runaway or Not," *International Photographer*, January 1962, 17.

106. Robert Surtees, "Location Filming in Africa For 'King Solomon's Mines,'" *American Cinematographer*, April 1950, 122–23, 136.

107. "Small Is Making 'Cagliostro' Adds," *Daily Variety*, May 21, 1948, 1.

108. Roger Corman examines the pros and cons of shooting a mid-budget production abroad in "Foreign Production for the Medium-Budget Producer," *Journal of the Screen Producers Guild* 6, no. 7 (December 1960): 19–20, 30.

109. Quoted in Antoine De Baecque, ed., *Paris by Hollywood* (Paris: Flammarion, 2012), 11.

110. Ruth Vasey, *The World According to Hollywood, 1918–1939* (Madison: University of Wisconsin Press, 1997), 116–18.

111. "Sam Zimbalist Cites 'Quo' as Costliest Yet; 300,000 Cast," *Daily Variety*, November 28, 1950, 1, 3.

112. Quoted in "Plan to Make 'Cleo' in England 'Idiotic' Says Mankiewicz," *Daily Variety*, April 24, 1961, 1, 10.

113. Darryl F. Zanuck, "Shoot It Where You Find It," *Journal of the Screen Producers Guild* 6, no. 7 (December 1960): 5, 31.

114. "Pressures Induce O'Seas Prod'n," *Daily Variety*, December 11, 1953, 1, 8.

115. "Resolution on Runaway Production," February 9, 1961, Hollywood AFL Film Council File, AMPTP Papers, AMPAS Library.

116. "20th's Foreign Sked Big," *Daily Variety*, October 25, 1948, 1, 11; "20th's European Story Ed Huddles with Zanuck," *Daily Variety*, December 1, 1954, 2.

117. "MGM's MacKenna to Scour Europe for Film Yarns," *Daily Variety*, September 29, 1955, 12.

118. "Billy Wilder en Route," *Daily Variety*, June 25, 1948, 1; "Wilder Off to Deepest Europe on Yarn-Hunt," *Daily Variety*, November 8, 1950, 10; "Wallis Hunts Tale for British Pic," *Daily Variety*, January 3, 1950, 2; "Hornblow to Paris," *Daily Variety*, April 25, 1950, 2; "Sol Lesser Back from Europe; Preps 'Tarzan and Vampire,'" *Daily Variety*, July 29, 1952, 2.

119. Neal Moses Rosendorf, "'Hollywood in Madrid': American Film Producers and the Franco Regime, 1950–1970," *Historical Journal of Film, Radio and Television* 27, no. 1 (March 2007): 77–109.

120. See correspondence in *The Inn of the Sixth Happiness*, Twentieth Century-Fox Production Files and Mark Robson Papers, Performing Arts Special Collections, UCLA, Los Angeles; Fox press release, *The Inn of the Sixth Happiness* (clipping file), AMPAS Library.

121. "The Story behind the Ban" press release, *The Roman Spring of Mrs. Stone* (press releases), Warner Archive.

122. William Ornstein, "'Runaway' Issue Boils at IA Meet," *Daily Variety*, September 13, 1962, 1, 4.

123. Kirk Douglas, "All Roads Lead to ... Hollywood," *Journal of the Screen Producers Guild* 6, no. 7 (December 1960): 5.

124. AFL advertisement, *Daily Variety*, July 8, 1960, 7. Neal Rosendorf suggests that the majority of the *Spartacus* shoot took place in the United States because the story's proletarian hero did not sit well with the Franco dictatorship, which prompted the production to film its less controversial scenes in Spain. Neal Moses Rosendorf, "'Hollywood in Madrid,'" 87–88. Also, while Douglas publicly supported domestic shooting for productions that did not need authentic foreign locations, he produced the US-British coproduction *The Devil's Disciple* (1959), a film that was set in revolutionary New England but shot in Britain.

125. "AFL-CIO Helps Sell 'Spartacus' Tix as Part of Its 'Runaway' Campaign," *Daily Variety*, January 18, 1961, 3. H. O'Neil Shanks to AFL-CIO unions, February 9, 1961, Hollywood AFL Film Council File, AMPTP Papers, AMPAS Library.

126. Thomas M. Pryor, "'Runaway' Runaround Crisis," *Daily Variety*, November 15, 1961, 4; Thomas M. Pryor, "Many Roads Open to 'Runaway' Trend; All Lead to Dead-End for H'wood," *Daily Variety*, November 16, 1961, 4.

127. "SEG's 'Greatest' Victory in 'Runaway' Fight," *Daily Variety*, May 16, 1962, 1, 7.

128. "'Sitting Bull' Filming in Mexico Is Protested," *Hollywood Reporter*, February 17, 1954, 3; "IATSE Local Stirs up Sioux to Protest Shooting of 'Sitting Bull' in Mexico," *Daily Variety*, February 23, 1954, 1, 3; "Bob Goldstein May Save Scalp of 'Sitting Bull,'" *Daily Variety*, February 23, 1954, 1, 3.

129. "Ask AFL-CIO Boycott of 'Dan Boone,'" *Daily Variety*, March 29, 1956, 1, 2.

130. "2 Producers Blast Unions on 'Unfair' Runaway Charge," *Hollywood Reporter*, August 16, 1955, 11. Gannaway eventually signed a collective bargaining contract with studio unions. See "AFL Lifts Its Boycott off 'Boone,'" *Daily Variety*, April 26, 1956, 1, 4.

131. Quoted in "2 Producers Blast Unions on 'Unfair' Runaway Charge," *Hollywood Reporter*, August 16, 1955, 11.

132. "AFL Boycott over 'Jones' Threatened," *Daily Variety*, March 31, 1958, 1, 4.

133. "'Jones' Not Filming U.S. Scenes O'seas, Bronston Aide Says," *Daily Variety*, April 1, 1958, 4.

134. "Bronston Bows to Film Council; Filming 'Jones' Partly in U.S.," *Daily Variety*, April 21, 1958, 1, 3.

135. "Film Council Seeks to Oust Herb Aller," *Daily Variety*, June 16, 1958, 1, 4; "Aller 'Subpoenas' Meany for Trial by AFL Film Council," *Daily Variety*, July 7, 1958, 1, 2.

136. Robert J. Landry, "'Runaway': What They Say and Do," *Variety*, November 2, 1960, 4.

137. One *Daily Variety* article proclaimed that certain studios, such as Warner Bros. and Paramount, had to cut back foreign operations because they were short on releases: "20th Lot Sale Brings $57–60 Mil," *Daily Variety*, March 4, 1959, 1, 4.

138. "WB Sells Teddington Studios in London," *Daily Variety*, August 26, 1958, 1; "WB Closing All British Exchanges," *Daily Variety*, March 10, 1958, 1.

139. "MGM Unloading Dubbing Studios in Paris, Rome," *Daily Variety*, February 12, 1958, 3; "MGM's British Studio on Block," *Hollywood Reporter*, March 18, 1958, 1; "Loew's May Hold British Studios," *Daily Variety*, March 25, 1958, 1, 4. MGM did not actually close its British studios until 1970. Patricia Warren, *British Film Studios: An Illustrated History* (London: B. T. Batsford, 2001), 88.

140. "RKO Toppers Meet on Big O'Seas Cuts," *Daily Variety*, February 19, 1958, 2; "RKO O'Seas Admin. Work to Rank Org," *Daily Variety*, March 26, 1958, 1, 18.

141. "Britain Thaws All H'Wood Coin," *Hollywood Reporter*, June 29, 1960, 1, 6.

142. Robert F. Hawkins, "Roamin' in Rome," *Daily Variety*, March 3, 1958, 6; "Italy Dangles Pic Imports to Halt U.S. Co. Layoffs," *Daily Variety*, April 2, 1958, 4.

143. "Record H'wood Prod'n Abroad," *Daily Variety*, April 14, 1960, 1, 4; "'Runaway' Film Prod'n Trend Is Increasing," *Daily Variety*, August 9, 1962, 3; Murray Schumach, "Paramount Gives Hollywood Hope," *New York Times*, September 25, 1962, 32.

144. "20th's British Prod'n Splurge," *Daily Variety*, November 1, 1960, 1, 4.

145. "'Have Talent, Will Travel Retorts Tiomkin to Critics of 'Runaway,'" *Daily Variety*, August 31, 1962, 8; George F. Custen, *Twentieth Century's Fox: Darryl F. Zanuck and the Culture of Hollywood* (New York: Basic Books, 1997), 367.

146. "'Back to Hollywood' Upbeat," *Film Daily*, October 17, 1962, 1, 4.

147. "H'wood Hits Alltime Prod'n Low," *Daily Variety*, December 10, 1962, 1, 4.

148. Daniel Steinhart, "The Making of Hollywood Production: Televising and Visualizing Global Filmmaking in 1960s Promotional Featurettes," *Cinema Journal* 57, no. 4 (Summer 2018): 96–119.

CASE STUDY. TAX EVASION, RED-BAITING, AND THE
WHITE WHALE: *MOBY DICK* (1956)

1. Quoted in Peter S. Greenberg, "Saints and Stinkers: The 'Rolling Stone' Interview," *Rolling Stone*, February 19, 1981, 25.

2. John Huston, "Home Is Where the Heart Is—and So Are Films," *Journal of the Screen Producers Guild* 10, no. 3 (March 1963): 3.

3. John Huston, "Home Is Where the Heart Is," 4.

4. "'Moby Dick' Cruises to $4,100,000 Negative Cost over 18-Month Span," *Daily Variety*, November 3, 1955, 3.

5. John Huston, *An Open Book* (New York: Knopf, 1980), 251.

6. John Huston, *An Open Book*, 163; Thomas Schatz, *The Genius of the System: Hollywood Filmmaking in the Studio Era* (New York: Metropolitan Books, 1996), 434.

7. The film's aspect ratio was 1.66:1 or 1.75:1.

8. "Add Another $1,000,000; Pick Madeira Locale for Huston's 'Moby Dick,'" *Variety*, October 20, 1954, 3, 18.

9. "Moulin-ABC-WB in Deal on 'Moby,'" *Hollywood Reporter*, February 19, 1954, 1.

10. The production is also analyzed in Briton C. Busch, "Fiction, Film, and Fact: John Huston's Trying-out of *Moby Dick*," *American Neptune* 61, no. 4 (2001): 379–95.

11. Quoted in Arthur Knight, "The Director," *Saturday Review*, June 9, 1956, 30.

12. Unsigned (presumably John Huston) to Gregory Peck, September 13, 1954, *Moby Dick* (Gregory Peck), John Huston Papers, Margaret Herrick Library, Academy of Motion Picture Arts and Sciences, Beverly Hills (hereafter AMPAS Library).

13. Huston recalled that some interior work was also done at Shepperton Studios. John Huston, *An Open Book*, 253.

14. Charles Hamblett, "We Solve the 'Moby' Mystery," *Picture Post*, April 21, 1956, 38–41. Hamblett, a dialogue writer along for part of the production, authored a number of press accounts. Warner Bros. press releases, *Moby Dick* (Carbon Press), Warner Bros. Archive, University of Southern California, Los Angeles (hereafter Warner Archive).

15. "Huston Lavishly Lauds Prod'n Facilities Abroad," *Daily Variety*, December 23, 1952, 15. On the British press's treatment of these films as British productions see Paul Holt, "Ha! A Bit of Film Magic!," *Daily Herald*, March 11, 1953, n.p., *Moulin Rouge* clipping file; "New Film Serial 'Beat the Devil,'" *Picture Post*, August 8, 15, and 22, 1953, *Beat the Devil* clipping file, both in the British Film Institute Library, London. Cinematographer Oswald Morris, who began working with the director at the time of *Moulin Rouge*, confirmed that in England these films were considered British in origin. Oswald Morris, interview with author, April 21, 2011, Fontmell Magna, England.

16. Harold Mirisch to John Huston, December 24, 1953, *Moby Dick* (Harold Mirisch), John Huston Papers, AMPAS Library.

17. John Huston to David Harries, November 16, 1954, *Moby Dick* (Correspondence 1947–1954), John Huston Papers, AMPAS Library.

18. Robert Stone, "Report on Las Palmas—Canary Island," *Moby Dick* (Locations), John Huston Papers, AMPAS Library.

19. Unsigned (presumably John Huston) to Alfred Crown, February 15, 1956, *Moby Dick* (Publicity Correspondence), John Huston Papers, AMPAS Library.

20. A similar argument was made for not entering *Moby Dick* into competition at the Venice Film Festival. See Alfred Crown to Lee Katz, August 9, 1956, *Moby Dick* (Correspondence 1955–1972), John Huston Papers, AMPAS Library.

21. Jympson Harman, "Peg-Leg Peck May Be a Jonah," *Evening News*, November 8, 1956, 6D.

22. John Huston recounts these international experiences in *An Open Book*. Huston's military experience is detailed in Mark Harris, *Five Came Back: A Story of Hollywood and the Second World War* (New York: Penguin, 2014).

23. Axel Madsen, *John Huston: A Biography* (Garden City, NY: Doubleday, 1978), 10–11. Jeffrey Meyers also emphasizes Huston's Hemingway-like character in *John Huston: Courage and Art* (New York: Crown Archetype, 2010).

24. John Huston to Morgan Maree, March 13, 1952, Correspondence (Morgan Maree 1952), John Huston Papers, AMPAS Library.

25. "Brewer Lists 21 Names as Seeking Tax-Exempt Assignments Overseas," *Daily Variety*, January 27, 1953, 1, 11.

26. "Pressures Induce O'Seas Prod'n," *Daily Variety*, December 11, 1953, 1, 8; Eric Hoyt, "Hollywood and the Income Tax, 1929–1955," *Film History* 22, no. 1 (2010): 15–16.

27. Morgan Maree to John Huston, February 27, 1952, *Moby Dick* (Morgan Maree 1952), John Huston Papers, AMPAS Library; "Only Huston and Spiegel, of All Filmsters Who Tried, Get 18-Mo. Tax-Free Ride," *Daily Variety*, July 24, 1953, 1, 12.

28. Jeffrey Meyers, *John Huston*, 164.

29. "Ray Bradbury Helping Huston Script 'Moby'," *Daily Variety*, November 25, 1953, 6.

30. Quoted in Eric Hoyt, "Hollywood and the Income Tax, 1929–1955," 16. Original correspondence comes from John Huston to Paul Kohner, October 25, 1955, Correspondence (Paul Kohner 1954–1960), John Huston Papers, AMPAS Library.

31. Ernest Anderson, "Bulletin No. 1 from Youghal, Country Cork, Eire," n.d., *Moby Dick* (Publicity), John Huston Papers, AMPAS Library; Various Warner Bros. press releases, *Moby Dick* (Carbon Press), Warner Archive.

32. Harold J. Mirisch to John Huston, December 4, 1953, *Moby Dick* (Harold Mirisch), John Huston Papers, AMPAS Library.

33. "They're Taking Years off Youghal!," *Times Pictorial*, July 3, 1954, 5; Charles Hamblett, "On Launching 'Moby Dick' in Eire," *New York Times*, August 15, 1954, X5; Jeanie Sims to "The Curator, The Seamen's Bethel in New Bedford," April 29, 1954, *Moby Dick* (Ralph Brinton), John Huston Papers, AMPAS Library.

34. Unsigned (presumably Lorraine Sherwood) to Lee Katz, December 21, 1954; Lee Katz to John Huston, July 5, 1955, *Moby Dick* (Lee Katz), John Huston Papers, AMPAS Library.

35. "Huston Builds Irish Studio for the End," *Daily Mail*, June 2, 1955, *Moby Dick* (Clippings 1952–55), John Huston Papers, AMPAS Library.

36. Larry Ceplair and Steven Englund, *The Inquisition in Hollywood: Politics in the Film Community, 1930–1960* (Urbana: University of Illinois Press, 2003), 275–77; Thomas Schatz, *Boom and Bust: American Cinema in the 1940s* (Berkeley: University of California Press, 1997), 309–11.

37. "We Were Strangers" review, *Hollywood Reporter*, April 22, 1949, 3–4.

38. John Huston, *An Open Book*, 137.

39. "AFL Nixes 'Unfriendly' Pix Project," *Daily Variety*, August 26, 1952, 3; "UA Undetermined on Handling 'Encounter,'" *Daily Variety*, August 27, 1952, 6.

40. "'Wildcat' Legionnaires Picket 'Rouge' Preem," *Daily Variety*, December 23, 1952, 1, 8; "'Moulin Rouge' Premiere Picketed by Legion Men," *Los Angeles Times*, December 24, 1952, 1, 9. The Legion had a practice of picketing cinemas and boycotting films. See Peter Lev, *The Fifties: Transforming the Screen 1950–1959* (Berkeley: University of California Press, 2003), 70–71.

41. "Legion May Lift 'Moulin Rouge' Ban Following Talks with Huston, Ferrer," *Daily Variety*, December 30, 1952, 1, 6.

42. Paul Kohner to John Huston, November 26, 1952, *Moulin Rouge* (Correspondence), John Huston Papers, AMPAS Library.

43. "Am. Legion Commander to Huddle with AMPP; 'Rouge' Rap Mystifies," *Daily Variety*, December 29, 1952, 1, 4.

44. "Brewer Lists 21 Names as Seeking Tax-Exempt Assignments Overseas," *Daily Variety*, January 27, 1953, 1, 11.

45. "AFL Stiffens Attitude on Film Prod'n Abroad," *Daily Variety*, January 21, 1953, 1, 14; "Legion Fights 'Red' Pix Imports," *Daily Variety*, January 22, 1953, 1, 14.

46. For his anti-communist labor campaigns in Europe, Brown was denounced as a CIA agent by the Communist press. Glenn Fowler, "Irving Brown, 77, U.S. Specialist on International Labor Movement," *New York Times*, February 11, 1989, 33.

47. An expense report shows that political leader and ex-Communist turncoat Ignazio Silone was also present at these meetings on January 27 and 28, 1953. See Jeanie Sims to Ron Allday, February 1, 1953, Correspondence (Morgan Maree 1953), John Huston Papers, AMPAS Library.

48. Humphrey Bogart as Told to Joe Hyams, "Movie Making Beats the Devil," *Cue*, November 28, 1953, 14–15.

49. "John Huston Reports Red Film Unions Losing Their Grip in Europe," *Daily Variety*, August 19, 1953, 1, 10.

50. Paul Kohner to John Huston, January 8, 1953, Correspondence (Paul Kohner 1942–1953), John Huston Papers, AMPAS Library; Jeffrey Meyers, *John Huston*, 132–33.

51. Paul Kohner to John Huston, January 29, 1953, Correspondence (Paul Kohner 1942–1953), John Huston Papers, AMPAS Library.

52. "John Huston Buys Film Rights to 'Matador,'" *Daily Variety*, August 21, 1952, 4.

53. Paul Kohner to John Huston, March 26, 1953, Correspondence (Paul Kohner 1942–1953), John Huston Papers, AMPAS Library, emphasis in original.

54. "John Huston Reports Red Film Unions Losing Their Grip in Europe," *Daily Variety*, August 19, 1953, 1.

1. Thomas Schatz, *Boom and Bust: American Cinema in the 1940s* (Berkeley: University of California Press, 1997), 337–38.

2. "Back from France: Real Locations Used for 'To the Victor,'" *New York Times*, September 21, 1947, X3; *To the Victor* review, *Time*, April 19, 1948, 94.

3. Jerry Wald to Delmer Daves, July 25, 1947, *To the Victor*, Warner Bros. Archive, University of Southern California, Los Angeles (hereafter Warner Archive).

4. Jerry Wald to Delmer Daves, August 1, 1947, *To the Victor*, Warner Archive.

5. Jerry Wald to Delmer Daves, July 30, 1947, *To the Victor*, Warner Archive.

6. Delmer Daves to Jerry Wald, July 19, 1947; Jerry Wald to René Clair, July 5, 1947, *To the Victor*, Warner Archive.

7. Jerry Wald to Delmer Daves, August 9, 1947, *To the Victor*, Warner Archive.

8. *Variety* called the film a "major disappointment" in "National Box Office Survey," *Variety*, April 21, 1948, 3. Film critic Bosley Crowther criticized the film as "artificial and contrived" in "The Screen," *New York Times*, April 17, 1948, 11.

9. Janet Staiger, "The Hollywood Mode of Production: Its Conditions of Existence," in David Bordwell, Janet Staiger, and Kristin Thompson, *The Classical Hollywood Cinema: Film Style and Mode of Production to 1960* (New York: Columbia University Press, 1985), 87–95.

10. Janet Staiger, "The Package-Unit System: Unit Management after 1955," in *The Classical Hollywood Cinema*, 334.

11. In 1919, Famous Players-Lasky, the parent company of Paramount, converted a power station into a twin-stage studio outside of London in Islington, but then sold the facility in 1924 to concentrate its production operations in Hollywood. Patricia Warren, *British Film Studios: An Illustrated History* (London: B. T. Batsford, 2001), 104.

12. Paramount London Office (1951–1962), Hal Wallis Papers, Margaret Herrick Library, Academy of Motion Picture Arts and Sciences, Beverly Hills (hereafter AMPAS Library); C. O. Erickson, interview with author, December 17, 2011, Las Vegas; Oswald Morris, interview with author, April 21, 2011, Fontmell Magna, England.

13. Paramount Paris Office (1951–1962) and Paramount Rome Office (1951–1962), Hal Wallis Papers, AMPAS Library.

14. Various foreign production records from Twentieth Century-Fox Production Files, Performing Arts Special Collections, UCLA, Los Angeles (hereafter UCLA Arts).

15. Henry Anderson to Pilade Levi, May 11, 1949; Jack Saper to Russell Holman, May 24, 1949, *September Affair* (Production Department Files), Paramount Pictures Production Records, AMPAS Library.

16. Richard McWhorter to Richard Blaydon, July 5 and 11, 1949, *September Affair* (Production Department Files), Paramount Pictures Production Records, AMPAS Library.

17. Herbert Coleman to Richard Mealand, January 31, 1955; Kathleen Selby to Herbert Coleman, March 29, 1955, *The Man Who Knew Too Much* (Location 1954–55), Alfred Hitchcock Papers, AMPAS Library.

18. Alfred Hitchcock to Edouard de Segonzac, January 31, 1955, *The Man Who Knew Too Much* (Location 1954–55), Alfred Hitchcock Papers, AMPAS Library.

19. Edouard de Segonzac to Alfred Hitchcock, February 5, 1955, *The Man Who Knew Too Much* (Location 1954–55), Alfred Hitchcock Papers, AMPAS Library.

20. C. O. Erickson, interview with author, December 17, 2011.

21. William Perlberg to Bing Crosby, July 29, 1952, *Little Boy Lost* (Production 1952), Paramount Pictures Production Records. AMPAS Library.

22. C. O. Erickson to Hugh Brown, June 18, 1954, *To Catch a Thief* (Production Location 1954), Paramount Pictures Production Records, AMPAS Library.

23. Herbert Coleman to Alfred Hitchcock, March 17, 1955, *The Man Who Knew Too Much* (Production 1955–56), Alfred Hitchcock Papers, AMPAS Library.

24. "20th's Foreign Sked Big," *Daily Variety*, October 25, 1948, 1, 11.

25. Various correspondence for *A Certain Smile*, Twentieth Century-Fox Production Files, UCLA Arts.

26. Sid Rogell to Edward Leggewie, January 24, 1958, *A Certain Smile*, Twentieth Century-Fox Production Files, UCLA Arts.

27. Sid Rogell to Edward Leggewie, July 17, 1959, *Seven Thieves*, Twentieth Century-Fox Production Files, UCLA Arts.

28. Saul Wurtzel to Sid Rogell, August 7, 1959, *Seven Thieves*, Twentieth Century-Fox Production Files, UCLA Arts.

29. Edward T. Long to the Department of State, September 9, 1955, Italy Motion Pictures (1955–1959), State Department Files, National Archives and Records Administration, College Park, Maryland (hereafter NARA).

30. Richard Mealand to Russell Holman, March 27, 1952, *Little Boy Lost* (Production 1952), Paramount Pictures Production Records, AMPAS Library.

31. Russell Holman to Y. Frank Freeman, February 25, 1954, *To Catch a Thief* (Pre-production Location 1953–1954), Paramount Pictures Production Records, AMPAS Library; Rebecca Prime, *Hollywood Exiles in Europe: The Blacklist and Cold War Film Culture* (New Brunswick, NJ: Rutgers University Press, 2014), 44–45.

32. Oswald Morris, interview with author, April 21, 2011.

33. "Otto Preminger Opens London Prod'n Office," *Daily Variety*, August 16, 1956, 12.

34. Various correspondence, *Quo Vadis* (Correspondence 1947–1950), MGM British Production Records, AMPAS Library.

35. International Film Service brochure, *Rome Adventure*, Delmer Daves Papers, Department of Special Collections and University Archives, Stanford University, Stanford, California.

36. Jean Negulesco recommended the International Film Service to Vincente Minnelli. Negulesco to Minnelli, May 14, 1961, General Files (N—Miscellaneous 1961–1966), Vincente Minnelli Papers, AMPAS Library.

37. "Production Service Firm Formed in Rome," *Daily Variety*, March 6, 1962, 4.

38. Janet Wasko, "Financing and Production: Creating the Hollywood Film Commodity," in *The Contemporary Hollywood Film Industry*, ed. Paul McDonald and Janet Wasko (Malden, MA: Blackwell, 2008), 55–56.

39. Kristin Thompson, *Exporting Entertainment: America in the World Film Market 1907–34* (London: BFI, 1985).

40. Allen J. Scott, *On Hollywood: The Place, The Industry* (Princeton, NJ: Princeton University Press, 2005), 6–8.

41. *The Film Industry in Great Britain: Some Facts and Figures* (London: British Film Academy, 1950), 4–5.

42. In various dispatches to the State Department, the US Embassy in London made the case for how Hollywood's British productions supported the ailing British studios. See for example "Motion Picture Industry in the United Kingdom—1949," January 30, 1950, Great Britain Motion Pictures (1950–1954), State Department Records, NARA.

43. "British Ban Sale of Studios for Frozen Coin," *Daily Variety*, April 23, 1948, 3.

44. "Goetz, Mayer Will Talk Resumption of British Pix," *Daily Variety*, January 28, 1948, 6.

45. An overview of MGM's Borehamwood facilities is included in the studio agreement between MGM-British Studios and Capricorn Corp., June 9, 1948, *Under Capricorn* (Capricorn Corporation), Warner Archive.

46. "'Edward, My Son' Is Winding 9 Days Early," *Daily Variety*, July 29, 1948, 4.

47. Sue Harper and Vincent Porter, *British Cinema of the 1950s: The Decline of Deference* (Oxford: Oxford University Press, 2003), 117.

48. Oswald Morris, interview with author, April 21, 2011.

49. "Where Have We Gone Wrong?," *The Cine-Technician*, November–December 1948, 169.

50. "November Motion Picture Report—United Kingdom," December 8, 1950, Great Britain Motion Pictures (1950–1954), State Department Files, NARA.

51. Various correspondence, *The Flame and the Flesh* (Correspondence), MGM British Production Records, AMPAS Library.

52. "The General Council Decides ...," *The Cine-Technician*, March 1954, 47.

53. "Chinese City of Wangcheng, Herts," *Daily Telegraph*, May 2, 1958; Anthony Carthew, "This £80,000 City Even Smells Like the East," *Daily Herald*, May 2, 1958; "Wangcheng Is Ready for Official Opening" press release, *The Inn of the Sixth Happiness* clipping file, British Film Institute Library, London.

54. "WB British Studio Back in Production," *Daily Variety*, January 7, 1948, 1; "WB Closing Its Studio in London," *Daily Variety*, November 4, 1948, 1, 9. Before Warner leased Teddington to an aircraft company for storage space in 1952, the Hollywood studio managed to shoot parts of *The Crimson Pirate* there. See Teddington Studios press releases, Film & Television Production & Distribution Company Material, British Film Institute Library, London.

55. Patricia Warren, *Elstree: The British Hollywood* (London: Elm Tree, 1983), 89–93.

56. Vincent Sherman to Steve Trilling, November 7, 1948, *The Hasty Heart* (Steve Trilling Files), Warner Archive.

57. Vincent Sherman, *Studio Affairs: My Life as a Film Director* (Lexington: University Press of Kentucky, 1996), 185.

58. Production notes, *The Hasty Heart* (Production Notes), Warner Archive. Interestingly, Jack Warner suggested that the Burbank studio consider adopting the turntable technique. Jack Warner to Vincent Sherman, December 16, 1948, *The Hasty Heart* (Story-Memos and Correspondence), Warner Archive.

59. Vincent Sherman to Jack Warner, December 10, 1948, *The Hasty Heart* (Steve Trilling Files), Warner Archive.

60. Vincent Sherman to Jack Warner, December 12, 1948, *The Hasty Heart* (Story-Memos and Correspondence); Vincent Sherman to Steve Trilling, February 11 and 24, 1949, *The Hasty Heart* (Steve Trilling Files), Warner Archive.

61. Vincent Sherman to Steve Trilling, March 7, 1949, *The Hasty Heart* (Steve Trilling Files), Warner Archive. Decades later, Sherman offered a somewhat favorable depiction of the *Hasty Heart* working experience in his memoir *Studio Affairs*, 176–94, 256–66.

62. Robert Siodmak to Steve Trilling, December 3, 1951, *The Crimson Pirate* (Steve Trilling Files), Warner Archive.

63. Alex T. Boyd to Steve Trilling, May 30, 1949, *The Hasty Heart* (Steve Trilling Files), Warner Archive.

64. Sue Harper and Vincent Porter discuss these various productions in *British Cinema of the 1950s*, 115–17.

65. Steve Chibnall, *Quota Quickies: The Birth of the British "B" Film* (London: BFI, 2007), 23, 70.

66. "Skouras Will Survey 20th's British Studio Situation," *Daily Variety*, March 22, 1948, 10; Patricia Warren, *British Film Studios*, 182–84.

67. "Korda en Route for Coast Talks on Production," *Daily Variety*, April 30, 1948, 6; "20th Switching from Korda to Rank," *Daily Variety*, March 20, 1950, 1, 8.

68. "Transmittal of FIEC Statement," February 21, 1956, Great Britain Motion Pictures (1955–1959), State Department Files, NARA.

69. David Lewis to Arthur M. Loew, October 17, 1947, *Quo Vadis* (Correspondence 1947–1950), MGM British Production Records, AMPAS Library.

70. Eventually in 1954 Scalera would be converted into a studio for the growing Titanus operation. Pauline Small, "Producer *and* Director? Or 'Authorship' in 1950s Italian Cinema," in *Beyond the Bottom Line: The Producer in Film and Television Studies*, ed. Andrew Spicer, A. T. McKenna, and Christopher Meir (New York: Bloomsbury, 2014), 113.

71. David Lewis to Arthur M. Loew, October 17 and 22, 1947; Dora Wright, "Report on Survey of Possible Film Production in Italy," January 23, 1948, *Quo Vadis* (Correspondence 1947–1950), MGM British Production Records, AMPAS Library.

72. Noa Steimatsky, "The Cinecittà Refugee Camp (1944–1950)," *October* 128 (Spring 2009): 23–55; David Forgacs and Stephen Gundle, *Mass Culture and Italian*

Society from Fascism to the Cold War (Bloomington: Indiana University Press, 2007), 131.

73. Dora Wright, "Report on Survey of Possible Film Production in Italy," January 23, 1948, *Quo Vadis* (Correspondence 1947–1950), MGM British Production Records, AMPAS Library.

74. A cost estimate for constructing a four-stage studio in Rome is included in Dave Lewis to Arthur M. Loew, October 17, 1947, *Quo Vadis* (Correspondence 1947–1950), MGM British Production Records, AMPAS Library.

75. Hugh Gray, "When in Rome . . . ," *Quarterly of Film Radio and Television* 10, no. 3 (Spring 1956): 266.

76. Robert L. Surtees, "The Filming of 'Quo Vadis' in Italy," *American Cinematographer*, October 1951, 417. *Quo Vadis* art director Edward Carfagno also remembered the studio as being run-down, with many of its soundstages in need of repair. "An Oral History with Edward Carfagno," interview by Barbara Hall (Beverly Hills, CA: AMPAS Oral History Program, 1991), 87–88.

77. Henry Henigson, Cinecittà studio survey, March 7, 1949, *Quo Vadis* (Miscellaneous), John Huston Papers, AMPAS Library.

78. Robert L. Surtees, "The Filming of 'Quo Vadis' in Italy," *American Cinematographer*, October 1951, 419.

79. Production conference notes, January 11, 1954, *Barefoot Contessa* (Production 1953–1954), Joseph L. Mankiewicz Papers, AMPAS Library.

80. Dave Lewis to Arthur M. Loew, October 17, 1947, *Quo Vadis* (Correspondence 1947–1950), MGM British Production Records, AMPAS Library.

81. Fred Zinnemann, *A Life in the Movies: An Autobiography* (New York: Charles Scribner's Sons, 1992), 91.

82. "'Cleo' Crowds Wald 'Adventures' out of Rome Studios," *Daily Variety*, July 17, 1961, 1, 4.

83. *Ben-Hur* advertisement, *Daily Variety*, November 24, 1959, 13.

84. In 1930 Paramount bought and expanded Saint-Maurice Studios to produce multilingual versions until the studio shifted its operations from production to dubbing just a few years later. See Colin Crisp, *The Classic French Cinema, 1930–1960* (Bloomington: Indiana University Press, 1993), 22–24; Harry Waldman, *Paramount in Paris: 300 Films Produced at the Joinville Studios, 1930–1933, with Credits and Biographies* (Lanham, MD: Scarecrow, 1998).

85. For overviews of French studios see "Motion Picture Theater Equipment—France," September 26, 1950, France Motion Pictures (1950–1954), State Department Files, NARA; "Les Studios Français" supplement in *La Technique Cinématographique*, April 1953, 99–113.

86. "French Costs Kill H'wd But Own Industry Booms," *Hollywood Reporter*, May 9, 1949, 3.

87. Christian Ferry, interview with author, February 18, 2011, Paris; Colin Crisp, *The Classic French Cinema, 1930–1960*, 121–28. For an overview of French studio facilities and equipment see various years, *Annuaire du Cinéma*.

88. "Signes précurseurs de crise?," *La Technique Cinématographique*, December 30, 1948, 515.

89. W. Irvin Brennan, "Paris Letter," *American Cinematographer*, December 1947, 437. The French industry publication *La Technique Cinématographique* took issue with this assessment. See "Un Américain à Paris," *La Technique Cinématographique*, February 19, 1948, 63. About a year later, producer Irving Allen described equipment available in France as modern, owing to imported equipment from the United States and the UK: "French Costs Kill H'wd but Own Industry Booms," *Hollywood Reporter*, May 9, 1949, 3.

90. "Don't Shoot 'American' in Paris, Warns Krasna," *Daily Variety*, March 7, 1956, 1, 3.

91. "Assistance Rendered American Motion Picture Company by Embassy," February 4, 1949, France Motion Pictures (1945–1949), State Department Files, NARA; interview with Stanley Cortez, "Filming 'The Man on the Eiffel Tower,'" *American Cinematographer*, February 1949, 46–47; Stanley Cortez, "Filming 'The Man on the Eiffel Tower,'" *International Photographer*, February 1949, 5–6; "Paris Power Blinks Out on 'Tower,'" *Daily Variety*, November 3, 1948, 1.

92. Colin Crisp, *The Classic French Cinema, 1930–1960*, 123–25.

93. "MGM Cooling Stations for 'Solomon' Footage," *Daily Variety*, September 13, 1949, 9; "Filming on the Dark Continent," *International Photographer*, January 1950, 12.

94. "20th Flies 'Prince' Rushes from Italy to Preserve Density," *Daily Variety*, October 21, 1948, 3.

95. Carl Foreman, "To Film or Not Abroad—That Is Not the Question," *Journal of the Screen Producers Guild* 6, no. 7 (December 1960): 11.

96. Bill Mull to Frank Caffey, December 16, 1952, *Little Boy Lost* (Production 1952–53), Paramount Pictures Production Records, AMPAS Library.

97. "Cinecolor Getting Site in London," *Daily Variety*, March 3, 1949, 2; "Cinecolor Sets Up Lab to Process Pix in Britain," *Daily Variety*, April 13, 1949, 5. The US firm and subtractive color process Cinecolor should not be confused with Britain's additive Cinecolor process. See Sarah Street, *Colour Films in Britain: The Negotiation of Innovation 1900–55* (London: Palgrave Macmillan, 2013), 266–68.

98. For an overview of Technicolor in Great Britain see Sarah Street, *Colour Films in Britain*; Sarah Street, "'Colour Consciousness': Natalie Kalmus and Technicolor in Britain," *Screen* 50, no. 2 (Summer 2009): 191–215.

99. Robert L. Surtees, "The Filming of 'Quo Vadis' in Italy, Part Two," *American Cinematographer*, November 1951, 473. MGM likely made a special arrangement with Italy's director-general of Kinematography, since Italian law forbade exporting exposed undeveloped negatives. Dora Wright, "Report on Survey of Possible Film Production in Italy," January 23, 1948, *Quo Vadis* (Correspondence 1947–1950), MGM British Production Records, AMPAS Library.

100. Sarah Street, *Colour Films in Britain*, 112.

101. Sue Harper and Vincent Porter, *British Cinema of the 1950s,* 208. Colin Crisp points out (in *The Classic French Cinema*, 140–41) that the Technicolor Paris lab shut down in 1959 due to lack of demand.

102. Robert F. Hawkins, "Roamin' in Rome," *Daily Variety,* November 29, 1956, 3.

103. William Wyler to Don Hartman, July 26, 1952, *Roman Holiday* (Paramount), William Wyler Papers, AMPAS Library.

104. Vincente Minnelli with Hector Arce, *I Remember It Well* (London: Angus and Robertson, 1975), 313; Jean Domarchi and Jean Douchet, "Rencontre avec Vincente Minnelli," *Cahiers du Cinéma,* February 1962, 4; Vanessa Schwartz, *It's So French! Hollywood, Paris, and the Making of Cosmopolitan Film Culture* (Chicago: University of Chicago Press, 2007), 46.

105. Frederick Foster, "High Key vs. Low Key," *American Cinematographer,* August 1957, 533.

106. "'Grass' Not Only Greener in Britain, Donen Says Foreign Stock Turns It Blue," *Daily Variety,* May 5, 1960, 3.

107. "Zanuck Finds New Eastman Film Makes Ould Sod Green Enuf For Hibernians," *Daily Variety,* June 28, 1960, 6.

108. "$1,000,000 Film Production Gear Shipped Abroad," *Daily Variety,* February 14, 1950, 8.

109. "Leo Packs for 'Quo Vadis' Trek," *Daily Variety,* March 8, 1950, 4; Piero Cavazzuti, "Technical Problems in the Rome Studios," January 19, 1948, *Quo Vadis* (Correspondence 1947–1950), MGM British Production Records, AMPAS Library.

110. William A. McFadden to the Department of State, June 27, 1950, Italy Motion Pictures (1950–1954), State Department Files, NARA.

111. Bill Mull to Frank Caffey, December 16, 1952, *Little Boy Lost* (Production 1952), Paramount Pictures Production Records, AMPAS Library.

112. Various correspondence in *September Affair* (Production Department Files), *Roman Holiday* (Correspondence 1952), *Little Boy Lost* (Production 1952), *To Catch a Thief* (Pre-Production Location 1953–1954), Paramount Pictures Production Records, AMPAS Library.

113. Robert Gardiner, ed., *The Shipping Revolution: The Modern Merchant Ship* (Annapolis, MD: Naval Institute Press, 1992), 42–62, 105–6.

114. Frank Caffey to Harry Caplan, July 4, 1956, *Funny Face* (Movement and Shipping), Paramount Pictures Production Records, AMPAS Library.

115. Jack Karp to Henry Henigson, April 16, 1952, *Roman Holiday* (Correspondence 1952), Paramount Pictures Production Records, AMPAS Library.

116. Bill Mull to Frank Caffey, August 26, 1952, *Little Boy Lost* (Production 1952), Paramount Pictures Production Records, AMPAS Library.

117. David Bordwell, *Reinventing Hollywood: How 1940s Filmmakers Changed Movie Storytelling* (Chicago: University of Chicago Press, 2017), 29–35.

118. "Italian Threat to Ban U.S. Film Techs Is Overcome," *Daily Variety,* July 22, 1949, 3.

119. Dora Wright, "Report on Survey of Possible Film Production in Italy," January 23, 1948, *Quo Vadis* (Correspondence 1947–1950), MGM British Production Records, AMPAS Library; William A. McFadden to the Department of State, July 13, 1950, Italy Motion Pictures (1950–1954), State Department Files, NARA.

120. Advertisement, *American Cinematographer*, December 1962, 727.

121. Frank Caffey to Russell Holman, April 6, 1955, *The Man Who Knew Too Much* (Production Department Files), Paramount Pictures Production Records, AMPAS Library.

122. Production notes, *The Hasty Heart* (Production Notes), Warner Archive.

123. "Christopher Challis BECTU Oral History," interview by Kevin Gough Yates, (London: BECTU History Project, October 11, 1988).

124. Jack Cardiff, "The Problem of Lighting and Photographing 'Under Capricorn,'" *American Cinematographer*, October 1949, 382.

125. "Equipments [*sic*] Offered by Our Advertisers," *La Technique Cinématographique*, April 1951, 125–26.

126. Interview with Stanley Cortez, "Filming 'The Man on the Eiffel Tower,'" *American Cinematographer*, February 1949, 47.

127. Arthur E. Gavin, "Location-Shooting in Paris for 'Gigi,'" *American Cinematographer*, July 1958, 425.

128. Susan Christopherson and Michael Storper, "Flexible Specialization: A Critique and Case Study" (Los Angeles: UCLA Graduate School of Architecture and Urban Planning, 1986); Susan Christopherson and Michael Storper, "The Effects of Flexible Specialization on Industrial Politics and the Labor Market: The Motion Picture Industry," *Industrial and Labor Relations Review* 42, no. 3 (April 1989): 331–47; Janet Staiger, "The Package-Unit System," 330–37.

3. LUMIÈRE, CAMERA, AZIONE!: THE PERSONNEL AND PRACTICES OF HOLLYWOOD'S MODE OF INTERNATIONAL PRODUCTION

1. Jean Negulesco to Vincente Minnelli, May 14, 1961, General Files (N—Miscellaneous 1961–1966), Vincente Minnelli Papers, Margaret Herrick Library, Academy of Motion Picture Arts and Sciences, Beverly Hills (hereafter AMPAS Library), emphasis in original.

2. Janet Staiger, "The Producer-Unit System: Management by Specialization after 1931," in David Bordwell, Janet Staiger, and Kristin Thompson, *The Classical Hollywood Cinema: Film Style and Mode of Production to 1960* (New York: Columbia University Press, 1985), 324.

3. "An Oral History with C. O. Erickson," interview by Douglas Bell (Beverly Hills, CA: AMPAS Oral History Program, 2006), 203, emphasis in original.

4. C. O. Erickson to Hugh Brown, February 12, 1954, *To Catch a Thief* (Pre-Production Location 1953–1954), Paramount Pictures Production Records, AMPAS Library.

5. C. O. Erickson to Frank Caffey, May 23, 1954, *To Catch a Thief* (Pre-Production Location 1953–1954), Paramount Pictures Production Records, AMPAS Library.

6. Hugh Brown to C. O. Erickson, May 28, 1954, *To Catch a Thief* (Pre-Production Location 1953–1954), Paramount Pictures Production Records, AMPAS Library.

7. Bill Mull to Frank Caffey, August 18, 1952, *Little Boy Lost* (Production 1952), Paramount Pictures Production Records, AMPAS Library.

8. Various correspondence for *Crack in the Mirror*, Twentieth Century-Fox Production Files, Performing Arts Special Collections, UCLA, Los Angeles (hereafter UCLA Arts).

9. "Chas. Vidor Urges Taking Crews for Foreign Production," *Hollywood Reporter*, May 21, 1953, 1, 4.

10. Robert L. Surtees, "The Filming of 'Quo Vadis' in Italy, Part Two," *American Cinematographer*, November 1951, 448.

11. "AFL Gets 'Tough' on Runaway Pix," *Daily Variety*, April 6, 1955, 1, 4; "Lensers Demand H'wood Crews on U.S.-Originated Pix O'Seas," *Daily Variety*, March 21, 1958, 6.

12. Vic Heutschy, "From Any Angle," *International Photographer*, December 1954, 22; Vic Heutschy, "From Any Angle," *International Photographer*, January 1955, 8; Robert Tobey, "Letter from Cairo," *International Photographer*, February 1955, 12.

13. Darryl Zanuck to Fox staff, September 14, 1948, Miscellaneous (Correspondence), Charles Schlaifer Collection, AMPAS Library.

14. "Metro Agrees to Stop Using H'Wood Techs in Britain," *Daily Variety*, June 15, 1948, 3.

15. Jonathan Stubbs, "'Blocked' Currency, Runaway Production in Britain and *Captain Horatio Hornblower* (1951)," *Historical Journal of Film, Radio and Television* 28, no. 3 (August 2008): 335.

16. Oswald Morris, interview with author, April 21, 2011, Fontmell Magna, England.

17. "Is Hollywood Right?," *The Cine-Technician*, January–February 1948, 17–20; "Unemployment Highest for 10 Years," *The Cine-Technician*, March–April 1948, 63, 65.

18. "Art Directors Sign Pact on Jobs with British Union," *Daily Variety*, April 26, 1948, 1, 15; "No Ban on H'd Art Directors in England," *Daily Variety*, July 1, 1948, 4; "British Pinch U.S. Talent," *Daily Variety*, February 28, 1950, 1, 8.

19. "June Motion Picture Report—United Kingdom," July 7, 1950, Great Britain Motion Pictures (1950–1954), State Department Files, National Archives and Records Administration, College Park, Maryland (hereafter NARA).

20. Quoted in Joseph Ruttenberg, "Assignment Overseas," *American Cinematographer*, October 1950, 355.

21. "Johnston Trying to Break British Ban on H'd Execs," *Daily Variety*, April 7, 1948, 1, 9.

22. The British actors' union tried but ultimately failed to block the casting of US actress Virginia Mayo in a starring role in *Captain Horatio Hornblower*. "WB, British Equity War over Mayo in Star Role," *Daily Variety*, January 20, 1950, 1, 11; "Britain Will Grant Permits to U.S. Artists," *Daily Variety*, March 24, 1950, 52; Jonathan Stubbs, "'Blocked' Currency, Runaway Production in Britain and *Captain Horatio Hornblower* (1951)," 343–44.

23. Joseph Ruttenberg, "Assignment Overseas," *American Cinematographer*, October 1950, 346.

24. "Brit Union Eases Limitation on U.S. Directors, Prods," *Daily Variety*, August 13, 1957, 1, 11; Robert B. Parke to the Department of State, August 20, 1957, Great Britain Motion Pictures (1955–1959), State Department Records, NARA.

25. W. P. Robinson, "The American Producer in England," in *Syllabus and Forms on American Motion Picture Production in Foreign Countries* (Los Angeles: Beverly Hills Bar Association and USC School of Law, May 9, 1959), 7–8, 47.

26. William G. Gibson to the Department of State, July 14, 20, and 24, 1953, Great Britain Motion Pictures (1950–1954), State Department Records, NARA; "Extras Strike All British Pix," *Daily Variety*, July 10, 1953, 1, 9.

27. Richard Kuisel, *Seducing the French: The Dilemma of Americanization* (Berkeley: University of California Press, 1993).

28. Rebecca Prime, *Hollywood Exiles in Europe: The Blacklist and Cold War Film Culture* (New Brunswick, NJ: Rutgers University Press, 2014), 37–41, 44–45; Colin Crisp, *The Classic French Cinema, 1930–1960* (Bloomington: Indiana University Press, 1993), 73–75.

29. "French Certify Franc Thaws," *Daily Variety*, August 30, 1949, 5; British Film Producers Association, "British Location Units Working in France," n.d., *Captain Horatio Hornblower* (Story–Memos & Correspondence), Warner Bros. Archive, University of Southern California, Los Angeles (hereafter Warner Archive); Christian Ferry, interview with author, February 18, 2011, Paris.

30. Edouard de Segonzac to Richard Mealand, June 16, 1952, *Little Boy Lost* (Production 1952), Paramount Pictures Production Records, AMPAS Library.

31. "Don't Shoot 'American' in Paris, Warns Krasna," *Daily Variety*, March 7, 1956, 1, 3; Sylvette Baudrot, interview with author, December 18, 2010, Paris; Christian Ferry, interview with author, February 18, 2011.

32. "Italian Threat to Ban U.S. Film Techs Is Overcome," *Daily Variety*, July 22, 1949, 3.

33. Gianni Manca, "Certain Relevant Aspects of the Production of Films in Italy by Foreign Producers," in *Syllabus and Forms on American Motion Picture Production in Foreign Countries*, 20.

34. Sergio Salvati, interview with author, March 16, 2011, Rome. David Forgacs and Stephen Gundle discuss how Italian workers benefited from the technical and organizational training on these Hollywood films in *Mass Culture and Italian Society from Fascism to the Cold War* (Bloomington: Indiana University Press, 2007), 140.

35. W. N. Walmsley Jr. to the secretary of state, June 11, 1949, Italy Motion Pictures (1945–1949), State Department Files, NARA.

36. Hugh Gray, "When in Rome . . . ," *Quarterly of Film Radio and Television* 10, no. 3 (Spring 1956): 271.

37. Robert F. Hawkins, "Rome Union Asks Italy 'Freeze' 20th Prod'n; 'Cleo' Beef," *Daily Variety*, June 28, 1962, 1, 4.

38. John C. Fuess to the Department of State, April 4, 1962, Italy Motion Pictures (1960–1963), State Department Files, NARA; "AFL-CIO Charges 20th Used Italo Commie Union, Refused to Change, in Making 'Cleo,'" *Daily Variety*, July 16, 1962, 1, 4.

39. Christian Ferry, interview with author, February 18, 2011; Sergio Salvati, interview with author, March 16, 2011; C. O. Erickson, interview with author, December 17, 2011, Las Vegas.

40. Quoted in Antoine De Baecque, ed., *Paris by Hollywood* (Paris: Flammarion, 2012), 184.

41. Sue Harper and Vincent Porter, *British Cinema of the 1950s: The Decline of Deference* (Oxford: Oxford University Press, 2003), 216; Colin Crisp, *The Classic French Cinema, 1930–1960*, 266–323; David Forgacs and Stephen Gundle, *Mass Culture and Italian Society from Fascism to the Cold War*, 124–40; Pauline Small, "Producer *and* Director? Or 'Authorship' in 1950s Italian Cinema," in *Beyond the Bottom Line: The Producer in Film and Television Studies*, ed. Andrew Spicer, A. T. McKenna, and Christopher Meir (New York: Bloomsbury, 2014), 111; Dora Wright, "Report on Survey of Possible Film Production in Italy," January 23, 1948, *Quo Vadis* (Correspondence 1947–1950), MGM British Production Records, AMPAS Library.

42. Janet Staiger, "The Package-Unit System: Unit Management after 1955," in *The Classical Hollywood Cinema*, 333–34.

43. Christian Ferry, interview with author, February 18, 2011.

44. Joseph Ruttenberg, "Assignment Overseas," *American Cinematographer*, October 1950, 352–53.

45. For a brief overview of this situation in France see Gene Moskowitz, "In Paris," *Daily Variety*, April 25, 1958, 3.

46. Joseph Ruttenberg, "Assignment Overseas," *American Cinematographer*, October 1950, 353.

47. Edward Dmytryk, *On Filmmaking* (Boston: Focal, 1986), 203.

48. Of course, language barriers were rarely a problem in the UK, one reason why Hollywood was attracted to working in that region, so my analysis mainly focuses on communication in Italy and France.

49. William Perlberg, "What Do You Mean? Run-Away Production!," *Journal of the Screen Producers Guild* 6, no. 7 (December 1960): 33.

50. Hazel Flynn, "General Josh and 'Fanny,'" *Beverly Hills Citizen*, July 7, 1960, 5.

51. "A List of Motion-Picture Technical Terms in Five Languages," *Journal of the Society of Motion Picture and Television Engineers*, February 1956, 85–91, subsequently reprinted in *American Cinematographer Manual*, ed. Joseph V. Mascelli (Hollywood, CA: American Society of Cinematographers, 1960), 434–50.

52. C. Ryle Gibbs, *Dictionnaire technique du cinéma: français-anglais, anglais-français* (Paris: Nouvelles éditions film et technique, 1959).

53. Jack Saper to Paul Nathan, August 10, 1949, *September Affair* (Production Department Files), Paramount Pictures Production Records, AMPAS Library.

54. Interview with Stanley Cortez, "Filming 'The Man on the Eiffel Tower,'" *American Cinematographer*, February 1949, 64.

55. See Josef von Sternberg's comments on the problems of communication with a Japanese crew on his Japanese production of *The Saga of Anatahan* (1953) in his memoir, *Fun in a Chinese Laundry* (New York: Macmillan, 1965), 286.

56. Edward Dmytryk, *On Filmmaking*, 205.

57. "English-Speaking Pix Talent Pool on Tap in Rome," *Daily Variety*, April 14, 1954, 4.

58. Edouard de Segonzac to Richard Mealand, June 16, 1952, *Little Boy Lost* (Production 1952), Paramount Pictures Production Records, AMPAS Library.

59. List of French personnel, June 7, 1952, *Little Boy Lost* (Production 1952), Paramount Pictures Production Records, AMPAS Library.

60. Giuseppe Rotunno, interview with author, March 22, 2011, Rome.

61. See for example Sylvette Baudrot's French-English production materials for *Atoll K* (1951) and *Lust for Life* (1956) in the Sylvette Baudrot-Guilbaud collection, Bibliothèque du film, Cinémathèque française, Paris. Also, assistant director Bernard Quatrehomme's bilingual materials for *The Longest Day* (1962) in the Bernard Quatrehomme collection, Bibliothèque du film, Cinémathèque française, Paris.

62. Henry Henigson to William Wyler, April 12, 1952, *Roman Holiday* (Henry Henigson), William Wyler Papers, AMPAS Library.

63. Berlitz advertisement, *Daily Variety*, April 29, 1955, 7.

64. Gladwin Hill, "Film People Study Languages for Fun, Work and Therapy," *New York Times*, November 22, 1960, 39.

65. Alberto Morin to John Huston, February 4, 1949, *Quo Vadis* (Staff), John Huston Papers, AMPAS Library. In the end, Morin does not seem to have worked on *Quo Vadis*.

66. *Act of Love* actor Kirk Douglas learned French in order to play in both English and French versions. Kirk Douglas, *The Ragman's Son: An Autobiography* (London: Simon and Schuster, 1988), 214–15.

67. Herb A. Lightman, "Decision before Dawn," *American Cinematographer*, February 1952, 84.

68. "An Oral History with C. O. Erickson," 262.

69. "Mankiewicz Finds European Meggers Eager Beavers," *Daily Variety*, August 24, 1950, 4.

70. Mark Evans, "The Production Side"; "Bob" Attwooll, "Production Routine"; and George Hill, "Effects Department," *The Cine-Technician*, January–February 1948, 20–22.

71. See for example Charles G. Clarke, "Practical Techniques for 3-D and Wide Screen Filming," *The Cine-Technician*, May-June 1953, 54–56; Joseph Ruttenberg, "Overhead Lighting for Overall Set Illumination," *The Cine-Technician*, May–June

1953, 68–69; Charles G. Clarke, "Effets de nuit réalisés en plein jour," *La Technique Cinématographique*, March 1957, 65–66. The July 1953 issue of *La Technique Cinématographique* was devoted to US wide-screen systems.

72. Not until the 1960s and 1970s did some European filmmakers come to the United States to shoot "European" productions and Euro-US coproductions, including Franco Rossi's *Smog* (1962), Michael Pfleghar's *Dead Woman from Beverly Hills* (1964), Jacques Demy's *Model Shop* (1969), Agnés Varda's *Lions Love (. . . and Lies)* (1969), Michelangelo Antonioni's *Zabriskie Point* (1970), and Jacques Deray's *The Outside Man* (1972).

73. Quoted in "Hitchcock Sees British Techs Learning Yanks' Pix Tricks," *Daily Variety*, October 26, 1948, 1, 5.

74. "Rapid 'Quo Vadis' Progress Reported by Film's Scribe," *Daily Variety*, July 14, 1950, 10.

75. Robert L. Surtees, "The Filming of 'Quo Vadis' in Italy, Part Two," *American Cinematographer*, November 1951, 448, 473.

76. See Robert Surtees, "Location Filming in Africa for 'King Solomon's Mines,'" *American Cinematographer*, April 1950, 122–23, 136; Frederick Foster, "Assignment in India," *American Cinematographer*, June 1952, 252, 260; Hilda Black, "Filming 'Return to Paradise' in Samoa," *American Cinematographer*, April 1953, 156–57, 188–89, 191.

77. Bill Mull to Frank Caffey, September 19, September 26, and December 16, 1952, *Little Boy Lost* (Production 1952), Paramount Pictures Production Records, AMPAS Library.

78. Wm. N. Williams, "Shooting 'Second Unit' in Europe," *American Cinematographer*, August 1953, 390–91.

79. "An Oral History with Edward Carfagno," interview by Barbara Hall (Beverly Hills, CA: AMPAS Oral History Program, 1991), 90, 96.

80. For the schedule negotiations of *Quo Vadis* see Hugh Gray, "When in Rome . . . ," 266–67. For *Helen of Troy* see "WB Shooting 'Troy' in 2 Work Shifts," *Daily Variety*, July 15, 1954, 6. For *The Hasty Heart* see Vincent Sherman to Steve Trilling, March 3, 1949, *The Hasty Heart* (Steve Trilling Files), Warner Archive.

81. Vincent Sherman to Jack Warner, December 12, 1948, *The Hasty Heart* (Story—Memos and Correspondence), Warner Archive. Vincent Sherman later recounted the tea break ritual in his memoir, *Studio Affairs: My Life as a Film Director* (Lexington: University Press of Kentucky, 1996), 183.

82. Bertram Tuttle to Steve Trilling, April 27, 1950, *Captain Horatio Hornblower* (Steve Trilling Files), Warner Archive.

83. Roger Corman, "Foreign Production for the Medium-Budget Producer," *Journal of the Screen Producers Guild* 6, no. 7 (December 1960): 20.

84. John Thornton Caldwell, *Production Culture: Industrial Reflexivity and Critical Practice in Film and Television* (Durham, NC: Duke University Press, 2008), 145–46.

85. Unsigned (probably Steve Trilling) to Jack Warner, December 23, 1948; Jack Warner to Steve Trilling, January 12, 1948, *The Hasty Heart* (Steve Trilling Files), Warner Archive.

86. Jack Warner to Steve Trilling, February 11, 1949, *The Hasty Heart* (Steve Trilling Files), Warner Archive.

87. "An Oral History with C. O. Erickson," 133–34.

88. "Operations World Wide," *Journal of the Screen Producers Guild* 6, no. 4 (December 1959): 13.

89. Various correspondence and studio surveys, *Quo Vadis* (Correspondence 1947–1950), MGM British Production Records, AMPAS Library.

90. Advice from Jacques Becker relayed in Edouard de Segonzac to Alfred Hitchcock, February 5, 1955, *The Man Who Knew Too Much* (Location 1954–55), Alfred Hitchcock Papers, AMPAS Library.

91. Richard McWhorter to R. L. Johnston, July 15, 1949, *September Affair* (Production Department Files), Paramount Pictures Production Records, AMPAS Library.

92. "20th Suspends All British Prod'n for a Year, Till Techs Can Be Briefed on CinemaScope," *Daily Variety*, August 31, 1953, 1, 3.

93. "Zanuck to London for Prod'n Parley," *Daily Variety*, November 19, 1954, 1, 3. However, the first CinemaScope production in Britain was MGM's *Knights of the Round Table* (1954).

94. Derek Hill, "Jack Cardiff's VistaVision Venture," *American Cinematographer*, December 1956, 733.

95. Interdepartmental memo, February 1950, *Quo Vadis* (Production), Turner/ MGM Scripts, AMPAS Library. Coaxial cables that better amplified telephone communication were laid underwater starting in the 1950s. See Nicole Starosielski, *The Undersea Network* (Durham, NC: Duke University Press, 2015), 38–44.

96. Humphrey Bogart shares an anecdote about the difficulties of trying to communicate by phone from the Italian town of Ravello during the production of *Beat the Devil* (1954) in Humphrey Bogart as told to Joe Hyams, "Movie Making Beats the Devil," *Cue*, November 28, 1953, 15.

97. Jerry Wald to Delmer Daves, August 1, 1947, *To The Victor*, Warner Archive.

98. Cable correspondence between David O. Selznick and Sid Rogell, June 20 and July 15, 1957, *A Farewell to Arms*, Twentieth Century-Fox Production Files, UCLA Arts.

99. Bill Mull to Frank Caffey, December 16, 1952, *Little Boy Lost* (Production 1952), Paramount Pictures Production Records, AMPAS Library.

100. C. O. Erickson to Hugh Brown, February 12, 1954, *To Catch a Thief* (Pre-Production Location 1953–1954), Paramount Pictures Production Records, AMPAS Library.

101. C. O. Erickson, interview with author, December 17, 2011.

102. Jean Negulesco to Vincente Minnelli, May 14, 1961, General Files (N— Miscellaneous 1961–1966), Vincente Minnelli Papers, AMPAS Library.

103. For an account of how studios supervised the work of contracted Hollywood directors see John Huston, *An Open Book* (New York: Knopf, 1980), 83. For the benefits and drawbacks of a newfound autonomy that some exiled blacklisted Hollywood filmmakers experienced in Europe see Rebecca Prime, *Hollywood Exiles in Europe*, 178–79.

104. C. O. Erickson, interview with author, December 17, 2011.

105. C. O. Erickson, interview with author, December 17, 2011. An *American Cinematographer* profile on MGM's *Across the Wide Missouri* (1951) explains that the film's location unit working in the Colorado Rockies had "walkie-talkie-cum-telephone" communication with the studio. William Mellor, "No Time for Weather," *American Cinematographer*, May 1951, 178–79, 199.

106. Oswald Morris, interview with author, April 21, 2011.

107. Oswald Morris, *Huston, We Have a Problem: A Kaleidoscope of Filmmaking Memories* (Lanham, MD: Scarecrow, 2006), 69–70; "Oswald Morris BECTU Oral History," interview by Alan Lawson (London: BECTU History Project, July 21, 1987), 31–32. Sarah Street points out that opposition to Technicolor by British cinematographers was prevalent in the technical discourse in part to elevate their status. Sarah Street, "'Colour Consciousness': Natalie Kalmus and Technicolor in Britain," *Screen* 50, no. 2 (Summer 2009): 209. Street also discusses *Moulin Rouge*'s technical and stylistic innovation in *Colour Films in Britain: The Negotiation of Innovation 1900–55* (London: Palgrave Macmillan, 2013), 200–204.

108. Mark Robson to Buddy Adler, April 23, 1958, *The Inn of the Sixth Happiness*, Mark Robson Papers, UCLA Arts, capitals in original.

109. Aida A. Hozic, *Hollyworld: Space, Power, and Fantasy in the American Economy* (Ithaca, NY: Cornell University Press, 2001), 97.

110. Ben Goldsmith and Tom O'Regan, *The Film Studio: Film Production in the Global Economy* (Lanham, MD: Rowman and Littlefield, 2005), 11.

111. "20th Frozen Coin for 5 Pix Abroad," *Daily Variety*, June 27, 1949, 1, 9; "Zanuck Abroading to Survey 20th Prod'n," *Daily Variety*, January 29, 1951, 1, 7.

112. "Jack Warner to Eye Rome Prod'n Progress," *Daily Variety*, June 23, 1954, 1; "Republic Sets 'Watch' for Global Filming," *Daily Variety*, November 23, 1954, 2; "Mirisch Abroading to Eye AA Prod'n," *Daily Variety*, August 31, 1956, 10.

113. "20th Boardmen Eye Progress on 'Cleo' in Rome," *Daily Variety*, October 12, 1961, 1, 4; Murray Schumach, "Hollywood Leave," *New York Times*, February 11, 1962, 115. Aubrey Solomon suggests that these frequent set visits contributed to the film's bloated budgets in *Twentieth Century Fox: A Corporate and Financial History* (Metuchen, NJ: Scarecrow, 1988), 143; Murray Schumach, "'Cleopatra' Cost Explained at Fox," *New York Times*, August 21, 1962, 36; Joe Hyams, "Cleopatra: Hollywood's Most Expensive Girl Friend," *Los Angeles Times*, November 25, 1962, TW8.

114. "Krim Going to Europe on 3-Week Look-See of United Artists Pix," *Daily Variety*, August 6, 1952, 1, 7.

115. Various correspondence, *A Farewell to Arms*, Twentieth Century-Fox Production Files, UCLA Arts.

116. "Eddie Mannix Returning; Half 'Vadis' Footage Shot," *Daily Variety*, July 18, 1950, 3.

117. "Mannix Returns from 'Ben-Hur' O'seas Task," *Daily Variety*, April 1, 1958, 1; "Vogel Quits Rome after Week's O.O. on 'Ben-Hur' Work," *Daily Variety*, July 1, 1958, 3; "Sol Siegel Plans 10-Day Europe Trek," *Daily Variety*, September 2, 1958, 1.

118. "An Oral History with Edward Carfagno," 168.

119. Various correspondence, *Captain Horatio Hornblower* (Steve Trilling Files) and *The Crimson Pirate* (Steve Trilling Files), Warner Archive.

120. Frank Caffey to Bill Mull, August 13, 1952, *Little Boy Lost* (Production 1952), Paramount Pictures Production Records, AMPAS Library.

121. "20th Flies 'Prince' Rushes from Italy to Preserve Density," *Daily Variety*, October 21, 1948, 3.

122. C. O. Erickson, interview with author, December 17, 2011.

123. Frank Caffey to C. O. Erickson, June 5, 1954, *To Catch a Thief* (Production Location 1954), Paramount Pictures Production Records, AMPAS Library.

124. Frank Caffey to C. O. Erickson, May 29, 1954, *To Catch a Thief* (Pre-Production Location 1953–1954), Paramount Pictures Production Records, AMPAS Library.

125. Robert Burks's concern was relayed in C. O. Erickson to Frank Caffey, June 1, 1954, *To Catch a Thief* (Production Location 1954), Paramount Pictures Production Records, AMPAS Library.

126. Herb A. Lightman, "Hitchcock Talks about Lights, Camera, Action," *American Cinematographer*, May 1967, 333.

127. Frank Caffey to C O. Erickson, June 11, 1954, *To Catch a Thief* (Production Location 1954), Paramount Pictures Production Records, AMPAS Library.

128. Various cables from Frank Caffey, June 1954, *To Catch a Thief* (Production Location 1954), Paramount Pictures Production Records, AMPAS Library.

129. C. O. Erickson to Hugh Brown, June 18, 1954, *To Catch a Thief* (Production Location 1954), Paramount Pictures Production Records, AMPAS Library.

130. C. O. Erickson to Frank Caffey, June 13, 1954, *To Catch a Thief* (Production Location), Paramount Pictures Production Records, AMPAS Library. This is a point made in Robert R. Shandley, *Runaway Romances: Hollywood's Postwar Tour of Europe* (Philadelphia: Temple University Press, 2009), 97.

131. C. O. Erickson, interview with author, December 17, 2011.

132. See Barry Salt's shot-scale database on Cinemetrics: http://www.cinemetrics .lv/saltdb.php.

133. "U.S. Locations Hurt Italian Production Rosselini [*sic*] Says," *Hollywood Reporter*, January 18, 1949, 4.

134. "20th Accused of Raising Film Costs in Italy," *Daily Variety*, September 13, 1948, 4. However, in his interview with this author (March 22, 2011, Rome), veteran set dresser Bruno Schiavi remembered that Italian unions set the wage scales, which avoided the potential for inflated payments. This regulation was possibly instituted well after 1948.

135. Quoted in "20th Saving $3 Million on 'Foxes' in Italy, Says Zanuck," *Daily Variety*, September 14, 1948, 3.

136. L. C. Algrant to Henry Henigson, April 7, 1949, *Quo Vadis* (Correspondence), John Huston Papers, AMPAS Library.

137. Henry Henigson to William Wyler, May 2, 1952, *Roman Holiday* (Henry Henigson), William Wyler Papers, AMPAS Library.

138. David Forgacs and Stephen Gundle, *Mass Culture and Italian Society from Fascism to the Cold War*, 140.

139. "Italian Pix Prod'n Costs Soar 20–40% Since '50 for American Film-makers," *Daily Variety*, August 8, 1952, 1, 5.

140. "Lopert Complains of Soaring Italo Production Costs," *Daily Variety*, November 16, 1954, 2.

141. "Prod'n Costs in Europe Now Par U.S.; Rossen Reports; Italo Bubble Bursts," *Daily Variety*, February 22, 1956, 3.

142. "The Italian Movie Industry," April 18, 1958, Italy Motion Pictures (1955–1959), State Department Files, NARA.

143. However, various Italian industry organizations called the attacks by the newspapers, *Il Messaggero* and *Corriere d'Informazione*, "vicious and completely unjustified." Robert F. Hawkins, "Italo Sneak Attack on H'wood," *Daily Variety*, August 6, 1962, 1, 23.

144. For a summary of these arguments see Gene Moskowitz, "In Paris," *Daily Variety*, December 22, 1955, 3; Gerald M. Mayer to the Department of State, December 26, 1951, France Motion Pictures (1950–1954), State Department Files, NARA; Rebecca Prime, *Hollywood Exiles in Europe*, 37–46.

CASE STUDY. WHEN IN ROME: *ROMAN HOLIDAY* (1953)

1. Henry Henigson to William Wyler, April 12, 1952, *Roman Holiday* (Henry Henigson), William Wyler Papers, Margaret Herrick Library, Academy of Motion Picture Arts and Sciences, Beverly Hills (hereafter AMPAS Library).

2. Henry Henigson to William Wyler, April 12, 1952, *Roman Holiday* (Henry Henigson), William Wyler Papers, AMPAS Library.

3. Mark Harris, *Five Came Back: The Story of Hollywood and the Second World War* (New York: Penguin, 2014).

4. Robert R. Shandley, *Runaway Romances: Hollywood's Postwar Tour of Europe* (Philadelphia: Temple University Press, 2009), chapter 2.

5. Quoted in Axel Madsen, *William Wyler: The Authorized Biography* (New York: Thomas Y. Crowell, 1973), 306. The original shooting-time estimates for production at Paramount Studios support the fact that the film was initially envisioned as being made in Hollywood. See William Wyler to Don Hartman, August 9, 1952, William Wyler Papers, AMPAS Library.

6. "Transcripts of proceedings held at the Warner Brothers [*sic*] Beverly Hills Theater," February 24, 1954, *Roman Holiday* (Transcripts and Interviews), William Wyler Papers, Performing Arts Special Collections, UCLA, Los Angeles.

7. "Transcripts of proceedings held at the Warner Brothers [*sic*] Beverly Hills Theater," February 24, 1954, *Roman Holiday* (Transcripts and Interviews), William Wyler Papers, Performing Arts Special Collections, UCLA, Los Angeles.

8. Production Cost Breakdowns, multiple dates, *Roman Holiday* (Costs 1952–57), Paramount Pictures Production Records, AMPAS Library.

9. Correspondence between Jacob Karp and Henry Henigson, June and July 1952, *Roman Holiday* (Correspondence) Paramount Pictures Production Records, AMPAS Library.

10. "Italian Pix Prod'n Costs Soar 20–40% Since '50 for American Film-makers," *Daily Variety*, August 8, 1952, 1, 5.

11. William Wyler to Jules Stein, July 16, 1953, General Files (MCA Artists 1952–1953), William Wyler Papers, AMPAS Library.

12. William Wyler to Mark M. Cohen, August 8, 1953, General Files (Mark Cohen 1953), William Wyler Papers, AMPAS Library; Eric Hoyt, "Hollywood and the Income Tax, 1929–1955," *Film History* 22, no. 1 (2010): 15; Camille K. Yale, "Runaway Film Production: A Critical History of Hollywood's Outsourcing Discourse" (PhD diss., University of Illinois at Urbana-Champaign, 2010), 67–68, 73–74. Gregory Peck didn't fare as well because he took a salary cut on *Roman Holiday* and instead opted for a percentage of the film's profits. See "Only Huston and Spiegel, of All Filmsters Who Tried, Get 18-Mo. Tax-Free Ride," *Daily Variety*, July 24, 1953, 12.

13. Wyler's reputation suffered during *Roman Holiday*'s postproduction when the *Hollywood Reporter* published a news brief that he and his wife Talli hosted a party at their home in Rome for members of the Hollywood community, including blacklisted screenwriter Leonardo Bercovici and exiled director Bernard Vorhaus. See "Rome," *Hollywood Reporter*, November 26, 1952, 4. The right-wing organization American Business Consultants picked up the story in their newsletter, *Counterattack*. The incident prompted Paramount to work with Wyler to devise a letter denouncing any affiliation with Communism and a list of activities in which he may have had dealings with known Communists. See various correspondence, Political Files (Personal 1952–1954), William Wyler Papers, AMPAS Library.

14. Louella O. Parsons, "Kathryn Grayson Gets Contract She Wants," *San Francisco Examiner*, September 9, 1952, *Roman Holiday* (Publicity), William Wyler Papers, AMPAS Library.

15. Henry Henigson to Jacob Karp, September 22, 1952, *Roman Holiday* (Henry Henigson), William Wyler Papers, AMPAS Library.

16. Louella O. Parsons, "Hollywood Greets Visitors from India," *Los Angeles Examiner*, October 1, 1952, *Roman Holiday* (Publicity), William Wyler Papers, AMPAS Library.

17. "Biographical Sketch," *Motion Picture News Booking Guide and Studio Directory*, October 1927, 90; "Henry Henigson Again Takes Up Duties as Associate Producer at the Big U," *Hollywood Filmograph*, December 23, 1933, 41; "Schulberg, Henigson, Bergerman, Kohn, Lighton in Studio Moves," *Motion Picture Herald*,

May 4, 1935, 15; "Henry Henigson to Handle Independents for Metro," *Boxoffice*, May 31, 1947, 58; Henry Henigson obituary, *Daily Variety*, January 15, 1973, 8.

18. "Goetz at Metro to Talk 'Quo Vadis' Plans," *Daily Variety*, March 21, 1949, 2. A written sample of Henigson's Cinecittà survey from March 7, 1949, can be found in *Quo Vadis* (Miscellaneous), John Huston Papers, AMPAS Library.

19. Quoted in "Henigson Gets Tribute as He Departs MGM," *Daily Variety*, March 8, 1951, 1, 2.

20. "An Oral History with Edward Carfagno," interview by Barbara Hall (Beverly Hills, CA: AMPAS Oral History Program, 1991), 155–56, 182.

21. Herbert Coleman, *The Man Who Knew Hitchcock: A Hollywood Memoir* (Lanham, MD: Scarecrow, 2003), 159–60, 162.

22. Christian Ferry, interview with author, February 18, 2011, Paris. This notion is supported by Austrian production accountant Siegfried Wallach (email to author, May 7, 2011), who served as administration head on *Quo Vadis*, *Roman Holiday*, and *Ben-Hur*, and says that Henigson "did indeed import a Hollywood style of management to M.G.M. (and other affiliated companies) work in Europe."

23. Henry Henigson to William Wyler, April 12, 1952, *Roman Holiday* (Henry Henigson), William Wyler Papers, AMPAS Library.

24. Henry Henigson to Walter Tyler, Charles Woolstenhulme, and Maurice Lodi-Fe, May 12, 1952, *Roman Holiday* (Henry Henigson), William Wyler Papers, AMPAS Library.

25. Henry Henigson to Jacob Karp, July 3, 1952, *Roman Holiday* (Henry Henigson), William Wyler Papers, AMPAS Library.

26. Henry Henigson to William Wyler, May 2, 1952, *Roman Holiday* (Henry Henigson), William Wyler Papers, AMPAS Library.

27. Henry Henigson obituary, *Daily Variety*, January 15, 1973, 8.

28. Thomas Schatz, *Boom and Bust: American Cinema in the 1940s* (Berkeley: University of California Press, 1997), 349. Although Paramount bought out Liberty, production cost breakdowns reveal that the independent entity was listed as a cofinancer of the film. *Roman Holiday* (Costs 1952–1957), Paramount Pictures Production Records, AMPAS Library.

29. Richard Mealand to William Wyler, October 12, 1951, *Roman Holiday* (Richard Mealand), William Wyler Papers, AMPAS Library.

30. Various cables, summer 1952, *Roman Holiday* (Richard Mealand), William Wyler Papers, AMPAS Library.

31. William Wyler to Pilade Levi, October 31, 1951, *Roman Holiday* (Correspondence 1951–1954), William Wyler Papers, AMPAS Library.

32. William Wyler to Charles Woolstenhulme, May 21, 1952, *Roman Holiday* (Production), William Wyler Papers, AMPAS Library.

33. Henry Henigson to various offices, September 16, 1952, *Roman Holiday* (Legal 1952), William Wyler Papers, AMPAS Library.

34. "Par's 1953 Budget $30,000,000," *Daily Variety*, November 11, 1952, 1, 8.

35. Frank Caffey to Henry Henigson, May 19, 1952, *Roman Holiday* (Correspondence 1952), Paramount Pictures Production Records, AMPAS Library.

36. Don Hartman to William Wyler, July 16, 1952, *Roman Holiday* (Paramount), William Wyler Papers, AMPAS Library.

37. Jacob Karp to Henry Henigson, August 4, 1952, *Roman Holiday* (Correspondence 1952), Paramount Pictures Production Records, AMPAS Library.

38. William Wyler to Don Hartman, August 7 and 9, 1952, *Roman Holiday* (Paramount), William Wyler Papers, AMPAS Library.

39. William Wyler to Mark M. Cohen, June 14, 1952, General Files (Mark Cohen 1952), William Wyler Papers, AMPAS Library.

40. Frank Caffey to Henry Henigson, May 10, 1952, *Roman Holiday* (Correspondence 1952), Paramount Pictures Production Records, AMPAS Library.

41. Loren Ryder and Charles F. West to Frank Caffey, April 18, 1952, *Roman Holiday* (Correspondence 1952), Paramount Pictures Production Records, AMPAS Library. This letter was then passed on to Henigson.

42. This explanation from John R. Bishop was included in a letter from Frank Caffey to Henry Henigson, April 24, 1952, *Roman Holiday* (Correspondence 1952), Paramount Pictures Production Records, AMPAS Library.

43. William Wyler to Y. Frank Freeman, December 13, 1952, *Roman Holiday* (Paramount), William Wyler Papers, AMPAS Library.

44. Herbert Coleman, *The Man Who Knew Hitchcock*, 165–66. Despite the slightly different European division of labor for cinematography, extant crew lists include an Italian gaffer, but it is unclear what his specific duties were. Correspondence also suggests that Planer's departure was due to falling ill during the production and his working difficulties with Wyler. See cable from William Wyler to Franz Planer, August 18, 1952, *Roman Holiday* (Staff and Crew), William Wyler Papers, AMPAS Library.

45. Henry Henigson to William Wyler, April 12, 1952, *Roman Holiday* (Henry Henigson), William Wyler Papers, AMPAS Library.

46. William Wyler to Don Hartman, July 26, 1952, *Roman Holiday* (Paramount), William Wyler Papers, AMPAS Library.

47. William Wyler to Don Hartman, August 7, 1952, *Roman Holiday* (Paramount 1952), William Wyler Papers, AMPAS Library.

48. William Wyler to Don Hartman, August 9, 1952, *Roman Holiday* (Paramount 1952), William Wyler Papers, AMPAS Library.

49. William Wyler speech, October 11, 1952, *Roman Holiday* (Production), William Wyler Papers, AMPAS Library.

50. Irving Hoffman, "Tales of Hoffman," *Hollywood Reporter*, March 10, 1952, 3.

51. Cesare Zavattini to William Wyler, January 15, 1952, *Roman Holiday* (Script), William Wyler Papers, AMPAS Library.

52. William Wyler to Don Hartman, August 7, 1952, *Roman Holiday* (Paramount), William Wyler Papers, AMPAS Library. Parts of this letter are quoted and analyzed in Robert R. Shandley, *Runaway Romances*, 35–36.

53. William Wyler to Don Hartman, July 26, 1952, *Roman Holiday* (Paramount), William Wyler Papers, AMPAS Library. Parts of this letter are quoted and analyzed in Robert R. Shandley, *Runaway Romances*, 34.

1. Michael Sragow, *Victor Fleming: An American Movie Master* (New York: Pantheon, 2008), 185.

2. Steven Bingen, Stephen X. Sylvester, and Michael Troyan, *MGM: Hollywood's Greatest Backlot* (Solana Beach, CA: Santa Monica Press, 2011), 118–19.

3. Rebecca Prime discusses Dassin's connection to Italian Neorealism in *Hollywood Exiles in Europe: The Blacklist and Cold War Film Culture* (New Brunswick, NJ: Rutgers University Press, 2014), 122–23.

4. Some scholars have argued that Italian Neorealism influenced Fred Zinnemann in MGM's *The Search* (1948). See Stephen Prince, "Historical Perspective and the Realist Aesthetic in *High Noon* (1952)," in *The Films of Fred Zinnemann: Critical Perspectives*, ed. Arthur Nolletti Jr. (Albany: SUNY Press, 1999), 81–82. This opinion is understandable given that Zinnemann used extensive location shooting and some nonprofessional actors to portray the friendship of a GI and a displaced boy amid the ruins of postwar Germany. The director himself expressed certain affinities with Neorealist filmmakers in his approach to the story. See Fred Zinnemann, "A Different Perspective," *Sight and Sound* 17, no. 67 (Autumn 1948): 113. However, Zinnemann, who had worked for documentary pioneer Robert Flaherty, said that the film "was influenced by Flaherty, not by the new realism in Italy." Brian Neve, "A Past Master of His Craft: An Interview with Fred Zinnemann," *Cineaste* 23, no. 1 (1997): 16.

5. David Bordwell, "Part One: The Classical Hollywood Style, 1917–60," in David Bordwell, Janet Staiger, and Kristin Thompson, *The Classical Hollywood Cinema: Film Style and Mode of Production to 1960* (New York: Columbia University Press, 1985), 1–84.

6. For examples see *Interlude* review, *Daily Variety*, May 7, 1957, 3; *Seven Hills of Rome* review, *Daily Variety*, January 8, 1958, 3.

7. My assessment of the functions of film style draws from David Bordwell, *Figures Traced in Light: On Cinematic Staging* (Berkeley: University of California Press, 2005), 33–35; as well as Patrick Keating, *Hollywood Lighting from the Silent Era to Film Noir* (New York: Columbia University Press, 2010), 5–6.

8. My analysis of the aesthetic development of location shooting is informed by Bordwell's problem-solution model of stylistic history. See David Bordwell, *On the History of Film Style* (Cambridge, MA: Harvard University Press, 1997), 149–57; David Bordwell, *Figures Traced in Light*, 249–54.

9. "An Oral History with C. O. Erickson," interview by Douglas Bell (Beverly Hills, CA: AMPAS Oral History Program, 2006), 134.

10. Quoted in Arthur E. Gavin, "Rural Route for Realism," *American Cinematographer*, September 1958, 553.

11. Quoted in Clifford Harrington, "Hollywood's Globetrotting Cameraman," *American Cinematographer*, December 1958, 34.

12. National Weather Institute Report, March 14, 1952, *Little Boy Lost* (Production 1952); National Weather Institute Report, November 18, 1953, *To Catch a Thief*

(Pre-Production Location 1953–1954), Paramount Pictures Production Records, Margaret Herrick Library, Academy of Motion Picture Arts and Sciences, Beverly Hills (hereafter AMPAS Library).

13. Janet Staiger, "The Division and Order of Production: The Subdivision of the Work from the First Years through the 1920s," in *The Classical Hollywood Cinema*, 148.

14. Norman Deming to Harold Hecht, February 2, 1951; unsigned (likely Norman Deming) to Harold Hecht, April 17, 1951, *The Crimson Pirate* (Steve Trilling Files), Warner Bros. Archive, University of Southern California, Los Angeles.

15. Charles Affron and Mirella Jona Affron, *Sets in Motion: Art Direction and Film Narrative* (New Brunswick, NJ: Rutgers University Press, 1995), 26; Merrill Schleier, "Postwar Hollywood, 1947–1967," in *Art Direction and Production Design*, ed. Lucy Fischer (New Brunswick, NJ: Rutgers University Press, 2015), 73–96.

16. Quoted in "Motion Picture Art Direction For Exterior Productions," *American Cinematographer*, February 1948, 48.

17. Joseph McMillan Johnson to Hal Pereira, May 18, 1954, *To Catch a Thief* (Pre-Production Location 1953–1954), Paramount Pictures Production Records, AMPAS Library.

18. Brian R. Jacobson, *Studios before the System: Architecture, Technology, and the Emergence of Cinematic Space* (New York: Columbia University Press, 2015), chapter 5.

19. Discussions of these improvements appear in Charles L. Anderson, "Background Projection Photography," *American Cinematographer*, August 1952, 359; Joe Henry, "The Science of Process Photography," *American Cinematographer*, January 1958, 37.

20. Patrick Keating, *Hollywood Lighting from the Silent Era to Film Noir*, 157.

21. Cinematographer Burnett Guffey discusses this method on *Me and the Colonel* in Arthur E. Gavin, "Rural Route for Realism," *American Cinematographer*, September 1958, 576.

22. For an overview of these technical challenges see Jack Taylor, "Dynamic Realism," *International Photographer*, September 1948, 6–7.

23. The planning of this scene is detailed in a transcript of a preproduction meeting between Hitchcock and production supervisor Fred Ahren. "Hitchcock Notes," n.d., *Stage Fright*, Robert Lennard Collection, British Film Institute Library, London.

24. For an analysis of rear-screen projection in *To Catch a Thief* and the technical discourse of rear-screen projection see Julie Turnock, "The Screen on the Set: The Problem of Classical-Studio Rear Projection," *Cinema Journal* 51, no. 2 (Winter 2012): 157–62.

25. Arthur E. Gavin, "Rural Route for Realism," *American Cinematographer*, September 1958, 577.

26. Various correspondence for *A Certain Smile*, 20th Century-Fox Production Files, Performing Arts Special Collections, UCLA, Los Angeles.

27. *Paris Blues* review, *Daily Variety*, September 26, 1961, 3.

28. Lisa Dombrowski, "Postwar Hollywood, 1947–1967," in *Cinematography*, ed. Patrick Keating (New Brunswick, NJ: Rutgers University Press, 2014), 66–68.

29. Frederick Foster, "Economy Lighting with Photofloods," *American Cinematographer*, January 1950, 10–11, 20.

30. Frederick Foster, "'Hitch' Didn't Want It Arty," *American Cinematographer*, February 1957, 113–14; Walter Strenge, "Realism in Real Sets and Locations," *American Cinematographer*, October 1957, 650; Joseph Mascelli, "Portable Lighting Equipment Sparks Trend toward More Location Filming," *American Cinematographer*, November 1957, 732–33, 749.

31. Hollis W. Moyse, "Latensification," *American Cinematographer*, December 1948, 409, 426–27; Phil Tannura, "The Practical Use of Latensification," *American Cinematographer*, February 1951, 54, 68–70.

32. Charles G. Clarke, "Getting a Lift from 'The Big Lift,'" *American Cinematographer*, May 1950, 172–73.

33. David Bordwell, "CinemaScope: The Modern Miracle You See without Glasses," in *Poetics of Cinema* (New York: Routledge, 2008), 296.

34. "Some Important Things to Remember When Shooting Exteriors," *American Cinematographer*, October 1961, 602, emphasis in original.

35. This decision-making process reflects the problem-solution model of style in David Bordwell, *On the History of Film Style*, 149.

36. Heinrich Wölfflin, *Principles of Art History: The Problem of the Development of Style in Later Art*, trans. M. D. Hottinger (New York: Dover, 1950), 73; David Bordwell, *On the History of Film Style*, 169–70.

37. Rudolf Arnheim, *The Power of the Center: A Study of Composition in the Visual Arts* (Berkeley: University of California Press, 1982), 145.

38. Charles Loring, "Pictorial Composition—Key Element in Cinematography," *American Cinematographer*, August 1962, 489.

39. Joseph V. Mascelli, "How and When to Frame a Scene," *American Cinematographer*, March 1958, 174.

40. John Alton, *Painting with Light* (1949; repr., Berkeley: University of California Press, 1995), 123, 125–27.

41. Patrick Keating, *Hollywood Lighting from the Silent Era to Film Noir*, 87–88.

42. See the production photos for *Beat the Devil* in Oswald Morris, *Huston, We Have a Problem: A Kaleidoscope of Filmmaking Memories* (Lanham, MD: Scarecrow, 2006), between pp. 44–45.

43. Vincente Minnelli with Hector Arce, *I Remember It Well* (London: Angus and Robertson, 1975), 314.

44. Vincente Minnelli with Hector Arce, *I Remember It Well*, 314; Arthur E. Gavin, "Location-Shooting in Paris for 'Gigi,'" *American Cinematographer*, July 1958, 442.

45. James Naremore, *The Films of Vincente Minnelli* (Cambridge, England: Cambridge University Press, 1993), 35.

46. Howard T. Souther, "Composition in Motion Pictures," *American Cinematographer*, March 1947, 85.

47. Charles Loring, "Techniques for Filming Exteriors," *American Cinematographer*, January 1953, 44. Although this article is aimed at the semiprofessional cinematographer, it summarizes some of the general conventions guiding composition in outdoor shooting.

48. Patrick Keating examines the functions and effects of glamour lighting at various points in *Hollywood Lighting from the Silent Era to Film Noir*.

49. "CinemaScope—What It Is; How It Works," *American Cinematographer*, March 1953, 134.

50. John Belton, *Widescreen Cinema* (Cambridge, MA: Harvard University Press, 1992), 194.

51. Charles G. Clarke discusses shooting this Scope travelogue in *Highlights and Shadows: The Memoirs of a Hollywood Cameraman*, ed. Anthony Slide (Metuchen, NJ: Scarecrow, 1989), 196–98, 216–22.

52. David Bordwell, "CinemaScope," 281–325.

53. Quoted in "Negulesco, Only 2-Campaign C'Scope Vet, Finds Process More Flexible," *Daily Variety*, October 1, 1953, 3.

54. Leon Shamroy, "Filming 'The Robe,'" in *New Screen Techniques*, ed. Martin Quigley Jr. (New York: Quigley, 1953), 180.

55. John Belton, *Widescreen Cinema*, chapter 9; David Bordwell, "CinemaScope," 286.

56. Mitchell Leisen, "The Dissidents Abroad," *Hollywood Reporter: Twenty-Fourth Anniversary Issue*, November 12, 1954, section II.

57. Charles Barr, "CinemaScope: Before and After," *Film Quarterly* 16, no. 4 (Summer 1963): 9.

58. Daniel Steinhart, "'Paris . . . as You've Never Seen It Before!!!': The U.S. Marketing of Hollywood Foreign Productions in the Postwar Era," *InMedia: The French Journal of Media Studies* 3 (2013): http://inmedia.revues.org/633.

59. Fred Zinnemann, *A Life in the Movies: An Autobiography* (New York: Charles Scribner's Sons, 1992), 90.

60. The film's themes are analyzed in Ralph Stern, "*The Big Lift* (1950): Image and Identity in Blockaded Berlin," *Cinema Journal* 46, no. 2 (Winter 2007): 66–90; Robert R. Shandley, *Runaway Romances: Hollywood's Postwar Tour of Europe* (Philadelphia: Temple University Press, 2009), 121–26; Barton Palmer, *Shot on Location: Postwar American Cinema and the Exploration of Real Place* (New Brunswick, NJ: Rutgers University Press, 2016), 4–15.

61. Brian Neve, "A Past Master of His Craft," 18.

62. Herb A. Lightman, "Shooting Black and White in Color," *American Cinematographer*, August 1959, 499.

63. I expand on these ideas in a case study of *The Nun's Story* in "Postwar Hollywood, 1945–1967, Part 2: Foreign Location Shooting," in *Hollywood on Location: An Industry History*, ed. Joshua Gleich and Lawrence Webb (New Brunswick, NJ: Rutgers University Press, 2019).

64. David Bordwell, *Narration in the Fiction Film* (Madison: University of Wisconsin Press, 1985), 160.

65. David Bass, "Insiders and Outsiders: Latent Urban Thinking in Movies of Modern Rome," in *Cinema and Architecture: Méliès, Mallet-Stevens, Multimedia*, ed. François Penz and Maureen Thomas (London: BFI, 1997), 85–86.

66. David Bordwell, *Reinventing Hollywood: How 1940s Filmmakers Changed Movie Storytelling* (Chicago: University of Chicago Press, 2017), 343, 348.

67. For analyses of Neorealism's narrative characteristics see André Bazin, "An Aesthetic of Reality: Neorealism," in *What Is Cinema?*, vol. 2, ed. and trans. Hugh Gray (Berkeley: University of California Press, 2005), 16–40; David Bordwell, *Narration in the Fiction Film*, 205–13.

68. Bordwell makes a similar point: "The Scope era may have been the last period of genuine stylistic variety." David Bordwell, "CinemaScope," 310.

CASE STUDY. MENTAL SPACES AND CINEMATIC PLACES: *LUST FOR LIFE* (1956)

1. John Houseman, *Front and Center* (New York: Simon and Schuster, 1979), 481.

2. John Houseman to J.J. Cohn, February 24, 1955, *Lust for Life* (Production), Vincente Minnelli Papers, Margaret Herrick Library, Academy of Motion Picture Arts and Sciences, Beverly Hills (hereafter AMPAS Library). Although only Houseman signed this letter, a subsequent piece of correspondence refers to the memo as containing information compiled by *both* Minnelli and Houseman. See William Kaplan to Vincente Minnelli, March 11, 1955, *Lust for Life* (Production), Vincente Minnelli Papers, AMPAS Library.

3. Irving Stone had been planning to make the film with director Jean Negulesco and Italian producers Carlo Ponti and Dino De Laurentiis. French director Jean Renoir was considering shooting his own van Gogh biopic. See "Stone Trying to Retrieve 'Lust' from MGM, Make van Gogh Biopic Abroad as Indie," *Daily Variety*, October 16, 1953, 1, 4; "Battle over Biopicting Van Gogh," *Daily Variety*, October 20, 1953, 1, 4.

4. John Houseman, *Front and Center*, 462–64.

5. Manny Farber, "Canadian Underground," *Artforum*, January 1969, 73.

6. Sylvette Baudrot, interview with author, December 18, 2010, Paris; Rapport de Montage, March–April 1955, *Lust for Life*, Sylvette Baudrot-Guilbaud collection, Bibliothèque du film, Cinémathèque française, Paris. Ruttenberg, Carfagno, and Baudrot did not continue working on the first-unit phase of the film.

7. John Houseman to William Kaplan, April 8, 1955, *Lust for Life* (Production), Vincente Minnelli Papers, AMPAS Library; Vincente Minnelli with Hector Arce, *I Remember It Well* (London: Angus and Robertson, 1975), 289. While it is unclear how much of the second-unit footage ended up in the final film, many ideas from Houseman and Minnelli influenced the production teams' approach to location shooting.

8. William Kaplan to J. J. Cohn, April 28 and May 6, 1955, *Lust for Life* (Production), Vincente Minnelli Papers, AMPAS Library.

9. Sylvette Baudrot, interview with author, December 18, 2010.

10. "Useful Addresses," n.d., *Lust for Life* (Research), Vincente Minnelli Papers, AMPAS Library.

11. *Lust for Life* advertisement, *Daily Variety*, August 8, 1955, 6–7.

12. John Houseman, *Front and Center*, 467–68. Stephen Harvey examines this location march with a production history of the film in *Directed by Vincente Minnelli* (New York: Museum of Modern Art, 1989), 221–47.

13. John Houseman, *Front and Center*, 475.

14. Vincente Minnelli, *I Remember It Well*, 292.

15. John Houseman, *Front and Center*, 477.

16. In his memoir (*I Remember It Well*, 287–88), Minnelli recalls that after initial "battles with the studio during pre-production," the location crew was left to its own devices.

17. In his memoir (*Front and Center*, 465), Houseman refers to the stock as AGFA. Ansco Color was actually a derivative of AGFA. "M-G-M's 'Lust For Life' Shot on New Ansco Color Film," *American Cinematographer*, January 1956, 44; Drew Casper, *Postwar Hollywood 1946–1962* (Malden, MA: Blackwell, 2007), 94. For info on Ansco Color see Barry Salt, *Film Style and Technology: History and Analysis* (London: Starwood, 1992), 241.

18. John Houseman, *Front and Center*, 465.

19. John Houseman, *Front and Center*, 465, 478; Vincente Minnelli, *I Remember It Well*, 288–89.

20. Vincente Minnelli, *I Remember It Well*, 288.

21. John Houseman, *Front and Center*, 466.

22. Vincente Minnelli, *I Remember It Well*, 290.

23. While scouting for locations, cinematographer Ruttenberg said that many bridges had been bombed during the war. Joseph Ruttenberg to Vincente Minnelli, April 31, 1955, *Lust for Life* (Production), Vincente Minnelli Papers, AMPAS Library.

24. "'Lust for Life' Test in Six Arties," *Variety*, August 22, 1956, 7.

25. Griselda Pollock, "Artists Mythologies and Media Genius, Madness and Art History," *Screen* 21, no. 3 (1980): 93, emphasis in original.

26. John Houseman to J. J. Cohn, February 24, 1955, *Lust for Life* (Production), Vincente Minnelli Papers, AMPAS Library.

27. John Houseman to J. J. Cohn, February 24, 1955, *Lust for Life* (Production), Vincente Minnelli Papers, AMPAS Library.

28. John Houseman to J. J. Cohn, February 24, 1955, *Lust for Life* (Production), Vincente Minnelli Papers, AMPAS Library.

29. John Houseman to J. J. Cohn, February 24, 1955, *Lust for Life* (Production), Vincente Minnelli Papers, AMPAS Library, emphasis in original.

30. Vincente Minnelli, *I Remember It Well*, 287.

1. Dan Barry, "Evoking 18th-Century Drama, a Tragedy on the Bounty," *New York Times*, November 4, 2012, A26; Matthew Shaer, "The Sinking of the Bounty," *Atavist Magazine*, no. 22 (2013): https://magazine.atavist.com/the-sinking-of-the-bounty.

2. "Reed Abandons MGM's 'Bounty,'" *Los Angeles Times*, February 28, 1961, A7; Hedda Hopper, "Studio Mutiny over 'Bounty' Film Quelled," *Los Angeles Times*, March 1, 1961, B7.

3. Bill Davidson, "The Mutiny of Marlon Brando," *Saturday Evening Post*, June 16, 1962, 18; Joel W. Finler, *The Hollywood Story* (London and New York: Wallflower, 2003), 154.

4. Tino Balio, *United Artists: The Company That Changed the Film Industry* (Madison: University of Wisconsin Press, 1987), 128.

5. Souvenir program, *Mutiny on the Bounty* clipping files, Margaret Herrick Library, Academy of Motion Picture Arts and Sciences, Beverly Hills (hereafter AMPAS Library).

6. Arthur Knight, "Money on the Bounty," *Show Business Illustrated*, September 5, 1961, 83.

7. "Hollywood Invades Tahiti for Prod. of 'Bounty' and Prices Go Sky-High," *Variety*, December 28, 1960, 2, 16.

8. Arthur Knight, "Money on the Bounty," *Show Business Illustrated*, September 5, 1961, 83.

9. Peter Manso, *Brando: The Biography* (New York: Hyperion, 1994), 550.

10. Murray Schumach, "'Bounty' Director Blames Timorous Management for Tumultuous Saga," *New York Times*, March 25, 1962, 125.

11. The director recorded some of his complaints about Brando in notes taken during the production. Lewis Milestone, "Anecdotes," n.d., *Mutiny on the Bounty* (Notes), Lewis Milestone Papers, AMPAS Library.

12. Bill Davidson, "The Mutiny of Marlon Brando," *Saturday Evening Post*, June 16, 1962, 18–23.

13. Bob Thomas, "Brando Gives His Side of 'Bounty' Trouble," *Los Angeles Times*, November 3, 1961, 24, 27; Marlon Brando with Robert Lindsey, *Brando: Songs My Mother Taught Me* (New York: Random House, 1994), 269.

14. Arthur Knight, "Money on the Bounty," *Show Business Illustrated*, September 5, 1961, 84.

15. Peter Manso, *Brando*, 542.

16. This trend is highlighted in "Top 1962 Show Biz News," *Daily Variety*, January 2, 1963, 1, 4.

17. "20th Backs 6 Latin Pix Abroad," *Daily Variety*, August 31, 1949, 1, 6.

18. Kristin Thompson, *The Frodo Franchise: "The Lord of the Rings" and Modern Hollywood* (Berkeley: University of California Press, 2007); Ben Goldsmith, Susan Ward, and Tom O'Regan, *Local Hollywood: Global Film Production and the Gold*

Coast (St. Lucia: University of Queensland Press, 2010); Aynne Kokas, *Hollywood Made in China* (Berkeley: University of California Press, 2017).

19. Myles McNutt, "Mobile Production: Spatialized Labor, Location Professionals, and the Expanding Geography of Television Production," *Media Industries Journal* 2, no. 1 (2015): http://dx.doi.org/10.3998/mij.15031809.0002.104.

20. Ben Goldsmith and Tom O'Regan, *The Film Studio: Film Production in the Global Economy* (Lanham, MD: Rowman and Littlefield, 2005), 8.

INDEX

Abbey, Eberbach, 163

ABPC (Associated British Picture Corporation), 18, 39, 41, 53, 80, 116; Elstree studio, 59, 63, 80–82, 154; *Moby Dick* coproduced by, 56, 58, 59, 60; union-sanctioned tea break in workday and, 114

Acheson, Dean, 33

Across the Wide Missouri (1951), 254n105

ACT (Association of Cine-Technicians), 79–80, 99, 101, 112

Act of Love (1953), 92, 111, 121, 251n66

Adler, Buddy, 120

adventure films, 5, 19, 57

AFL (American Federation of Labor), 8, 26, 44, 50–53; efforts to block import of films made with blacklisted talent, 65; Huston's cooperation with, 66; "un-Americanism" charged by, 52. *See also* Hollywood AFL Film Council

Africa, 43, 77, 178–79, 180. *See also* Belgian Congo; British East Africa

African Queen, The (1952), 57–58, 59–60, 61, 62, 64, 182

Agee, James, 6

Albert, Eddie, *131*

Aldrich, Robert, 174–75

Alekan, Henri, 136

Ali Baba et les quarante voleurs (1954), 116

Allen, Irving, 7, 38, 87, 245n89

Aller, Herb, 53

Allied Artists, 42, 121

Alton, John, 8, 159

Ambassador's Daughter (1956), 87

American Cinematographer (journal), 6, 87, 93, 105, 112, 113, 149; on backgrounds as distraction, 165; on CinemaScope, 169; colonialist imaginary in location shooting and, 179; on diagonal lines in compositions, 159; on problems of shooting exterior scenes, 158

American Film Institute Catalog, 9

American Legion, 64–65

Anglo-American Agreement, 31–32, 54

Ansco Color, 87, 188, 189, 265n17

Antonioni, Michelangelo, 11

architecture, film and geometry of, 159, *160,* 163, *163,* 166, *167, 168,* 172–73, *173,* 174–75, *174,* 177, *178,* 181, *181*

Arise, My Love (1940), 173

Arnheim, Rudolf, 158–59

Around the World in 80 Days (1956), 169, 182

Artists and Models Abroad (1938), 173

Associazione Nazionale Industrie Cinematografiche e Affini, 230n35

Australia, 29, 199

auteurism, 16

authenticity, 48, 52–53, 71, 143, 190; of place, 44, 156, 160, 187; process shots and lack of, 8, 129; as reason for filming overseas, 56; travelogue effect and, 180; visual markers of supposed authenticity, 146; wartime newsreels and, 17. *See also* foreign locations, authentic

Ford, Cecil, 60
Ford, John, 5, 43, 143, 146
Foreign Affair, A (1948), 111
foreign locations, approximate, 49–51
foreign locations, authentic, 7–8, 14, 24, 41,
    44, 46, 129, 189–90; definition of
    runaway productions and, 47–49;
    interiors filmed in, 42; studios' compe-
    tition with television and, 19; unions'
    view of, 26. *See also* authenticity
foreign locations, stand-in, 51–53,
    63, 66
Foreman, Carl, 11, 38, 43–44, 89, 226n37
Forgacs, David, 249n34
Four Horsemen of the Apocalypse, The (1921
    and 1962), 196
Fox, Fred, 117
France, 6, 11, 29, 71–72, 101, 125, 187; Com-
    munist Party in, 76; earnings of Hol-
    lywood studios in, 32; as favored loca-
    tion for Hollywood, 14–15, 18;
    Hollywood films shot entirely in, 42;
    production subsidies in, 34, 35; protec-
    tionist film policies in, 73; studios in,
    86–88
Frank, Charles, 36
Franstudios (Paris), 86–87
Freeman, Frank, 129
French Equatorial Africa, 143
French language, 35, 38, 107, 108, 111
frozen funds, xiv, 7, 14, 25, 28–34, 39–40;
    of MGM, 26, 85; of Twentieth Century-
    Fox, 26, 75; unblocked in Italy, 23, 129
Fulci, Lucio, xiii
Fuller, Samuel, 170
FULS (Federazione Unitaria Lavoratori
    dello Spettacolo), 102
Funny Face (1957), 75, 92, 103, 181

Gable, Clark, 143, *144, 145,* 146
gaffers, 105, 113, 259n44
Gangs of New York (2002), Cinecittà set
    from, *xiv, xv*
Gannaway, Al, 52
Gardner, Ava, 61
Garnelite lights, 157
Garson, Greer, 100
Gaumont Studios (London), 62

General Agreement on Tariffs and
    Trade, 37
General Film Production Service, 77
geography, 9, 17, 18, 19, 40–41, 54–55, 58, 78;
    distance of studios from satellite film
    sites, 74; films made abroad and state-
    side, 45–47; films made in a single for-
    eign country, 41–42; films made in
    multiple foreign countries, 43–45; inter-
    national mode of production and, 20
German language, 107, 111
Germany, 32, 42, 46, 72, 111, 132, 163, 176
Gigi (1958), 89, 93, 164–65, *164*
globalization, 12, 13, 73, 200
Godard, Jean-Luc, 11
Goldsmith, Ben, 120, 200
Goldwyn, Samuel, 31
Graetz, Paul, 39
Grass Is Greener, The (1961), 90
Gray, Hugh, 102
Greatest Story Ever Told, The (1965), 10, 51,
    198
Green Glove, The (1952), 39
GTC Labs (Paris), 89
Guback, Thomas, 34
Guffey, Burnett, 149
Gundle, Stephen, 249n34

Harlan, Russell, 187
Harper, Sue, 79
Hartman, Don, 134, 137
Haskin, Byron, 41–42
Hasty Heart, The (1950), 80, 81, 93, 114, 116
Hathaway, Henry, 6
Hecht, Ben, 138
Hecht, Harold, 39, 150
Helen of Troy (1956), 86, 99
Hemingway's Adventures of a Young Man
    (1962), 86
Henigson, Henry, 16, 19, 85, 130, *131;* career
    at MGM, 131–32, 258n22; Hollywood
    production practices and, 135, 136–37; as
    principal organizing force behind
    Roman Holiday, 131, 132–33, 134; on
    translation of scripts, 109; on working
    in Italy, 127
Hepburn, Audrey, 128, 134, *138*
historical epics, 19, 49, 50, 147, 169

Hitchcock, Alfred, 75, 97, 122–23, 150; on productivity of British technicians, 112–13; rear projection used by, 154; *Stage Fright,* 154, *155; Under Capricorn,* 93, 112, 116; VistaVision and, 173–74. See also *Man Who Knew Too Much, The; To Catch a Thief*

Hollywood: blacklist, 11, 45, 64–67, 138, 226n37; cultural imperialism of, 13; enduring attraction of foreign locations, 200; evolution of film colony in, 4; globalization of, 12; global power/reach of, 3, 14, 17; mixing of Hollywood and foreign personnel, 96, 99–106; past and present of international production, 3–15; postwar film style, 183–84; production culture of, 15–16; shifting international strategies of, 53–55; stylistic history, 16–17

Hollywood AFL Film Council, 8, 26, 27, 28, 34; anti-communist views of, 45, 64, 102; campaign against runaway productions, 64; on combined foreign and stateside filming, 45–46; criticism of filming interiors on foreign soundstages, 42, 44; foreign-made films set in United States opposed by, 51–52; *Hollywood at the Crossroads* report and, 36; on producers' claims for foreign locations, 49; tax exemption on foreign earnings opposed by, 61–62. *See also* AFL (American Federation of Labor)

Hollywood at the Crossroads (Bernstein, 1957), 8, 36

Hollywood Joint Labor-Management Committee on Foreign Film Production, 10, 225n27

Hollywood Reporter, 4, 8, 28, 45, 64

Hollywood Ten, 66

Hollyworld: Space, Power, and Fantasy in the American Economy (Hozic, 2001), 120

Hong Kong, 50, 107

Horizon Pictures, 38, 57

Hornblow, Arthur, Jr., 49

Houseman, John, 16, 185, 186, 187, 188–89, 194; on capturing experience of van Gogh's paintings on film, 191–92, 193; criticism of CinemaScope, 189

House of Bamboo (1955), 170–71, *171*

House on 92nd Street, The (1945), 6

How to Marry a Millionaire (1953), 170

Hozic, Aida, 120

HUAC (House Un-American Activities Committee), 64, 66, 76

Hunter, Ian McLellan, 138

Huston, John, 16, 18, *59,* 110, 119, 130, 152, 160, 186; FBI file of, 66; as "location man," 56; political risks of working overseas, 128; red-baiting and, 63–67; studios worked with, 57–58; taxes and, 61–63, 67. See also *African Queen, The; Beat the Devil; Moby Dick; Moulin Rouge; We Were Strangers*

IATSE (International Alliance of Theatrical Stage Employees), 34; *International Photographer* (IATSE publication), 46, 99, 112; Motion Picture Set Painters Union, 51

import quotas, 6–7, 13, 32

Independent Moving Pictures Company, 4

India, 180

infrastructure, 5, 7, 14, 30, 124, 125; foreign, 42, 54, 73, 90; French, 87; investment in, 11, 31; Italian, 83, 86; in London area, 82; in Los Angeles, 12, 73, 78, 127, 135; networks of, 94; rebuilt from destruction of World War II, 199

Inn of the Sixth Happiness, The (1958), 50, 80, 119–20

international (mode of) production, 17, 18, 20, 72–73, 126, 175, 185; influence on European film industries, 124–26; location production management and, 96–99; past and present of, 3–12; *Roman Holiday* as exemplar of, 128; satire of, 3; "supplemental," 26–27; transcultural nature of, 96, 183; US print media articles about, 23–24, *24–25*

International Film Service (IFS), 77, 241n36

International Photographer (IATSE publication), 46, 99, 112

Ireland, 4, 56, 58, 60, 62–63, 64

Irma la Douce (1963), 11

Isleworth Studios (London), 60, 82

South Pacific, 5, 20, 196–97
Spain, 50, 52, 56, 168, 235n124
Spanish Affair (1958), 92
Spanish language, 93, 107
Spartacus (1960), 10, 50–51, 235n124
Spiegel, Sam, 38, 57, 121
Stagecoach (1939), 5
Stage Fright (1950), 154, *155*
Staiger, Janet, 73
State Department, US, 12, 13, 31, 234n103
Stein, Jules, 130
Stevens, George, 51, 103, 133
Stone, Irving, 185, 186, 264n3
"straight" shots, visual continuity and, 154
Street, Sarah, 254n107
Stross, Raymond, 121
Stubbs, Jonathan, 99
Studio Francoeur (Paris), 87, 187
Studio Hamburg (Germany), 42
studios, foreign, 42, 78; British, 78–82, 242n42; French, 86–88; Italian, 83–86, *84*
studios, Hollywood: back lots, 5, 6, 8, 11, 143; foreign locations re-created in, 8; free-trade interests of, 33; frozen funds and, 28, 32; independent filmmakers' escape from supervision of, 118–23; infrastructure of, 5; location surveys and, 149; scaling back of foreign operations, 53–54, 236n137; subsidiaries and, 37; "trade knowledge" and, 115–18
Studios de Billancourt (Paris), 86, 87
Studios de Boulogne (Paris), 42, 86, 88
Studios de Butte-Chaumont (Paris), 86
Studios de Joinville (Paris), 86, 87
Studios de Marseille (France), 87
Studios de Neuilly (Paris), 86
Studios de Saint-Maurice (Paris), 86–87, 244n84
Studios La Victorine (Nice, France), 43, 87
studio system, Hollywood, 3, 15–16, 96, 123, 151, 157; production managers, 96–97; stable contracted labor in, 106; trade knowledge in, 115; Wyler and, 135, 139
subsidiaries, foreign, 11, 37–38
subsidies, foreign, 34–37
Sundowners, The (1960), 182
SuperScope, 174

Surtees, Robert, 85, 99, 113, 196
Sweden, 30, 43
Swink, Robert, 136

Tahiti, 14, 196, 197
Taiwan, 50
Tanganyika (1954), 151, *152*
Tarzan the Ape Man (1952), 143
taxes, 38, 58, 67; British ad valorem tax, 30–31, 72; Eady Levy, 35, 36, 37; eighteen-month tax clause, 34, 61–62, 66, 130; evasion of, 18, 62–63; import and export, 91; tax incentives, 3, 7, 200
Taylor, Elizabeth, 121
Taylor, Samuel, 109
Technicolor, 89, 93, 119, 122, 175, 254n107; lighting for, 90–91; postwar film style and, 183
Technique Cinématographique, La (journal), 93
Teddington Studios (London), 39, 53, 80, 82, 116; leased as storage space, 242n54; Warner Bros. Burbank studio in communication with, 121
television, 5, 7, 19, 53, 54, 88, 175
Ten Commandments, The (1956), 99
Teresa (1951), 86
Third Man, The (1950), 39
13 Rue Madeleine (1947), 6
Thirty Mile Zone (TMZ), 40, 232n80
This Is Cinerama (1952), 169
Thomas, Michel, 109
Three Coins in the Fountain (1954), 95, 166, *168*, 170; interplay of wide-screen and architecture, 172, *173*; travelogue effect in, 180
Tierney, Gene, 62
Titanus studio (Rome), 83, 243n70
To Catch a Thief (1955), 75, 76, 97, *98*, 118; location surveys and, 149, 150; processing of footage, 122; studio supervision of footage, 123; VistaVision shooting of, 103, 174
Todd, Michael, 169
Todd-AO format, 169
Tone, Franchot, 87
To the Victor (1948), 71, 72, 74, 94, 116, 154
Toulouse-Lautrec, Henri, 119, 186